PSYCHOLOGY OF LEARNING BEHAVIOUR

PSYCHOLOGY OF LEARNING BEHAVIOUR

Dr. Asha Rani

CENTRUM PRESS
NEW DELHI-110002 (INDIA)

CENTRUM PRESS

H.O.: 4360/4, Ansari Road, Daryaganj,
New Delhi-110002 (India)
Tel: 23278000, 23261597, 23255577, 23286875

B.O.: No. 1015, Ist Main Road, BSK IIIrd Stage,
IIIrd Phase, IIIrd Block, Bangalore-560085 (INDIA)
Tel: 080-41723429

Email: centrumpress@gmail.com
Visit us at: www.centrumpress.com

Psychology of Learning Behaviour

First Edition, 2011

ISBN 978-93-80921-59-4

PRINTED IN INDIA

Printed at Tarun Offset Printers, Delhi-110053

Contents

Preface

Behavioural psychology is one of the major topics taught in every introductory psychology course, yet many concepts that lie at the heart of this subject can be confusing for students. If you've ever found yourself confusing the unconditioned stimulus with the conditioned stimulus, this basic tutorial is for you. Learning is a process that depends on experience and leads to longterm changes in behaviour potential. Behaviour potential designates the possible behaviour of an individual, not actual behaviour. The main assumption behind all learning psychology is that the effects of the environment, conditioning, reinforcement, etc. provide psychologists with the best information from which to understand human behaviour. As opposed to *short term* changes in behaviour potential (caused e.g. by fatigue) learning implies *long term* changes.

As opposed to long term changes caused by *aging and development*, learning implies changes related directly to *experience*. Learning theories try to better understand how the learning process works. Major research traditions are behaviourism, cognitivism and self-regulated learning. Neurosciences have provided important insights into learning, too, even when using much simpler organisms than humans (aplysia). Distance learning, eLearning, online learning, blended learning and media psychology are dimensions of the psychology that are emerging and where research and literature are important in the 21st century.

In psychology and education, learning is commonly defined as a process that brings together cognitive, emotional, and environmental influences and experiences for acquiring, enhancing, or making changes in one's knowledge, skills, values, and world views. Learning as a process focuses on what happens when the learning takes place. Explanations of what happens constitute learning theories. A learning theory is an attempt to describe how people and animals learn, thereby helping us understand the inherently complex process of learning. Learning theories have two chief values according to Hill (2002). One is in providing us with vocabulary and a conceptual framework for interpreting the examples of learning that we observe. The other is in suggesting where to look for solutions to practical problems. The theories do not give us solutions, but they do direct our attention to those variables that are crucial in finding solutions. There are three main categories or philosophical frameworks under which learning theories fall: behaviourism, cognitivism, and constructivism. Behaviourism focuses only on the objectively observable aspects of learning. Cognitive theories look beyond behaviour to explain brain-based learning. And constructivism views learning as a process in which the learner actively constructs or builds new ideas or concepts.

Each chapter in the book is self contained and is consistent with the general aim of the book. No doubt, the chapters given in this book shall help the teachers, students and social scientists to understand and explore more in the subject.

—Dr. Asha Rani & Dr. Punam Singh

1

Introduction

Learning is acquiring new knowledge, behaviours, skills, values, preferences or understanding, and may involve synthesizing different types of information. The ability to learn is possessed by humans, animals and some machines. Progress over time tends to follow learning curves.

Human learning may occur as part of education, personal development, or training. It may be goal-oriented and may be aided by motivation. The study of how learning occurs is part of neuropsychology, educational psychology, learning theory, and pedagogy.

Learning may occur as a result of habituation or classical conditioning, seen in many animal species, or as a result of more complex activities such as play, seen only in relatively intelligent animals. Learning may occur consciously or without conscious awareness. There is evidence for human behavioural learning prenatally, in which habituation has been observed as early as 32 weeks into gestation, indicating that the central nervous system is sufficiently developed and primed for learning and memory to occur very early on in development.

Play has been approached by several theorists as the first form of learning. Children play, experiment with the world, learn the rules, and learn to interact. Vygotsky agrees that play is pivotal for children's development, since they make meaning of their environment through play.

While this article describes the different environments in which learning happens, there seems as yet to be no description of how a collection of neurons learns nor where, exactly, in this collection of neurons "memory" is located.

Types of Learning

Simple Non-associative Learning

Habituation

In psychology, habituation is an example of non-associative learning in which there is a progressive diminution of behavioural response probability with repetition stimulus. An animal first responds to a stimulus, but if it is neither rewarding nor harmful the animal reduces subsequent responses. One example of this can be seen in small song birds—if a stuffed owl (or similar predator) is put into the cage, the birds initially react to it as though it were a real predator. Soon the birds react less, showing habituation. If another stuffed owl is introduced (or the same one removed and re-introduced), the birds react to it again as though it were a predator, demonstrating that it is only a very specific stimulus that is habituated to (namely, one particular unmoving owl in one place). Habituation has been shown in essentially every species of animal, including the large protozoan *Stentor coeruleus*.

Sensitization

Sensitization is an example of non-associative learning in which the progressive amplification of a response follows repeated administrations of a stimulus. An everyday example of this mechanism is the repeated tonic stimulation of peripheral nerves that will occur if a person rubs his arm continuously. After a while, this stimulation will create a warm sensation that will eventually turn painful. The pain is the result of the progressively amplified synaptic response of the peripheral nerves warning the person that the stimulation is harmful. Sensitization is thought to underlie both adaptive as well as maladaptive learning processes in the organism.

Associative Learning

Associative learning is the process by which an element is taught through association with a separate, pre-occurring element. It is also referred to as classical conditioning.

Operant conditioning is the use of consequences to modify the occurrence and form of behaviour. *Operant conditioning* is distinguished from *Pavlovian conditioning* in that operant conditioning uses reinforcement/punishment to alter an action-outcome association. In contrast Pavlovian conditioning involves strengthening of the stimulus-outcome association. Behaviourism is a psychological movement that seeks to alter behaviour by arranging the environment to elicit successful changes and to arrange consequences to maintain or diminish a behaviour. Behaviourists study behaviours that can be measured and changed by the environment. However, they do not eliminate that there are thought processes that interact with those behaviours. Delayed discounting is the process of devaluing rewards based on the delay of time they are presented. This process is thought to be tied to impulsivity. Impulsivity is a core process for many behaviours (e.g., substance abuse, problematic gambling, OCD). Making decisions is an important part of everyday functioning. How we make those decisions is based on what we perceive to be the most valuable or worthwhile actions. This is determined by what we find to be the most reinforcing stimuli. So when teaching an individual a response, you need to find the most potent reinforcer for that person. This may be a larger reinforcer at a later time or a smaller immediate reinforcer.

Classical Conditioning

The typical paradigm for classical conditioning involves repeatedly pairing an unconditioned stimulus (which unfailingly evokes a reflexive response) with another previously neutral stimulus (which does not normally evoke the response). Following conditioning, the response occurs both to the unconditioned stimulus and to the other, unrelated stimulus (now referred to as the "conditioned stimulus"). The response to the conditioned stimulus is termed a *conditioned response.* The classic example is Pavlov and his dogs. Meat powder naturally will make a dog salivate when it is put into a dog's mouth; salivating is a reflexive response to the meat powder. Meat powder is the unconditioned stimulus (US) and the salivation is the unconditioned response (UR). Then Pavlov rang a bell before presenting the meat powder. The first time Pavlov rang the bell, the neutral stimulus, the dogs did not salivate, but once he put the meat powder in their mouths they began to salivate. After numerous pairings of the bell, and then food the dogs learned that the bell was a signal that the food was about to come and began to salivate just when the bell was rang. Once this occurs the bell becomes the conditioned stimulus (CS) and the salivation to the bell is the conditioned response (CR). Another influential person in the world of Classical Conditioning is John B. Watson. Watson's work was very influential and paved the way for B. F. Skinner's radical behaviourism. Watson's behaviourism (and philosophy of science) stood in direct contrast to Freud. Watson's view was that Freud's introspective method was too subjective, and that we should limit the study of human development to directly observable behaviours. In 1913, Watson published the article "Psychology as the Behaviourist Views," in which he argued that laboratory studies should serve psychology best as a science. Watson's most famous, and controversial, experiment, "Little Albert," where he demonstrated how psychologists can account for the learning of emotion through classical conditioning principles.

Imprinting

Imprinting is the term used in psychology and ethology to describe any kind of phase-sensitive learning (learning occurring at a particular age or a particular life stage) that is rapid and apparently independent of the consequences of behaviour. It was first used to describe situations in which an animal or person learns the characteristics of some stimulus, which is therefore said to be "imprinted" onto the subject.

Observational Learning

The learning process most characteristic of humans is imitation; one's personal repetition of an observed behaviour, such as a dance. Humans can copy three types of information simultaneously: the demonstrator's goals, actions and environmental outcomes. Through copying these types of information, (most) infants will tune into their surrounding culture.

Play

Play generally describes behaviour which has no particular end in itself, but improves performance in similar situations in the future. This is seen in a wide variety of vertebrates besides humans, but is mostly limited to mammals and birds. Cats are known to play with a ball of string when young, which gives them experience with catching prey. Besides inanimate objects, animals may play with other members of their own species or other animals, such as orcas playing with seals they have caught. Play involves a significant cost to animals, such as increased vulnerability to predators and the risk of injury and possibly infection. It also consumes energy, so there must be significant benefits associated with play for it to have evolved. Play is generally seen in younger animals, suggesting a link with learning. However, it may also have other benefits not associated directly with learning.

Enculturation

Enculturation is the process by which a person learns the requirements of their native culture by which he or she is surrounded, and acquires values and behaviours that are appropriate or necessary in that culture. The influences which as part of this process limit, direct or shape the individual, whether deliberately or not, include parents, other adults, and peers. If successful, enculturation results in competence in the language, values and rituals of the culture. (compare acculturation, where a person is within a culture different to their normal culture, and learns the requirements of this different culture).

Multimedia Learning

Multimedia learning is where a person uses both auditory and visual stimuli to learn information (Mayer 2001). This type of learning relies on dual-coding theory (Paivio 1971).

E-learning and Augmented Learning

Electronic learning or e-learning is a general term used to refer to Internet-based networked computer-enhanced learning. A specific and always more diffused e-learning is mobile learning (m-learning), which uses different mobile telecommunication equipment, such as cellular phones. When a learner interacts with the e-learning environment, it's called augmented learning. By adapting to the needs of individuals, the context-driven instruction can be dynamically tailored to the learner's natural environment. Augmented digital content may include text, images, video, audio (music and voice). By personalizing instruction, augmented learning has been shown to improve learning performance for a lifetime.

Rote Learning

Rote learning is a technique which avoids understanding the inner complexities and inferences of the subject that is being learned and instead focuses on memorizing the material so that it can be recalled by the learner exactly the way it was read or heard. The major practice involved in rote learning techniques is *learning by repetition*, based on the idea that one will be able to quickly recall the meaning of the material the more it is repeated. Rote learning is used in diverse areas, from mathematics to music to religion. Although it has been criticized by some schools of thought, rote learning is a necessity in many situations.

Informal Learning

Informal learning occurs through the experience of day-to-day situations. It is learning from life, during a meal at table with parents, play, exploring, etc.

Formal Learning

Formal learning is learning that takes place within a teacher-student relationship, such as in a school system.

Nonformal Learning

Nonformal learning is organized learning outside the formal learning system. For example: learning by coming together with people with similar interests and exchanging viewpoints, in clubs or in (international) youth organizations, workshops.

Nonformal Learning and Combined Approaches

The educational system may use a combination of formal, informal, and nonformal learning methods. The UN and EU recognize these different forms of learning. In some schools students can get points that count in the formal-learning systems if they get work done in informal-learning circuits. They may be given time to assist international youth workshops and training courses, on the condition they prepare, contribute, share and can proof this offered valuable new insight, helped to acquire new skills, a place to get experience in organizing, teaching, etc.

In order to learn a skill, such as solving a Rubik's cube quickly, several factors come into play at once:

- Directions help one learn the patterns of solving a Rubik's cube.
- Practicing the moves repeatedly and for extended time helps with "muscle memory" and therefore speed.
- Thinking critically about moves helps find shortcuts, which in turn helps to speed up future attempts.
- The Rubik's cube's six colours help anchor solving it within the head.
- Occasionally revisiting the cube helps prevent negative learning or loss of skill.

Tangential Learning

Tangential learning is the process by which some portion of people will self-educate if a topic is exposed to them in something that they already enjoy such as playing a musical instrument.

Dialogic Learning

Dialogic learning is a type of learning based on dialogue.

Domains of Learning

Benjamin Bloom has suggested three domains of learning:

- Cognitive – To recall, calculate, discuss, analyse, problem solve, etc.
- Psychomotor – To dance, swim, ski, dive, drive a car, ride a bike, etc.
- Affective – To like something or someone, love, appreciate, fear, hate, worship, etc.

These domains are not mutually exclusive. For example, in learning to play chess, the person will have to learn the rules of the game (cognitive domain); but he also has to learn how to set up the chess pieces on the chessboard and also how to properly hold and move a chess piece (psychomotor). Furthermore, later in the game the person may even learn to love the game itself, value its applications in life, and appreciate its history (affective domain).

The Psychology of Learning is a Theoretical Science

Learning is a process that depends on experience and leads to longterm changes in behaviour potential. Behaviour potential designates the possible behaviour of an individual, not actual behaviour. The main assumption behind all learning psychology is that the effects of the environment, conditioning, reinforcement, etc. provide psychologists with the best information from which to understand human behaviour.

As opposed to *short term* changes in behaviour potential (caused e.g. by fatigue) learning implies *long term* changes. As opposed to long term changes caused by *aging and development*, learning implies changes related directly to *experience*.

Learning theories try to better understand how the learning process works. Major research traditions are behaviourism, cognitivism and self-regulated learning. Neurosciences have provided important insights into learning, too, even when using much simpler organisms than humans (aplysia). Distance learning, eLearning, online learning, blended learning and media psychology are dimensions of the psychology that are emerging and where research and literature are important in the 21st century.

Theoretical Development

In psychology and education, learning is commonly defined as a process that brings together cognitive, emotional, and environmental influences and experiences for acquiring, enhancing, or making changes in one's knowledge, skills, values, and world views. Learning as a process focuses on what happens when the learning takes place. Explanations of what happens constitute learning theories. A learning theory is an attempt to describe how people and animals learn, thereby helping us understand the inherently complex process of learning. Learning theories have two chief values according to Hill (2002). One is in providing us with vocabulary and a conceptual framework for interpreting the examples of learning that we observe. The other is in suggesting where to look for solutions to practical problems. The theories do not give us solutions, but they do direct our attention to those variables that are crucial in finding solutions.

There are three main categories or philosophical frameworks under which learning theories fall: behaviourism, cognitivism, and constructivism. Behaviourism focuses only on the objectively observable aspects of learning. Cognitive theories look beyond behaviour to explain brain-based learning. And constructivism views learning as a process in which the learner actively constructs or builds new ideas or concepts.

Behaviourism

Behaviourism as a theory was primarily developed by B. F. Skinner. It loosely encompasses the work of people like Edward Thorndike, Tolman, Guthrie, and Hull. What characterizes these investigators are their underlying assumptions about the process of learning. In essence, three basic assumptions are held to be true. First, learning is manifested by a change in behaviour. Second, the environment shapes behaviour. And third, the principles of contiguity (how close in time two events must be for a bond to be formed) and reinforcement (any means of increasing the likelihood that an event will be repeated) are central to explaining the learning process. For behaviourism, learning is the acquisition of new behaviour through conditioning.

There are two types of possible conditioning:

1) Classical conditioning, where the behaviour becomes a reflex response to stimulus as in the case of Pavlov's Dogs. Pavlov was interested in studying reflexes, when he saw that the dogs drooled without the proper stimulus. Although no food was in sight, their saliva still dribbled. It turned out that the dogs were reacting

to lab coats. Every time the dogs were served food, the person who served the food was wearing a lab coat. Therefore, the dogs reacted as if food was on its way whenever they saw a lab coat. In a series of experiments, Pavlov then tried to figure out how these phenomena were linked. For example, he struck a bell when the dogs were fed. If the bell was sounded in close association with their meal, the dogs learned to associate the sound of the bell with food. After a while, at the mere sound of the bell, they responded by drooling.

2) Operant conditioning where there is reinforcement of the behaviour by a reward or a punishment. The theory of operant conditioning was developed by B.F. Skinner and is known as Radical Behaviourism. The word 'operant' refers to the way in which behaviour 'operates on the environment'. Briefly, a behaviour may result either in reinforcement, which increases the likelihood of the behaviour recurring, or punishment, which decreases the likelihood of the behaviour recurring. It is important to note that, a punishment is not considered to be applicable if it does not result in the reduction of the behaviour, and so the terms punishment and reinforcement are determined as a result of the actions. Within this framework, behaviourists are particularly interested in measurable changes in behaviour.

Educational approaches such as applied behaviour analysis, curriculum based measurement, and direct instruction have emerged from this model.

Cognitivism

The earliest challenge to the behaviourists came in a publication in 1929 by Bode, a gestalt psychologist. He criticized behaviourists for being too dependent on overt behaviour to explain learning. Gestalt psychologists proposed looking at the patterns rather than isolated events. Gestalt views of learning have been incorporated into what have come to be labeled *cognitive theories*. Two key assumptions underlie this cognitive approach: (1) that the memory system is an active organized processor of information and (2) that prior knowledge plays an important role in learning. Cognitive theories look beyond behaviour to explain brain-based learning. Cognitivists consider how human memory works to promote learning.

For example, the physiological processes of sorting and encoding information and events into short term memory and long term memory are important to educators working under the cognitive theory. The major difference between gestaltists and behaviourists is the locus of control over the learning activity: the individual learner is more key to gestaltists than the environment that behaviourists emphasize.

Once memory theories like the Atkinson-Shiffrin memory model and Baddeley's working memory model were established as a theoretical framework in cognitive psychology, new cognitive frameworks of learning began to emerge during the 1970s, 80s, and 90s. Today, researchers are concentrating on topics like cognitive load and information processing theory. These theories of learning play a role in influencing instructional design. Aspects of cognitivism can be found in learning how to learn, social role acquisition, intelligence, learning, and memory as related to age.

Constructivism

Constructivism is a theory of knowledge (epistemology) that argues that humans generate knowledge and meaning from an interaction between their experiences and their ideas. During infancy, it is an interaction between their experiences and their reflexes or behaviour-patterns.

Piaget called these systems of knowledge *schemata*. Constructivism is not a specific pedagogy, although it is often confused with constructionism, an educational theory developed by Seymour Papert, inspired by constructivist and experiential learning ideas of Jean Piaget. Piaget's theory of constructivist learning has had wide ranging impact on learning theories and teaching methods in education and is an underlying theme of many education reform movements. Research support for constructivist teaching techniques has been mixed, with some research supporting these techniques and other research contradicting those results.

History

In past centuries, constructivist ideas were not widely valued due to the perception that children's play was seen as aimless and of little importance. Jean Piaget did not agree with these traditional views, however. He saw play as an important and necessary part of the student's cognitive development and provided scientific evidence for his views. Today, constructivist theories are influential throughout much of the informal learning sector. One good example of constructivist learning in an informal setting is the Investigate Centre at The Natural History Museum, London. Here visitors are encouraged to explore a collection of real natural history specimens, to practice some scientific skills and make discoveries for themselves.

Some historical figures who influenced constructivism:

- Giambattista Vico (1668–1744)
- Immanuel Kant (1724–1804)
- John Dewey (1859–1952)
- Maria Montessori (1870–1952)
- Wshadysahaw Strzemiñski (1893–1952)
- Jean Piaget (1896–1980)
- Lev Vygotsky (1896–1934)
- Heinz von Foerster (1911–2002)
- Jerome Bruner (1915-)
- Herbert Simon (1916–2001)
- Paul Watzlawick (1921–2007)
- Ernst von Glasersfeld (1917-)
- Edgar Morin (1921-).

Constructivist Theory

Formalization of the theory of constructivism is generally attributed to Jean Piaget, who articulated mechanisms by which knowledge is internalized by learners. He suggested that through processes of *accommodation* and *assimilation*, individuals construct new knowledge from their experiences. When individuals assimilate, they incorporate the new experience into an already existing framework without changing that framework. This may occur when individuals' experiences are aligned with their internal representations of the world, but may also occur as a failure to change a faulty understanding; for example, they may not notice events, may misunderstand input from others, or may decide that an event is a fluke and is therefore unimportant as information about the world. In contrast, when individuals' experiences contradict their internal representations, they may change their perceptions of the experiences to fit their internal representations. According to the theory, accommodation is the process of reframing one's mental representation of the external world to fit new experiences. Accommodation can be understood as the mechanism by which failure leads to learning: when we act on the expectation that the world operates in one way and it violates our expectations, we often fail, but by accommodating this new experience and reframing our model of the way the world works, we learn from the experience of failure, or others' failure.

It is important to note that constructivism is not a particular pedagogy. In fact, constructivism is a theory describing how learning happens, regardless of whether learners are using their experiences to understand a lecture or following the instructions for building a model airplane. In both cases, the theory of constructivism suggests that learners construct knowledge out of their experiences. However, constructivism is often associated with pedagogic approaches that promote active learning, or learning by doing.

Constructivist Learning Intervention

The Nature of the Learner

The Learner as a Unique Individual

Social constructivism views each learner as a unique individual with unique needs and backgrounds. The learner is also seen as complex and multidimensional. Social constructivism not only acknowledges the uniqueness and complexity of the learner, but actually encourages, utilizes and rewards it as an integral part of the learning process (Wertsch 1997).

The Importance of the Background and Culture of the Learner

Social constructivism encourages the learner to arrive at his or her version of the truth, influenced by his or her background, culture or embedded worldview. Historical developments and symbol systems, such as language, logic, and mathematical systems, are inherited by the learner as a member of a particular culture and these are learned throughout the learner's life. This also stresses the importance of the nature of the learner's social interaction with knowledgeable members of the society. Without the social interaction with other more knowledgeable people, it is impossible to acquire social meaning of important symbol systems and learn how to utilize them. Young children develop their thinking abilities by interacting with other children, adults and the physical world. From the social constructivist viewpoint, it is thus important to take into account the background and culture of the learner throughout the learning process, as this background also helps to shape the knowledge and truth that the learner creates, discovers and attains in the learning process (Wertsch 1997).

The Responsibility for Learning

Furthermore, it is argued that the responsibility of learning should reside increasingly with the learner (Glasersfeld, 1989). Social constructivism thus emphasizes the importance of the learner being actively involved in the learning process, unlike previous educational viewpoints where the responsibility rested with the instructor to teach and where the learner played a passive, receptive role. Von Glasersfeld (1989) emphasizes that learners construct their own understanding and that they do not simply mirror and reflect what they read. Learners look for meaning and will try to find regularity and order in the events of the world even in the absence of full or complete information.

The Motivation for Learning

Another crucial assumption regarding the nature of the learner concerns the level and source of motivation for learning. According to Von Glasersfeld (1989) sustaining motivation to learn is strongly dependent on the learner's confidence in his or her potential for learning. These feelings of competence and belief in potential to solve new problems, are derived from first-hand experience of mastery of problems in the past and are much more powerful than any external acknowledgment and motivation. This links up with Vygotsky's "zone of proximal development" (Vygotsky 1978) where learners are challenged within close proximity to, yet slightly above, their current level of development. By experiencing the successful completion of challenging tasks, learners gain confidence and motivation to embark on more complex challenges.

The Role of the Instructor

Instructors as Facilitators

According to the social constructivist approach, instructors have to adapt to the role of facilitators and not teachers (Bauersfeld, 1995). Where a teacher gives a didactic lecture that covers the subject matter, a facilitator helps the learner to get to his or her own understanding of the content. In the former scenario the learner plays a passive role and in the latter scenario the learner plays an active role in the learning process. The emphasis thus turns away from the instructor and the content, and towards the learner. This dramatic change of role implies that a facilitator needs to display a totally different set of skills than a teacher. A teacher tells, a facilitator asks; a teacher lectures from the front, a facilitator supports from the back; a teacher gives answers according to a set curriculum, a facilitator provides guidelines and creates the environment for the learner to arrive at his or her own conclusions; a teacher mostly gives a monologue, a facilitator is in continuous dialogue with the learners. A facilitator should also be able to adapt the learning experience 'in mid-air' by taking the initiative to steer the learning experience to where the learners want to create value.

The learning environment should also be designed to support and challenge the learner's thinking (Di Vesta, 1987). While it is advocated to give the learner ownership of the problem and solution process, it is not the case that any activity or any solution is adequate. The critical goal is to support the learner in becoming an effective thinker. This can be achieved by assuming multiple roles, such as consultant and coach.

A few strategies for cooperative learning include

- Reciprocal Questioning: students work together to ask and answer questions
- Jigsaw Classroom: students become "experts" on one part of a group project and teach it to the others in their group
- Structured Controversies: Students work together to research a particular controversy.

The Nature of the Learning Process

Learning is an Active, Social Process

Social constructivism, strongly influenced by Vygotsky's (1978) work, suggests that knowledge is first constructed in a social context and is then appropriated by individuals. According to social constructivists, the process of sharing individual perspectives-called *collaborative elabouration*-results in learners constructing understanding together that wouldn't be possible alone.

Social constructivist scholars view learning as an active process where learners should learn to discover principles, concepts and facts for themselves, hence the importance of encouraging guesswork and intuitive thinking in learners. In fact, for the social constructivist, reality is not something that we can discover because it does not pre-exist prior to our social invention of it. Kukla (2000) argues that reality is constructed by our own activities and that people, together as members of a society, invent the properties of the world.

Other constructivist scholars agree with this and emphasize that individuals make meanings through the interactions with each other and with the environment they live in. Knowledge is thus a product of humans and is socially and culturally constructed. McMahon (1997) agrees that learning is a social process. He further states that learning is not a process that only takes place inside our minds, nor is it a passive development of our behaviours that is shaped by external forces and that meaningful learning occurs when individuals are engaged in social activities.

Vygotsky (1978) also highlighted the convergence of the social and practical elements in learning by saying that the most significant moment in the course of intellectual development occurs when speech and practical activity, two previously completely independent lines of development, converge. Through practical activity a child constructs meaning on an intrapersonal level, while speech connects this meaning with the interpersonal world shared by the child and her/his culture.

Dynamic Interaction between Task, Instructor and Learner

A further characteristic of the role of the facilitator in the social constructivist viewpoint, is that the instructor and the learners are equally involved in learning from each other as well. This means that the learning experience is both subjective and objective and requires that the instructor's culture, values and background become an essential part of the interplay between learners and tasks in the shaping of meaning. Learners compare their version of the truth with that of the instructor and fellow learners to get to a new, socially tested version of truth (Kukla 2000). The task or problem is thus the interface between the instructor and the learner (McMahon 1997). This creates a dynamic interaction between task, instructor and learner. This entails that learners and instructors should develop an awareness of each other's viewpoints and then look to their own beliefs, standards and values, thus being both subjective and objective at the same time (Savery 1994).

Some studies argue for the importance of mentoring in the process of learning. The social constructivist model thus emphasizes the importance of the relationship between the student and the instructor in the learning process.

Some learning approaches that could harbour this interactive learning include reciprocal teaching, peer collaboration, cognitive apprenticeship, problem-based instruction, web quests, anchored instruction and other approaches that involve learning with others.

Collaboration Among Learners

Learners with different skills and backgrounds should collaborate in tasks and discussions to arrive at a shared understanding of the truth in a specific field.

Most social constructivist models, such as that proposed by Duffy and Jonassen (1992), also stress the need for collaboration among learners, in direct contradiction to traditional competitive approaches. One Vygotskian notion that has significant implications for peer collaboration, is that of the zone of proximal development. Defined as the distance between the actual developmental level as determined by independent problem-solving and the level of potential development as determined through problem-solving under adult guidance or in collaboration with more capable peers, it differs from the fixed biological nature of Piaget's stages of development. Through a process of 'scaffolding' a learner can be extended beyond the limitations of physical maturation to the extent that the development process lags behind the learning process.

Learning by Teaching (LdL) as Constructivist Method

If students have to present and train new contents with their classmates, a non-linear process of collective knowledge-construction will be set up.

The Importance of Context

The social constructivist paradigm views the context in which the learning occurs as central to the learning itself (McMahon 1997).

Underlying the notion of the learner as an active processor is "the assumption that there is no one set of generalised learning laws with each law applying to all domains". Decontextualised knowledge does not give us the skills to apply our understandings to authentic tasks because, as Duffy and Jonassen (1992) indicated, we are not working with the concept in the complex environment and experiencing the complex interrelationships in that environment that determine how and when the concept is used. One social constructivist notion is that of authentic or situated learning, where the student takes part in activities directly relevant to the application of learning and that take place within a culture similar to the applied setting. Cognitive apprenticeship has been proposed as an effective constructivist model of learning that attempts to "enculturate students into authentic practices through activity and social interaction in a way similar to that evident, and evidently successful, in craft apprenticeship".

Assessment

Holt and Willard-Holt (2000) emphasize the concept of dynamic assessment, which is a way of assessing the true potential of learners that differs significantly from conventional tests. Here the essentially interactive nature of learning is extended to the process of assessment. Rather than viewing assessment as a process carried out by one person, such as an instructor, it is seen as a two-way process involving interaction between both instructor and learner. The role of the assessor becomes one of entering into dialogue with the persons being assessed to find out their current level of performance on any task and sharing with them possible ways in which that performance might be improved on a subsequent occasion. Thus, assessment and learning are seen as inextricably linked and not separate processes.

According to this viewpoint instructors should see assessment as a continuous and interactive process that measures the achievement of the learner, the quality of the learning experience and courseware. The feedback created by the assessment process serves as a direct foundation for further development.

The Selection, Scope and Sequencing of the Subject Matter

Knowledge should be Discovered as an Integrated Whole

Knowledge should not be divided into different subjects or compartments, but should be discovered as an integrated whole.

This also again underlines the importance of the context in which learning is presented. The world, in which the learner needs to operate, does not approach one in the form of different subjects, but as a complex myriad of facts, problems, dimensions and perceptions (Ackerman 1996).

Engaging and Challenging the Learner

Learners should constantly be challenged with tasks that refer to skills and knowledge just beyond their current level of mastery. This captures their motivation and builds on previous successes to enhance learner confidence (Brownstein 2001). This is in line with Vygotsky's zone of proximal development, which can be described as the distance between the actual developmental level (as determined by independent problem-solving) and the level of potential development (as determined through problem-solving under adult guidance or in collaboration with more capable peers) (Vygotsky 1978).

Vygotsky (1978) further claimed that instruction is good only when it proceeds ahead of development. Then it awakens and rouses to life an entire set of functions in the stage of maturing, which lie in the zone of proximal development. It is in this way that instruction plays an extremely important role in development.

To fully engage and challenge the learner, the task and learning environment should reflect the complexity of the environment that the learner should be able to function in at the end of learning. Learners must not only have ownership of the learning or problem-solving process, but of the problem itself (Derry 1999).

Where the sequencing of subject matter is concerned, it is the constructivist viewpoint that the foundations of any subject may be taught to anybody at any stage in some form. This means that instructors should first introduce the basic ideas that give life and form to any topic or subject area, and then revisit and build upon these repeatedly. This notion has been extensively used in curricula.

It is also important for instructors to realize that although a curriculum may be set down for them, it inevitably becomes shaped by them into something personal that reflects their own belief systems, their thoughts and feelings about both the content of their instruction and their learners. Thus, the learning experience becomes a shared enterprise. The emotions and life contexts of those involved in the learning process must therefore be considered as an integral part of learning. The goal of the learner is central in considering what is learned

The Structuredness of the Learning Process

It is important to achieve the right balance between the degree of structure and flexibility that is built into the learning process. Savery (1994) contends that the more structured the learning environment, the harder it is for the learners to construct meaning based on their conceptual understandings. A facilitator should structure the learning experience just enough to make sure that the students get clear guidance and parameters within which to achieve the learning objectives, yet the learning experience should be open and free enough to allow for the learners to discover, enjoy, interact and arrive at their own, socially verified version of truth.

Constructivism for Adult Learners

Adults learn in fundamentally different ways than children. Children have fewer experiences, so their brains are able to create new neurological structures when they learn. Adults have previously existing neurological structures due to their vast amount of experience, so new learning for adults requires new connections between already existing neurological structures. There are several processes that are important for working with adult learners: mechanisms for mutual planning, diagnosis of learner needs and interests, cooperative learning climate, sequential activities for achieving the objectives, formulation of learning objectives based on the diagnosed needs and interests, selection of methods, materials, and resources, and evaluation of learning. Adult learners should be informed why something is important to learn and be shown how to direct themselves through information. The topic being presented should be related to the learners' experiences. People tend not to learn until they are ready and motivated, and they may need help overcoming inhibitions, behaviours and beliefs about learning.

Personal relevance of the content, involvement of the learner in the process, and deeper understanding of underlying concepts are some of the intersections between emphases in constructivism and adult learning principles.

Final Remarks

A constructivist learning intervention is thus an intervention where contextualised activities (tasks) are used to provide learners with an opportunity to discover and collaboratively construct meaning as the intervention unfolds. Learners are respected as unique individuals, and instructors act as facilitators rather than as teachers.

Pedagogies based on Constructivism

In fact, there are many pedagogies that leverage constructivist theory. Most approaches that have grown from constructivism suggest that learning is accomplished best using a hands-on approach. Learners learn by experimentation, and not by being told what will happen. They are left to make their *own* inferences, discoveries and conclusions. It also emphasizes that learning is not an "all or nothing" process but that students learn the new information that is presented to them by building upon knowledge that they already possess. It is therefore important that teachers constantly assess the knowledge their students have gained to make sure that the students' perceptions of the new knowledge are what the teacher had intended. Teachers will find that since the students build upon already existing knowledge, when they are called upon to retrieve the new information, they may make errors. It is known as reconstruction error when we fill in the gaps of our understanding with logical, though incorrect, thoughts. Teachers need to catch and try to correct these errors, though it is inevitable that some reconstruction error will continue to occur because of our innate retrieval limitations.

In most pedagogies based on constructivism, the teacher's role is not only to observe and assess but to also engage with the students while they are completing activities, wondering aloud and posing questions to the students for promotion of reasoning. (ex: I wonder why the water does not spill over the edge of the full cup?) Teachers also intervene when there are conflicts that arise; however, they simply facilitate the students' resolutions and self-regulation, with an emphasis on the conflict being the students' and that they must figure things out for themselves. For example, promotion of literacy is accomplished by integrating the need to read and write throughout individual activities within print-rich classrooms. The teacher, after reading a story, encourages the students to write or draw stories of their own, or by having the students reenact a story that they may know well, both activities encourage the students to *conceive themselves* as reader and writers.

Specific approaches to education that are based on constructivism include:

- Constructionism
    - An approach to learning developed by Seymour Papert and his colleagues at MIT in Cambridge, Massachusetts. Papert had worked with Piaget at the latter's Institute in Geneva. Papert eventually called his approach "constructionism." It included everything associated with Piaget's constructivism, but went beyond it to assert that constructivist learning happens especially well when people are engaged in constructing a product, something external to themselves such as a sand castle, a machine, a computer program or a book. This approach is greatly facilitated by the ready availability of powerful 'constructing' applications on personal computers. Promoters of the use of computers in education see an increasing need for students to develop skills in Multimedia literacy in order to use these tools in constructivist learning.
- Reciprocal Learning
    - Two teach each other.
- Procedural Facilitations for Writing
- Critical Exploration: The two components of critical exploration are curriculum development and pedagogy. In this method teachers find ways to encourage their students to explore the subject matter and express their thoughts on the material(Duckworth).
- Cognitive Tutors

- Cognitively Guided Instruction
    - A research and teacher professional development program in elementary mathematics created by Thomas P. Carpenter, Elizabeth Fennema, and their colleagues at the University of Wisconsin-Madison. Its major premise is that teachers can use students' informal strategies (i.e., strategies students construct based on their understanding of everyday situations, such as losing marbles or picking flowers) as a primary basis for teaching mathematics in the elementary grades.
- Inquiry-based learning
- Problem-based learning
- Cognitive apprenticeships
- Various methods involving collaboration or group work
- Cooperative learning (reciprocal questioning, Jigsaw Classroom, structured controversies)
- Anchored Instruction (Bransford et al.)
    - Problems and approaches to solutions are embedded in a narrative environment.
- Cognitive Apprenticeship (Collins et al.)
    - Learning is achieved by integration into a specific implicit and explicit culture of knowledge.
        - Six features of cognitive apprenticeships: modeling of the performance, support through coaching/tutoring, scaffolding, students articulate knowledge, reflection on progress, exploration of new applications. (Woolfolk, 2010)
- Cognitive Flexibility (Sprio et al.)
- Constructive Alignment
    - A constructivist approach to curriculum design, in which the learning activities spelled out in the intended learning outcomes are built into the teaching methods and assessment tasks.
- Pragmatic Constructivism

- The Silent Way
    - o A constructivist approach to foreign language teaching and learning developed by Caleb Gattegno who worked with Piaget before WWII and in the late 1940s.

Research and Evidence Supporting Constructivism

Hmelo-Silver, Duncan, & Chinn cite several studies supporting the success of the constructivist problem-based and inquiry learning methods. For example, they describe a project called GenScope, an inquiry-based science software application. Students using the GenScope software showed significant gains over the control groups, with the largest gains shown in students from basic courses.

Hmelo-Silver et al. also cite a large study by Geier on the effectiveness of inquiry-based science for middle school students, as demonstrated by their performance on high-stakes standardized tests. The improvement was 14% for the first cohort of students and 13% for the second cohort. This study also found that inquiry-based teaching methods greatly reduced the achievement gap for African-American students.

Guthrie et al. (2004) compared three instructional methods for third-grade reading: a traditional approach, a strategies instruction only approach, and an approach with strategies instruction and constructivist motivation techniques including student choices, collaboration, and hands-on activities. The constructivist approach, called CORI (Concept-Oriented Reading Instruction), resulted in better student reading comprehension, cognitive strategies, and motivation.

Jong Suk Kim found that using constructivist teaching methods for 6th graders resulted in better student achievement than traditional teaching methods. This study also found that students preferred constructivist methods over traditional ones. However, Kim did not find any difference in student self-concept or learning strategies between those taught by constructivist or traditional methods. Doðru and Kalender compared science classrooms using traditional teacher-centred approaches to those using student-centred, constructivist methods. In their initial test of student performance immediately following the lessons, they found no significant difference between traditional and constructivist methods. However, in the follow-up assessment 15 days later, students who learned through constructivist methods showed better retention of knowledge than those who learned through traditional methods.

Criticism of Educational Constructivism

As with any theory it is important to consider opposing perspectives. Several cognitive psychologists and educators have questioned the central claims of constructivism. It is argued that constructivist theories are misleading or contradict known findings. Matthews (1993) attempts to sketch the influence of constructivism in current mathematics and science education, aiming to indicate how pervasive Aristotle's empiricist epistemology is within it and what problems constructivism faces on that account.

In the neo-Piagetian theories of cognitive development it is maintained that learning at any age depends upon the processing and representational resources available at this particular age. That is, it is maintained that if the requirements of the concept to be understood exceeds the available processing efficiency and working memory resources then the concept is by definition not learnable. Therefore, however active a child is in a leaning endeavour, to learn the child must operate in a learning environment that meets the developmental and individual learning constraints that are characteristic for the child's age and this child's possible deviations from her age's norm. If this condition is not met, construction goes astray.

Several educators have also questioned the effectiveness of this approach toward instructional design, especially as it applies to the development of instruction for novices. While some constructivists argue that "learning by doing" enhances learning, critics of this instructional strategy argue that little empirical evidence exists to support this statement given novice learners. Sweller and his colleagues argue that novices do not possess the underlying mental models, or "schemas" necessary for "learning by doing". Indeed, Mayer (2004) reviewed the literature and found that fifty years of empirical data do not support using the constructivist teaching technique of pure discovery; in those situations requiring discovery, he argues for the use of guided discovery instead.

Mayer (2004) argues that not all teaching techniques based on constructivism are efficient or effective for all learners, suggesting many educators misapply constructivism to use teaching techniques that require learners to be behaviourally active. He describes this inappropriate use of constructivism as the "constructivist teaching fallacy". "I refer to this interpretation as the constructivist teaching fallacy because it equates active learning with active teaching." Instead Mayer proposes learners should be "cognitively active" during learning and that instructors use "guided practice."

In contrast, Kirschner, et al. (2006) describe constructivist teaching methods as "unguided methods of instruction." They suggest more structured learning activities for learners with little to no prior knowledge. Perhaps because of this proposition the Kirschner, et al. (2006) article has been criticized by a number of authors for various reasons.

Criticisms of Kirschner, Sweller, and Clark

Critics argue that the article creates a false dilemma between "guided" and "unguided" instruction without recognizing the continuum of guidance and structure possible within constructivist, problem-based learning, and other methods. Kirschner et al. also group a number of learning theories together (Discovery, Problem-Based, Experiential, and Inquiry-Based learning), disregarding the differences and actual amount of structure and scaffolding included in the theories.

Hmelo-Silver, Duncan, & Chinn have stated that highly scaffolded constructivist teaching methods like problem-based learning and inquiry learning are effective, and the evidence does not support Kirschner, Sweller, and Clark's conclusion. Hmelo-Silver et al. argue that Kirschner et al. "overlooked" research favorable to problem-based learning. They include in their response a 2003 meta-analysis showing PBL has benefits for knowledge application over traditional curriculum. In addition, some critics state Kirschner, Sweller, and Clark focus more on learning as memorization rather than learning as behaviour change or action. For example, in their article they criticize a project-based learning experiment for medical students because students did not perform as well on a written test as traditionally taught students. The medical students demonstrated better clinical skills, but were less efficient, ordering more unnecessary tests during clinical tests. Nevertheless, some critics of Kirschner et al. have argued that they personally would prefer the better clinical skills, regardless of written test performance.

A Rebuttal to the Criticisms of Kirschner, Sweller, and Clark

While there are critics of the Kirschner, Sweller, and Clark article, Sweller and his associates have written in their articles about:

1. instructional designs for producing procedural learning (learning as behaviour change);
2. their grouping of seemingly disparate learning theories and;
3. a continuum of guidance beginning with worked examples that may be followed by practice, or transitioned to practice.

Kirschner et al. (2006) describe worked examples as an instructional design solution for procedural learning. Clark, Nguyen, and Sweller (2006) describe this as a very effective, empirically validated method of teaching learners procedural skill acquisition. Evidence for learning by studying worked-examples, is known as the worked-example effect and has been found to be useful in many domains [e.g. music, chess, athletics; concept mapping; geometry; physics, mathematics, or programming.

Kirschner et al. (2006) describe why they group a series of seemingly disparate learning theories (Discovery, Problem-Based, Experiential, and Inquiry-Based learning). The reasoning for this grouping is because each learning theory promotes the same constructivist teaching technique — "learning by doing." While they argue "learning by doing" is useful for more knowledgeable learners, they argue this constructivist teaching technique is not useful for novices. Mayer states that it promotes behavioural activity too early in the learning process, when learners should be cognitively active (Mayer, 2004).

In addition, Sweller and his associates describe a continuum of guidance, starting with worked examples to slowly fade guidance. This continuum of faded guidance has been tested empirically to produce a series of learning effects: the worked-example effect, the guidance fading effect, and the expertise-reversal effect.

Criticism of Discovery-based Teaching Techniques

> *"After a half century of advocacy associated with instruction using minimal guidance, there appears no body of research supporting the technique. In so far as there is any evidence from controlled studies, it almost uniformly supports direct, strong instructional guidance rather constructivist-based minimal guidance during the instruction of novice to intermediate learners. Even for students with considerable prior knowledge, strong guidance while learning is most often found to be equally effective as unguided approaches. Not only is unguided instruction normally less effective; there is also evidence that it may have negative results when student acquire misconceptions or incomplete or disorganized knowledge"*

— *Why Minimal Guidance During Instruction Does Not Work: An Analysis of the Failure of Constructivist, Discovery, Problem-Based, Experiential, and Inquiry-Based Teaching by Kirschner, Sweller, Clark*

Mayer (2004) argues against discovery-based teaching techniques and provides an extensive review to support this argument. Mayer's arguments are against pure discovery, and are not specifically aimed as constructivism: "Nothing in this article should be construed as arguing against the view of learning as knowledge construction or against using hands-on inquiry or group discussion that promotes the process of knowledge construction in learners. The main conclusion I draw from the three research literatures I have reviewed is that it would be a mistake to interpret the current constructivist view of learning as a rationale for reviving pure discovery as a method of instruction."

Mayer's concern is how one applies discovery-based teaching techniques. He provides empirical research as evidence that discovery-based teaching techniques are inadequate. Here he cites this literature and makes his point "For example, a recent replication is research showing that students learn to become better at solving mathematics problems when they study worked-out examples rather than when they solely engage in hands-on problem solving (Sweller, 1999). Today's proponents of discovery methods, who claim to draw their support from constructivist philosophy, are making inroads into educational practice. Yet a dispassionate review of the relevant research literature shows that discovery-based practice is not as effective as guided discovery."

Mayer's point is that people often misuse constructivism to promote pure discovery-based teaching techniques. He proposes that the instructional design recommendations of constructivism are too often aimed at discovery-based practice (Mayer, 2004). Sweller (1988) found evidence that practice by novices during early schema acquisition, distracts these learners with unnecessary search-based activity, when the learner's attention should be focused on understanding (acquiring schemas).

The Math Wars and Discovery-based Teaching Techniques

The math wars controversy in the United States is an example of the type of heated debate that sometimes follows the implementation of constructivist-inspired curricula in schools. In the 1990s, mathematics textbooks based on new standards largely informed by constructivism were developed and promoted with government support. Although constructivist theory does not require eliminating instruction entirely, some textbooks seemed to recommend this extreme. Some parents and mathematicians protested the design of textbooks that omitted or de-emphasized instruction of standard mathematical methods. Supporters responded that the methods were to be eventually discovered under direction by the teacher, but since this was missing or unclear, many insisted the textbooks were designed to deliberately eliminate instruction of standard methods. In one commonly adopted text, the standard formula for the area of a circle is to be derived in the classroom, but not actually printed in the student textbook as is explained by the developers of CMP: "The student role of formulating, representing, clarifying, communicating, and reflecting on ideas leads to an increase in learning. If the format of the texts included many worked examples, the student role would then become merely reproducing these examples with small modifications."

Similarly, this approach has been applied to reading with whole language and inquiry-based science that emphasizes the importance of *devising* rather than just performing hands-on experiments as early as the elementary grades (traditionally done by research scientists), rather than studying facts. In other areas of curriculum such as social studies and writing are relying more on "higher order thinking skills" rather than memorization of dates, grammar or spelling rules or reciting correct answers.

Constructivist Learning Environments?...for which Learners?

During the 1990s, several theorists began to study the cognitive load of novices (those with little or no prior knowledge of the subject matter) during problem solving. Cognitive load theory was applied in several contexts. Based on the results of their research, these authors do not support the idea of allowing novices to interact with ill-structured learning environments. Ill-structured learning environments rely on the learner to discover problem solutions (Jonassen, 1997). Jonassen (1997) also suggested that novices be taught with "well-structured" learning environments.

Jonassen (1997) also proposed well-designed, well-structured learning environments provide scaffolding for problem-solving. Finally both Sweller and Jonassen support problem-solving scenarios for more advanced learners.

Sweller and his associates even suggest well-structured learning environments, like those provided by worked examples, are not effective for those with more experience—this was later described as the "expertise reversal effect". Cognitive load theorists suggest worked examples initially, with a gradual introduction of problem solving scenarios; this is described as the "guidance fading effect". Each of these ideas provides more evidence for Anderson's ACT-R framework. This ACT-R framework suggests learning can begin with studying examples.

Finally Mayer states: "Thus, the contribution of psychology is to help move educational reform efforts from the fuzzy and unproductive world of educational ideology—which sometimes hides under the banner of various versions of constructivism—to the sharp and productive world of theory-based research on how people learn."

Confusion between Constructivist and Maturationist Views

Many people confuse constructivist with maturationist views. The constructivist (or cognitive-developmental) stream "is based on the idea that the dialectic or interactionist process of development and learning through the student's active construction should be facilitated and promoted by adults". Whereas, "The romantic maturationist stream is based on the idea that the student's naturally occurring development should be allowed to flower without adult interventions in a permissive environment". In other words, adults play an active role in guiding learning in constructivism, while they are expected to allow children to guide themselves in maturationism.

Social Constructivism

In recent decades, constructivist theorists have extended the traditional focus on individual learning to address collaborative and social dimensions of learning. It is possible to see *social constructivism* as a bringing together of aspects of the work of Piaget with that of Bruner and Vygotsky. The term *Communal constructivism* was introduced by Bryn Holmes in 2001. As described in an early paper, "in this model, students will not simply pass through a course like water through a sieve but instead leave their own imprint in the learning process."

Influence on Computer Science

Constructivism has influenced the course of programming and computer science. Some famous programming languages have been created, wholly or in part, for educational use, to support the constructionist theory of Seymour Papert. These languages have been dynamically typed, and reflective.

- Logo is a multi-paradigm language, which is an easier-to-read adaptation and dialect of Lisp, without the parentheses. Logo is known for its introduction of turtle graphics to elementary schoolchildren in the 1980s. Its creators were Wally Feurzeig, and Papert.
- Smalltalk is an object-oriented language that was designed and created at Xerox PARC by a team led by Alan Kay.
- Etoys is being developed since the 1990s under the direction of Alan Kay, most recently by the Viewpoints Research Institute, based on Morphic tile scripting. Etoys was initially targeted at primary school math and science education.
- Scratch was developed in the early 21st century at MIT Media Lab under Mitchel Resnick. Like Etoys, it is based on Morphic tile scripts. Scratch is initially targeted at programming interactive multimedia, in primary and secondary education.
- StarLogo TNG was developed by the MIT Scheller Teacher Education Program under Eric Klopfer. It combines a block programming interface with compelling 3D graphics. It is targeted at programming games and game-like simulations in middle and secondary schools.

Informal and Post-modern Theories

Informal theories of education may attempt to break down the learning process in pursuit of practicality. One of these deals with whether learning should take place as a building of concepts toward an overall idea, or the understanding of the overall idea with the details filled in later. Critics believe that trying to teach an overall idea without details (facts) is like trying to build a masonry structure without bricks. Other concerns are the origins of the drive for learning. Some argue that learning is primarily self-regulated, and that the ideal learning situation is one dissimilar to the modern classroom. Critics argue that students learning in isolation fail.

Other Learning Theories

Other learning theories have also been developed for more specific purposes than general learning theories.

Connectivism is a recent theory of Networked learning which focuses on learning as making connections.

Multimedia learning theory focuses on principles for the effective use of multimedia in learning.

Criticism

Criticism of learning theories that underlie traditional educational practices claims there is no need for such a theory. The attempt to comprehend the process of learning through theory construction has created more problems than it has solved. It further claims that in order to make up for the feeling of inadequacy in confronting a process that we don't really comprehend, we label something "learning" and measure it. Then we're comfortable, because at least then we have the feeling that we have a grasp on the problem.

We don't really follow the process, but in lieu of a profound understanding of what's going on, we find something and say, "Let's declare that to be learning, by consensus." This is basically what the entire educational system the world over has done: quantify learning by breaking it up into measurable pieces—curricula, courses, hours, tests, and grades.

The assumption is that psychologically one knows enough about the mind to identify aptitudes: the accepted (knowledge-based) conception of learning identifies four assumptions of the accepted view of learning: that (some) one knows *what* ought to be learned by people, *why* it ought to be learned, *how* it ought to be learned, and by *whom* each thing ought to be learned. Together these assumptions are the lenses through which people have been socialized in our culture to judge whether learning is occurring or not; and a further assumption is that once one knows aptitudes, one also knows how to track a person so he will in fact reach the goal that is being set out for him. The whole approach is the ultimate in pedagogical and psychological technology. The only trouble is that it is humanly absurd. In this society, such a process is exceptionally subtle, because it involves an authoritarian approach within a free culture. By employing a variety of ruses the system produces a process which allows it to inhibit personal freedom without really feeling that this is what is going on. The person doesn't feel that something arbitrary is being done to him—which is in fact what is happening.

Other Interests

Every well-constructed theory of education has at its centre a philosophical anthropology.

2

Pavlovian Theory of Conditioning Learning

Classical conditioning (also Pavlovian or respondent conditioning, Pavlovian reinforcement) is a form of associative learning that was first demonstrated by Ivan Pavlov (1927). The typical procedure for inducing classical conditioning involves presentations of a neutral stimulus along with a stimulus of some significance. The neutral stimulus could be any event that does not result in an overt behavioural response from the organism under investigation. Pavlov referred to this as a *conditioned stimulus* (CS). Conversely, presentation of the significant stimulus necessarily evokes an innate, often reflexive, response. Pavlov called these the *unconditioned stimulus* (US) and *unconditioned response* (UR), respectively. If the CS and the US are repeatedly paired, eventually the two stimuli become associated and the organism begins to produce a behavioural response to the CS. Pavlov called this the *conditioned response* (CR).

Popular forms of classical conditioning that are used to study neural structures and functions that underlie learning and memory include fear conditioning, eyeblink conditioning, and the foot contraction conditioning of *Hermissenda crassicornis*.

The original and most famous example of classical conditioning involved the salivary conditioning of Pavlov's dogs. During his research on the physiology of digestion in dogs, Pavlov noticed that, rather than simply salivating in the presence of meat powder (an innate response to food that he called the *unconditioned response*), the dogs began to salivate in the presence of the lab technician who normally fed them. Pavlov called these *psychic secretions*.

From this observation he predicted that, if a particular stimulus in the dog's surroundings were present when the dog was presented with meat powder, then this stimulus would become *associated* with food and cause salivation on its own. In his initial experiment, Pavlov used a bell to call the dogs to their food and, after a few repetitions, the dogs started to salivate in response to the bell.

Types

- Forward conditioning: During forward conditioning the onset of the CS precedes the onset of the US. Two common forms of forward conditioning are delay and trace conditioning.
  - Delay conditioning: In delay conditioning the CS is presented and is overlapped by the presentation of the US.
  - Trace conditioning: During trace conditioning the CS and US do not overlap. Instead, the CS is presented, a period of time is allowed to elapse during which no stimuli are presented, and then the US is presented. The stimulus free period is called the *trace interval*. It may also be called the *conditioning interval*.
- Simultaneous conditioning: During simultaneous conditioning, the CS and US are presented and terminated at the same time.
- Backward conditioning: Backward conditioning occurs when a conditioned stimulus immediately follows an unconditioned stimulus. Unlike traditional conditioning models, in which the conditioned stimulus precedes the unconditioned stimulus, the conditioned response tends to be inhibitory. This is because the conditioned stimulus serves as a signal that the unconditioned stimulus has ended, rather than a reliable method of predicting the future occurrence of the unconditioned stimulus.

- Temporal conditioning: The US is presented at regularly-timed intervals, and CR acquisition is dependent upon correct timing of the interval between US presentations. The background, or context, can serve as the CS in this example.
- Unpaired conditioning: The CS and US are not presented together. Usually they are presented as independent trials that are separated by a variable, or pseudo-random, interval. This procedure is used to study non-associative behavioural responses, such as sensitization.
- CS-alone extinction: The CS is presented in the absence of the US. This procedure is usually done after the CR has been acquired through "Forward conditioning" training. Eventually, the CR frequency is reduced to pre-training levels.

Procedure Variations

In addition to the simple procedures described above, some classical conditioning studies are designed to tap into more complex learning processes. Some common variations are discussed below.

Classical Discrimination/Reversal Conditioning

In this procedure, two CSs and one US are typically used. The CSs may be the same modality (such as lights of different intensity), or they may be different modalities (such as auditory CS and visual CS). In this procedure, one of the CSs is designated CS+ and its presentation is always followed by the US. The other CS is designated CS" and its presentation is never followed by the US. After a number of trials, the organism learns to *discriminate* CS+ trials and CS" trials such that CRs are only observed on CS+ trials.

During *Reversal Training*, the CS+ and CS" are reversed and subjects learn to suppress responding to the previous CS+ and show CRs to the previous CS".

Classical ISI Discrimination Conditioning

This is a discrimination procedure in which two different CSs are used to signal two different interstimulus intervals.

For example, a dim light may be presented 30 seconds before a US, while a very bright light is presented 2 minutes before the US. Using this technique, organisms can learn to perform CRs that are appropriately timed for the two distinct CSs.

Latent Inhibition Conditioning

Latent inhibition is a technical term used in Classical conditioning. A stimulus that has not had any significance in the past takes longer to acquire meaning (as a signal) than a new stimulus. It is "a measure of reduced learning about a stimulus to which there has been prior exposure without any consequence." This tendency to disregard or even inhibit formation of memory, by preventing associative learning of observed stimuli, is an unconscious response and is assumed to prevent sensory overload. Latent inhibition is observed in many species, and is believed to be an integral part of learning, enabling an organism to interact successfully in an environment (e.g., social).

Low Latent Inhibition

Most people are able to ignore the constant stream of incoming stimuli, but this capability is reduced in those with low latent inhibition. It is hypothesized that a low level of latent inhibition can cause either psychosis or a high level of creative achievement or both, which is usually dependent on the subject's intelligence. Those of above average intelligence are thought to be capable of processing this stream effectively, enabling their creativity. Those with less than average intelligence, on the other hand, are less able to cope, and so as a result are more likely to suffer from mental illness.

High levels of the neurotransmitter dopamine (or its agonists) in the brain have been shown to decrease latent inhibition. Certain dysfunctions of the neurotransmitters glutamate, serotonin and acetylcholine have also been implicated,

Low latent inhibition is not a mental disorder but an observed personality trait, and a description of how an individual absorbs and assimilates data or stimuli. Furthermore, it does not necessarily lead to mental disorder or creative achievement—this is, like many other factors of life, a case of environmental and predispositional influences, whether these be positive (e.g., education) or negative (e.g., abuse) in nature.

In this procedure, a CS is presented several times before paired CS-US training commences. The pre-exposure of the subject to the CS before paired training slows the rate of CR acquisition relative to organisms that are not CS pre-exposed.

Conditioned Inhibition Conditioning

Three phases of conditioning are typically used:

Phase 1: A CS (CS+) is paired with a US until asymptotic CR levels are reached.

Phase 2: CS+/US trials are continued, but interspersed with trials on which the CS+ in compound with a second CS, but not with the US (i.e., CS+/CS" trials). Typically, organisms show CRs on CS+/US trials, but suppress responding on CS+/CS" trials.

Phase 3: In this retention test, the previous CS" is paired with the US. If conditioned inhibition has occurred, the rate of acquisition to the previous CS" should be impaired relative to organisms that did not experience Phase 2.

Blocking

This form of classical conditioning involves two phases.

Phase 1: A CS (CS1) is paired with a US.

Phase 2: A compound CS (CS1+CS2) is paired with a US.

Test: A separate test for each CS (CS1 and CS2) is performed. The blocking effect is observed in a lack of conditioned response to CS2, suggesting that the first phase of training blocked the acquisition of the second CS.

Applications

Little Albert

John B. Watson, founder of behaviourism, demonstrated classical conditioning empirically through experimentation using the Little Albert experiment in which a child ("Albert") was presented with a white rat (CS). After a control period in which the child reacted normally to the presence of the rat, the experimentors paired the presence of the rat with a loud, jarring noise caused by clanging two pipes together behind the child's head (US). As the trials progressed, the child began showing signs of distress at the sight of the rat, even when unaccompanied by the frightening noise. Furthermore, the child demonstrated generalization of stimulus associations, and showed distress when presented with any white, furry object—even such things as a rabbit, dog, a fur coat, and a Santa Claus mask with hair.

Behavioural Therapies

In human psychology, implications for therapies and treatments using classical conditioning differ from operant conditioning. Therapies associated with classical conditioning are aversion therapy, flooding and systematic desensitization.

Classical conditioning is short-term, usually requiring less time with therapists and less effort from patients, unlike humanistic therapies. The therapies mentioned are designed to cause either aversive feelings toward something, or to reduce unwanted fear and aversion.

Theories of Classical Conditioning

There are two competing theories of how classical conditioning works. The first, stimulus-response theory, suggests that an association to the unconditioned stimulus is made with the conditioned stimulus within the brain, but without involving conscious thought. The second, stimulus-stimulus theory involves cognitive activity, in which the conditioned stimulus is associated to the concept of the unconditioned stimulus, a subtle but important distinction.

Stimulus-response theory, referred to as S-R theory, is a theoretical model of behavioural psychology that suggests humans and other animals can learn to associate a new stimulus, the conditioned stimulus (CS), with a pre-existing stimulus, the unconditioned stimulus (US), and can think, feel or respond to the CS as if it were actually the US.

The opposing theory, put forward by cognitive behaviourists, is stimulus-stimulus theory (S-S theory). S-S theory is a theoretical model of classical conditioning that suggests a cognitive component is required to understand classical conditioning and that S-R theory is an inadequate model. It proposes that a cognitive component is at play. S-R theory suggests that an animal can learn to associate a conditioned stimulus (CS) such as a bell, with the impending arrival of food termed the unconditioned stimulus, resulting in an observable behaviour such as salivation. S-S theory suggests that instead the animal salivates to the bell because it is associated with the concept of food, which is a very fine but important distinction.

To test this theory, psychologist Robert Rescorla undertook the following experiment. Rats learned to associate a loud noise as the unconditioned stimulus, and a light as the conditioned stimulus. The response of the rats was to freeze and cease movement. What would happen then if the rats were habituated to the US? S-R theory would suggest that the rats would continue to respond to the CS, but if S-S theory is correct, they would be habituated to the concept of a loud sound (danger), and so would not freeze to the CS. The experimental results suggest that S-S was correct, as the rats no longer froze when exposed to the signal light. His theory still continues and is applied in everyday life.

Instrumental Learning

The consequence of responding is the most important element in instrumental learning. In this type of learning, the behaviour is instrumental in producing a change in the environment, and that environmental change in turn affects the probability of the behaviour that produced it.

Thorndike on Outcomes

Questions about the nature of instrumental processes began with Edward Thorndike. According to Thorndike's casual observations in his "cat in the puzzle box" experiments, inappropriate emotional responses aimed at escaping gave way to solution-oriented responses that produced reward. Thorndike theorized that it is the connection between a stimulus and a response that determines behavioural probability. The mechanisms for habit growth are contained in the law of effect.

This principle states that it is the effect of a response on the environment that determines whether or not the stimulus-response connection will form. The law of effect corresponds to positive reinforcement and punishment.

Skinner and Operant Conditioning

B.F. Skinner's version of instrumental conditioning, called operant conditioning, involves environmental control of responses. In his experiments involving a rat being placed in a Skinner box, the light is viewed as a discriminative stimulus because it serves as a cue to indicate the particular conditions under which response will be reinforced. Reinforcement controls responding by selectively strengthening behaviours that act on the environment to produce change. The key is that the outcome of responding determines the future probability of behaviour. The best conditioning occurs when reinforcers are given immediately.

Shaping

Through the process of shaping, experimenters involved with training animals to perform can decrease the time required to learn the task. Shaping is achieved by reinforcing approximations to a goal behaviour in a step-by-step fashion.

Basic Training Behaviours

In positive reinforcement, also known as reward training, the emission of an operant response is followed by stimuli called positive reinforcers that make the actions that produce them more probable. When a response results in the production of an aversive stimulus, the conditioning procedure is called punishment. The effect of punishment is to suppress responses that have led to it.

Omission training is one alternative to the use of punishment. In this procedure, a positive reinforcer is given as long as an unwanted behaviour does not occur. When the unwanted behaviour occurs, it results in the omission of the next scheduled reward. Negative reinforcement is a training procedure wherein operant behaviours terminate or postpone the delivery of aversive stimuli. Response probability increases.

Stimulus Control

Generalization and discrimination are also of concern in operant conditioning, but they are usually dealt with as special cases of stimulus control. This concept presumes that only certain environmental events become defining features in conditioning.

Secondary Reinforcement

Because reinforcers such as food and water are natural and have biological relevance, they are called primary reinforcers. They tend to be few in number, and they generally operate uniformly across species. When an event acquires reinforcing properties because of an association with a primary reinforcer, the event is labeled a secondary reinforcer.

Generalized Reinforcers

Generalized reinforcers are secondary reinforcers that are associated with a wide variety of other reinforcers such as food, clothing, shelter, and luxury items. A major advantage is that motivation to respond is almost guaranteed.

Chaining

Chaining occurs when a subject performs several different behaviours in sequence in order to obtain a reward. One example is that of a rat having to performs a series of tasks before a reward is available. Chains can often be very complex and complicated.

Schedules of Reinforcement

The schedule of reinforcement is probably the most heavily researched topic in all of operant conditioning. The significance of schedule variables comes from the fact that unique rates and patterns of responding are produced by selected schedule conditions. The two major types of reinforcement schedules are continuous reinforcement and intermittent reinforces. Continuous schedules are defined as schedules that reinforce the occurrence of every operant behaviour that satisfies an accepted criterion. There are basically four types of intermittent schedules.

In a fixed-ratio schedule, behaviour is rewarded after a fixed number of responses have been made. An example of a FR schedule is an industrial worker whose wages are adjusted according to unit output.

In a fixed-interval schedule, the subject is rewarded for the first response that occurs after a specified period of time has elapsed. One example of a fixed-interval schedule is waiting for a fruit to ripen on a tree.

Under variable-ratio schedule conditions, the number of responses required for reinforcement changes, depending on where the subject is in the schedule. A familiar example of a VR schedule is provided by slot machines at gambing casinos.

As one of the most widely used schedules in basic operant conditioning research, variable-interval schedules reward responses that occur after one given interval of time, then a different time interval, and still a different time interval until the end of training has been reached. Generally, ratio schedules occasion higher rates than fixed schedules. This pattern still holds when the subject is placed on operant extinction. All intermittent schedules will lead to greater resistance to extinction than a continuous reinforcement schedule. This phenomenon is often called the partial reinforcement effect.

The Premack Principle

David Premack has stressed that reinforcers may be better seen as responses. Premack's claimed that reinforcers are relative, being effective with some responses and not others. This expression is referred to as the Premack principle. Implicit in this statement is that reinforcers can be moved up and down a hierarchy by environmental manipulation. Most any behaviour can be made highly probable or improbable if the external conditions are structured properly.

3

Operant Learning Behaviour

Operant conditioning is the use of a behaviour's antecedent and/or its consequence to influence the occurrence and form of behaviour. Operant conditioning is distinguished from classical conditioning (also called respondent conditioning) in that operant conditioning deals with the modification of "voluntary behaviour" or operant behaviour. Operant behaviour "operates" on the environment and is maintained by its consequences, while classical conditioning deals with the conditioning of reflexive (reflex) behaviours which are elicited by antecedent conditions. Behaviours conditioned via a classical conditioning procedure are not maintained by consequences.

Reinforcement, Punishment, and Extinction

Reinforcement and punishment, the core tools of operant conditioning, are either positive (delivered following a response), or negative (withdrawn following a response). This creates a total of four basic consequences, with the addition of a fifth procedure known as extinction (i.e. no change in consequences following a response).

It's important to note that actors are not spoken of as being reinforced, punished, or extinguished; it is the actions that are reinforced, punished, or extinguished. Additionally, reinforcement, punishment, and extinction are not terms whose use is restricted to the laboratory. Naturally occurring consequences can also be said to reinforce, punish, or extinguish behaviour and are not always delivered by people.

- Reinforcement is a consequence that causes a behaviour to occur with greater frequency.
- Punishment is a consequence that causes a behaviour to occur with less frequency.
- Extinction is the lack of any consequence following a behaviour. When a behaviour is inconsequential, producing neither favorable nor unfavorable consequences, it will occur with less frequency. When a previously reinforced behaviour is no longer reinforced with either positive or negative reinforcement, it leads to a decline in the response.

Four Contexts of Operant Conditioning

Here the terms *positive* and *negative* are not used in their popular sense, but rather: *positive* refers to addition, and *negative* refers to subtraction.

What is added or subtracted may be either reinforcement or punishment. Hence *positive punishment* is sometimes a confusing term, as it denotes the "addition" of a stimulus or increase in the intensity of a stimulus that is aversive (such as spanking or an electric shock). The four procedures are:

1. Positive reinforcement (Reinforcement): occurs when a behaviour (response) is followed by a stimulus that is appetitive or rewarding, increasing the frequency of that behaviour. In the Skinner box experiment, a stimulus such as food or sugar solution can be delivered when the rat engages in a target behaviour, such as pressing a lever.
2. Negative reinforcement (Escape): occurs when a behaviour (response) is followed by the removal of an aversive stimulus, thereby increasing that behaviour's frequency. In the Skinner box experiment, negative reinforcement can be a loud noise continuously sounding inside the rat's cage until it engages in the target behaviour, such as pressing a lever, upon which the loud noise is removed.
3. Positive punishment (Punishment) (also called "Punishment by contingent stimulation"): occurs when

a behaviour (response) is followed by a stimulus, such as introducing a shock or loud noise, resulting in a decrease in that behaviour.

4. Negative punishment (Penalty) (also called "Punishment by contingent withdrawal"): occurs when a behaviour (response) is followed by the removal of a stimulus, such as taking away a child's toy following an undesired behaviour, resulting in a decrease in that behaviour.

Also:

- Avoidance learning is a type of learning in which a certain behaviour results in the cessation of an aversive stimulus. For example, performing the behaviour of shielding one's eyes when in the sunlight (or going indoors) will help avoid the aversive stimulation of having light in one's eyes.
- Extinction occurs when a behaviour (response) that had previously been reinforced is no longer effective. In the Skinner box experiment, this is the rat pushing the lever and being rewarded with a food pellet several times, and then pushing the lever again and never receiving a food pellet again. Eventually the rat would cease pushing the lever.
- Noncontingent reinforcement refers to delivery of reinforcing stimuli regardless of the organism's (aberrant) behaviour. The idea is that the target behaviour decreases because it is no longer necessary to receive the reinforcement. This typically entails time-based delivery of stimuli identified as maintaining aberrant behaviour, which serves to decrease the rate of the target behaviour. As no measured behaviour is identified as being strengthened, there is controversy surrounding the use of the term noncontingent "reinforcement".
- Shaping is a form of operant conditioning in which the increasingly accurate approximations of a desired response are reinforced.
- Chaining is an instructional procedure which involves reinforcing individual responses occurring in a sequence to form a complex behaviour.

Thorndike's Law of Effect

Operant conditioning, sometimes called *instrumental conditioning* or *instrumental learning*, was first extensively studied by Edward L. Thorndike (1874–1949), who observed the behaviour of cats trying to escape from home-made puzzle boxes. When first constrained in the boxes, the cats took a long time to escape. With experience, ineffective responses occurred less frequently and successful responses occurred more frequently, enabling the cats to escape in less time over successive trials. In his law of effect, Thorndike theorized that successful responses, those producing *satisfying* consequences, were "stamped in" by the experience and thus occurred more frequently. Unsuccessful responses, those producing *annoying* consequences, were *stamped out* and subsequently occurred less frequently. In short, some consequences *strengthened* behaviour and some consequences *weakened* behaviour. Thorndike produced the first known learning curves through this procedure. B.F. Skinner (1904–1990) formulated a more detailed analysis of operant conditioning based on reinforcement, punishment, and extinction. Following the ideas of Ernst Mach, Skinner rejected Thorndike's mediating structures required by "satisfaction" and constructed a new conceptualization of behaviour without any such references. So, while experimenting with some homemade feeding mechanisms, Skinner invented the operant conditioning chamber which allowed him to measure rate of response as a key dependent variable using a cumulative record of lever presses or key pecks.

Biological Correlates of Operant Conditioning

The first scientific studies identifying neurons that responded in ways that suggested they encode for conditioned stimuli came from work by Mahlon deLong and by R.T. "Rusty" Richardson. They showed that nucleus basalis neurons, which release acetylcholine broadly throughout the cerebral cortex, are activated shortly after a conditioned stimulus, or after a primary reward if no conditioned stimulus exists. These neurons are equally active for positive and negative reinforcers, and have been demonstrated to cause plasticity in many cortical regions. Evidence also exists that dopamine is activated at similar times. There is considerable evidence that dopamine participates in both reinforcement and aversive learning. Dopamine pathways project much more densely onto frontal cortex regions. Cholinergic projections, in contrast, are dense even in the posterior cortical regions like the primary visual cortex. A study of patients with Parkinson's disease, a condition attributed to the insufficient action of dopamine, further illustrates the role of dopamine in positive reinforcement. It showed that while off their medication, patients learned more readily with aversive consequences than with positive reinforcement. Patients who were on their medication showed the opposite to be the case, positive reinforcement proving to be the more effective form of learning when the action of dopamine is high.

Factors that Alter the Effectiveness of Consequences

When using consequences to modify a response, the effectiveness of a consequence can be increased or decreased by various factors. These factors can apply to either reinforcing or punishing consequences.

1. Satiation/Deprivation: The effectiveness of a consequence will be reduced if the individual's "appetite" for that source of stimulation has been satisfied. Inversely, the effectiveness of a consequence will increase as the individual becomes deprived of that stimulus. If someone is not hungry, food will not be an effective reinforcer for behaviour. Satiation is generally only a potential problem with primary reinforcers, those that do not need to be learned such as food and water.
2. Immediacy: After a response, how immediately a consequence is then felt determines the effectiveness of the consequence. More immediate feedback will be more effective than less immediate feedback. If someone's license plate is caught by a traffic camera for speeding and they receive a speeding ticket in the mail a week later, this consequence will not be very effective against speeding. But if someone is speeding and is caught in the act by an officer who pulls them

over, then their speeding behaviour is more likely to be affected.

3. Contingency: If a consequence does not contingently (reliably, or consistently) follow the target response, its effectiveness upon the response is reduced. But if a consequence follows the response consistently after successive instances, its ability to modify the response is increased. The schedule of reinforcement, when consistent, leads to faster learning. When the schedule is variable the learning is slower. Extinction is more difficult when learning occurs during intermittent reinforcement and more easily extinguished when learning occurs during a highly consistent schedule.
4. Size: This is a "cost-benefit" determinant of whether a consequence will be effective. If the size, or amount, of the consequence is large enough to be worth the effort, the consequence will be more effective upon the behaviour. An unusually large lottery jackpot, for example, might be enough to get someone to buy a one-dollar lottery ticket (or even buying multiple tickets). But if a lottery jackpot is small, the same person might not feel it to be worth the effort of driving out and finding a place to buy a ticket. In this example, it's also useful to note that "effort" is a punishing consequence. How these opposing expected consequences (reinforcing and punishing) balance out will determine whether the behaviour is performed or not.

Most of these factors exist for biological reasons. The biological purpose of the Principle of Satiation is to maintain the organism's homeostasis. When an organism has been deprived of sugar, for example, the effectiveness of the taste of sugar as a reinforcer is high. However, as the organism reaches or exceeds their optimum blood-sugar levels, the taste of sugar becomes less effective, perhaps even aversive.

The Principles of Immediacy and Contingency exist for neurochemical reasons. When an organism experiences a reinforcing stimulus, dopamine pathways in the brain are activated. This network of pathways "releases a short pulse of dopamine onto many dendrites, thus broadcasting a rather global reinforcement signal to postsynaptic neurons." This results in the plasticity of these synapses allowing recently activated synapses to increase their sensitivity to efferent signals, hence increasing the probability of occurrence for the recent responses preceding the reinforcement. These responses are, statistically, the most likely to have been the behaviour responsible for successfully achieving reinforcement. But when the application of reinforcement is either less immediate or less contingent (less consistent), the ability of dopamine to act upon the appropriate synapses is reduced.

Operant Variability

Operant variability is what allows a response to adapt to new situations. Operant behaviour is distinguished from reflexes in that its response topography (the form of the response) is subject to slight variations from one performance to another. These slight variations can include small differences in the specific motions involved, differences in the amount of force applied, and small changes in the timing of the response. If a subject's history of reinforcement is consistent, such variations will remain stable because the same successful variations are more likely to be reinforced than less successful variations. However, behavioural variability can also be altered when subjected to certain controlling variables.

Avoidance Learning

Avoidance learning belongs to negative reinforcement schedules. The subject learns that a certain response will result in the termination or prevention of an aversive stimulus. There are two kinds of commonly used experimental settings: discriminated and free-operant avoidance learning.

Discriminated Avoidance Learning

In discriminated avoidance learning, a novel stimulus such as a light or a tone is followed by an aversive stimulus such as a shock (CS-US, similar to classical conditioning). During the first trials (called escape-trials) the animal usually experiences both the CS (Conditioned Stimulus) and the US (Unconditioned Stimulus), showing the operant response to terminate the aversive US. During later trials, the animal will learn to perform the response already during the presentation of the CS thus preventing the aversive US from occurring. Such trials are called "avoidance trials."

Free-operant Avoidance Learning

In this experimental session, no discrete stimulus is used to signal the occurrence of the aversive stimulus. Rather, the aversive stimulus (mostly shocks) are presented without explicit warning stimuli. There are two crucial time intervals determining the rate of avoidance learning. This first one is called the S-S-interval (shock-shock-interval). This is the amount of time which passes during successive presentations of the shock (unless the operant response is performed). The other one is called the R-S-interval (response-shock-interval) which specifies the length of the time interval following an operant response during which no shocks will be delivered. Note that each time the organism performs the operant response, the R-S-interval without shocks begins anew.

Two-process Theory of Avoidance

This theory was originally established to explain learning in discriminated avoidance learning. It assumes two processes to take place:

Classical conditioning of fear: During the first trials of the training, the organism experiences both CS and aversive US (escape-trials). The theory assumed that during those trials classical conditioning takes place by pairing the CS with the US. Because of the aversive nature of the US the CS is supposed to elicit a conditioned emotional reaction (CER) – fear. In classical conditioning, presenting a CS conditioned with an aversive US disrupts the organism's ongoing behaviour.

Reinforcement of the operant response by fear-reduction: Because during the first process, the CS signaling the aversive US has itself become aversive by eliciting fear in the organism, reducing this unpleasant emotional reaction serves to motivate the operant response. The organism learns to make the response during the US, thus terminating the aversive internal reaction elicited by the CS. An important aspect of this theory is that the term "avoidance" does not really describe what the organism is doing. It does not "avoid" the aversive US in the sense of anticipating it. Rather the organism escapes an aversive internal state, caused by the CS.

Verbal Behaviour

In 1957, Skinner published *Verbal Behaviour*, a theoretical extension of the work he had pioneered since 1938. This work extended the theory of operant conditioning to human behaviour previously assigned to the areas of language, linguistics and other areas. *Verbal Behaviour* is the logical extension of Skinner's ideas, in which he introduced new functional relationship categories such as intraverbals, autoclitics, mands, tacts and the controlling relationship of the audience. All of these relationships were based on operant conditioning and relied on no new mechanisms despite the introduction of new functional categories.

Four Term Contingency

Applied behaviour analysis, which is the name of the discipline directly descended from Skinner's work, holds that behaviour is explained in four terms: conditional stimulus (S^C), a discriminative stimulus (S^d), a response (R), and a reinforcing stimulus (S^{rein} or S^r for reinforcers, sometimes S^{ave} for aversive stimuli).

Operant Hoarding

Operant hoarding is a referring to the choice made by a rat, on a compound schedule called a multiple schedule, that maximizes its rate of reinforcement in an operant conditioning context. More specifically, rats were shown to have allowed food pellets to accumulate in a food tray by continuing to press a lever on a continuous reinforcement schedule instead of retrieving those pellets. Retrieval of the pellets always instituted a one-minute period of extinction during which no additional food pellets were available but those that had been accumulated earlier could be consumed. This finding appears to contradict the usual finding that rats behave impulsively in situations in which there is a choice between a smaller food object right away and a larger food object after some delay.

An Alternative to the Law of Effect

However, an alternative perspective has been proposed by R. Allen and Beatrix Gardner. Under this idea, which they called "feedforward," animals learn during operant conditioning by simple pairing of stimuli, rather than by the consequences of their actions. Skinner asserted that a rat or pigeon would only manipulate a lever if rewarded for the action, a process he called "shaping" (reward for approaching then manipulating a lever). However, in order to prove the necessity of reward (reinforcement) in lever pressing, a control condition where food is delivered without regard to behaviour must also be conducted.

Skinner never published this control group. Only much later was it found that rats and pigeons do indeed learn to manipulate a lever when food comes irrespective of behaviour. This phenomenon is known as autoshaping. Autoshaping demonstrates that consequence of action is not necessary in an operant conditioning chamber, and it contradicts the law of effect. Further experimentation has shown that rats naturally handle small objects, such as a lever, when food is present. Rats seem to insist on handling the lever when free food is available (contra-freeloading) and even when pressing the lever leads to less food (omission training). Whenever food is presented, rats handle the lever, regardless if lever pressing leads to more food. Therefore, handling a lever is a natural behaviour that rats do as preparatory feeding activity, and in turn, lever pressing cannot logically be used as evidence for reward or reinforcement to occur. In the absence of evidence for reinforcement during operant conditioning, learning which occurs during operant experiments is actually only Pavlovian (classical) conditioning. The dichotomy between Pavlovian and operant conditioning is therefore an inappropriate separation.

Discrimination Learning

In psychology, discrimination learning is the process by which animals or people learn to make different responses to different stimuli. It was a classic topic in the psychology of learning from the 1920s to the 1970s, and was particularly investigated within:

- comparative psychology, where a key issue was whether continuous or discontinuous learning processes were concerned in the acquisition of discriminations
- human cognitive psychology
- the experimental analysis of behaviour, where a key issue was whether discriminations could be trained without the necessity for the subject to make errors
- developmental psychology, where a key issue was the changes that occur in the process of discrimination as a function of age
- cross-cultural psychology, where a key issue was the role that the cultural appropriateness of the stimuli to be discriminated played in the rate of acquisition of effective discrimination
- mathematical psychology, where attempts were made to formalise the distinctions being drawn in other branches of psychology.

While interest in the learning of discriminations has continued in all those fields, from about 1980 onwards the phrase "discrimination learning" was used less often as the main description either of individual studies or of a field of investigation. Instead, investigations of the learning of discriminations have tended to be described in other terms such as pattern recognition or concept discrimination. This change partly reflects the increasing diversity of studies of discrimination, and partly the general expansion of the topic of cognition within psychology, so that learning is not now the central organizing topic that it was in the mid-20th century.

The term *discrimination learning*—learning to respond differentially to different stimuli—encompasses a diverse range of different types of learning, such as perceptual learning, concept learning, and language learning. The practical goal of discrimination training often involves complex discriminations, such as when pilots learn to recognize potentially hazardous patterns on complicated instrument panels. The greatest challenge in discrimination training—aside from the initial problem of perceiving differences between categories—is to accomplish long-term learning that transfers across situations and stimuli. Training techniques that produce good performance can be misleading; difficult training is sometimes more effective than easier training in the long term.

Discrimination learning occurs at many levels, such as perceptual learning, higher level concept and category learning, and language learning. A baby experiences all three types of learning: She has to learn basic perceptual categories (e.g., discriminating between "ba" versus "ga"), higher-level concepts (e.g., friends and relatives versus strangers) and linguistic labels for these categories and concepts (e.g., "dog" refers to furry pets, but not cats).

Learning to discriminate often involves a process of differentiation and unitization. Differentiation involves learning to separate similar stimuli into different categories (e.g., ravens versus crows); unitization involves learning to group stimuli into larger units and to discriminate based on the unit (e.g., seeing a whole face instead of separate facial features). Unitization and differentiation may appear to be opposite processes, but both involve learning to perceive information at the appropriate level of representation.

Real-world Applications

In real-world applications, the usual goal of discrimination training is to teach people or animals complex discriminations. For example, drug-sniffing dogs learn to discriminate among complex odor compounds in order to respond appropriately. Athletes, such as quarterbacks in American football, goalkeepers in hockey, and batters in baseball, need to be able to discriminate very complex and fast-moving patterns of stimuli and respond appropriately. In athletics and more generally, perceptual learning works in concert with motor learning, which requires discriminating among internal sensations, such as the proprioceptive feeling of an ace tennis serve versus a serve that goes into the net.

In school, learning occurs primarily via direct instruction—books and teachers provide information, and students try to understand and remember that information. Direct instruction alone is not sufficient to promote many types of discrimination learning, however, which often requires a combination of instruction and experience. Verbal descriptions of a genre of music, for example, may be of little help compared with actual experience listening to the music.

Factors Affecting Discrimination Learning

In most cases, the goal of discrimination training is long-term transfer—that is, teaching learners in a way that will be relevant when they encounter novel stimuli and new situations. For example, a soldier taught to distinguish enemy soldiers from civilians during basic training needs to be able to transfer that learning to the battlefield. Training techniques that make training conditions difficult—and thereby decrease performance levels during training—often increase long-term learning and transfer. Such techniques are referred to as *desirable difficulties*. In learning to recognize patterns, for example, increasing the variability between members of a category during training decreases training performance but positively affects transfer.

Trainers and trainees often mistake short-term performance during training as evidence of long-term learning, and therefore perceive difficulty during training as an impediment when it is actually an advantage. For example, people think they learn artists' styles best when the artists are presented for study one at a time, whereas in reality mixing various artists' paintings together enhances categorization of novel paintings. It is important not to be fooled by training techniques that enhance short-term training performance at the expense of long-term learning and transfer.

Although difficult training can be vital, especially if the goal is to train difficult discriminations, too much difficulty can prevent learners from identifying categories' essential features. For that reason, perceptual training often begins with easy discriminations that adaptively increase in difficulty during training. However, discrimination learning can also occur when discrimination is impossibly difficult; asking people to discriminate between physically identical tones, for example, enhances transfer to a discrimination task on which tones vary.

At relatively early stages of perceptual processing, such as learning to make fine distinctions between lines at various orientations, transfer is frequently difficult to accomplish.

Learning does not necessarily even transfer when an old task is presented in a new spatial or retinal location. However, long-term training can increase basic sensitivity in a way that can be transferred; for example, violinists show more activity in the sensory cortex when touched on their left hand (i.e., the violin neck hand) than when touched on their right hand (i.e., the bow hand).

Avoidance Learning

An individual's response to avoid an unpleasant or stressful situation; also known as escape learning.

Avoidance learning is the process by which an individual learns a behaviour or response to avoid a stressful or unpleasant situation. The behaviour is to avoid, or to remove oneself from, the situation. Researchers have found avoidance behaviour challenging to explain, since the reinforcement for the behaviour is to not experience the negative reinforcer, or punishment. In other words, the reinforcement is the absence of punishment.

An individual's response to avoid an unpleasant or stressful situation; also known as escape learning.

Avoidance learning is the process by which an individual learns a behaviour or response to avoid a stressful or unpleasant situation. The behaviour is to avoid, or to remove oneself from, the situation. Researchers have found avoidance behaviour challenging to explain, since the reinforcement for the behaviour is to not experience the negative reinforcer, or punishment. In other words, the reinforcement is the absence of punishment. To explain this, psychologists have proposed two stages of learning: in stage one, the learner experiences classical conditioning; a warning, or stimulus, paired with a punishment. The learner develops a fear response when he experiences the stimulus. In stage two, the learner experiences operant conditioning; whereby he realizes that an action response to the stimulus eliminates the stressful outcome.

In a common laboratory experiment conducted to demonstrate avoidance learning, a rat is placed in a confined space with an electrified floor. A warning signal is given, followed by an electric current passing through the floor. To avoid being shocked, the rat must find an escape, such as a pole to climb or a barrier to jump over onto a nonelectric floor. At first, the rat responds only when the shock begins, but as the pattern is repeated, the rat learns to avoid the shock by responding to the warning signal. An example of avoidance learning in humans is the situation when a person avoids a yard where there is a barking dog. This learning is particularly strong in individuals who have been attacked by a dog.

Skill of Acquisition

A skill is the learned capacity to carry out pre-determined results often with the minimum outlay of time, energy, or both. Skills can often be divided into domain-general and domain-specific skills.

For example, in the domain of work, some general skills would include time management, teamwork and leadership, self motivation and others, whereas domain-specific skills would be useful only for a certain job. Skill usually requires certain environmental stimuli and situations to assess the level of skill being shown and used.

People need a broad range of skills in order to contribute to a modern economy and take their place in the technological society of the twenty-first century. An ASTD study showed that through technology, the workplace is changing, and so are the skills that employees must have to be able to change with it. The study identified 16 basic skills (Carnevale, 1990) that the workplace of the future would need in the employee of the future.

General Skills

Learning to Learn

Learning is an integral part of everyday life. The skill of knowing how to learn is a must for everybody and is the key to acquiring new skills and sharpening the ability to think through problems face challenges. It opens the door to other learning. Study smarter-not harder. A secondary benefit of learning how to learn is that it empowers the learner's ability to develop a measurable task repeatedly.

Foundation Skills

From the employer's perspective, the skill of knowing how to learn is cost-effective because it can mitigate the cost of retraining efforts. When workers use efficient learning strategies, they absorb and apply training more quickly, saving their employers money and time. When properly prepared, employees can use learning-to-learn techniques to distinguish between essential and nonessential information, discern patterns in information, and pinpoint the actions necessary to improve job performance. Many employers-particularly those dealing with rapid technological change see the learning-to-learn skill as an urgent necessity. Productivity, innovation, and competitiveness all depend on developing the workers' learning capability. Machinery and processes are transferable between companies and countries, but it is the application of human knowledge to technology and systems that provides the competitive edge.

Basic Skills Competence

The inability of large numbers of new workers to meet reading, writing, or computational (simple mathematics) standards is an economic and competitive issue. This forces employers to spend more on these critical competence skills. The majority of workers are literate and numerate but frequently, cannot use these skills effectively because they are rusty when called upon to use mathematical principles they have not used for 20 years, because they must use the skills in a context different from the one in which they originally learned them, or because they do not understand how to expand or apply the skill.

Reading

Reading has historically been considered the fundamental vocational skill for a person to get, keep, get ahead, or to change jobs. One educational assessment by Kirsch and Jungeblut in 1986, indicates that there is a large nationwide population of intermediate literates who only have fourth to eighth grade literacy equivalency (but are high school graduates) and who have not obtained a functional or employable literacy level.

Writing

Writing is consistently ranked among the highest priorities for job applicants and employees. One study states that more than 50 percent of the business respondents identified writing skill deficiencies in secretarial, skilled, managerial, supervisory, and bookkeeping personnel.

Computation

Because of technology, simple mathematical computation is important as employers focus on an employee's ability to compute at higher levels of sophistication. The introduction of sophisticated management and quality control approaches demand higher mathematical skills. Ironically, as occupational skill-level requirements climb, higher educational dropout rates and worsening worker deficiencies in computational skills are appearing. Employers complain particularly about miscalculations of decimals and fractions, resulting in expensive production errors. Employees must calculate correctly to conduct inventories, complete accurate reports of production levels, measure machine parts or specifications so that medium-to-high levels of mathematics skills are required across job categories. The business effect of math skill deficiencies is bottom line losses.

Communication Skills

Formal education in communication has been directed at reading and writing skills that are used least in the workplace. Most have only one or two years in speech related courses and no formal training in listening. Workers who can express their ideas orally and who understands verbal instructions make fewer mistakes, adjust more easily to change, and more readily absorb new ideas than those who do not. Thus career development is enhanced by training in oral communication and listening because these skills contribute to an employee's success in all of the following areas: interviewing, making presentations at or conducting meetings; negotiating and resolving conflict; selling; leading; being assertive; teaching or coaching others; working in a team; giving supervisors feedback about conversations with customers; and retraining. Employees spend most of the day communicating, and the time they spend will increase as robots, computers, and other machines take over mundane, repetitive jobs.

Oral

Skill in oral communication is a key element of good customer service. More than 76 million workers (in the USA) are in the service sector and companies that provide excellent service tend to stay far ahead of their competitors. To provide good service, all employees (not just designated sales and marketing employees) must learn how to talk and listen to customers, handle complaints and solve their problems.

Listening

As workers go up the corporate ladder, the listening time increases so that top managers spend as much as 65 percent of their day listening (Keefe, 1971). Because most people have had no training in this critical skill, poor listening habits cost hundreds of millions of dollars each year in productivity lost through misunderstandings and mistakes. At the rate of one $15 mistake per U.S. employee per year, the annual cost of poor listening would be more than a billion dollars.

Problem-solving

Problem-solving skills include the ability to recognize and define problems, invent and implement solutions, and track and evaluate results. Creative thinking not only requires the ability to understand problem-solving techniques, but also to transcend logical and sequential thinking, making the leap to innovation. Unresolved problems create dysfunctional relationships in the workplace. Ultimately, they become impediments to flexibility and in dealing with strategic change in an open-ended and creative way.

Creative Thinking

New approaches to problem-solving, organizational design, and product development all spring from the individual capacity for creative thinking. At work, creative thinking is generally expressed through the process of creative problem solving. Increasingly, companies are identifying creative problem solving as critical to their success and are instituting structured approaches to problem identification, analysis, and resolution. Creative solutions help the organization to move forward toward strategic goals. Organizational strategy is an example of creative thinking.

Self-esteem

Another key to effectiveness is good personal management. Self-esteem, motivation/goal setting, and employability/career development skills are critical because they impact individual morale which in turn plays a significant role in an institutions ability to achieve bottom line results. Employers have felt the pressure to make provisions to address perceived deficiencies in these skill areas because they realize that a work force without such skills is less productive. Conversely, solid personal management skills are often manifested by efficient integration of new technology or processes, creative thinking, high productivity, and a pursuit of skill enhancement. Unfortunately, problems related to these skill areas have increased primarily because entry-level applicants are arriving with deficiencies in personal management skills. On the job, the lack of personal management skills affects hiring and training costs, productivity, quality control, creativity, and ability to develop skills to meet changing needs. This presents a series of roadblocks that slow or halt an organizations progress. An organization with such difficulties cannot plan accurately for its future to integrate new technology, establish new work structures, or implement new work processes.

Motivation/Goal Setting

Motivation is the combination of desire, values, and beliefs that drives you to take action. These three motivating factors, and/or lack of them, are at the root of why people behave the way they do. Because you ultimately control your values, beliefs, and desires, you can influence your motivations. This means, if you consider something important and assign value to it, you are more likely to do the work it takes to attain the goal. When motivation originates from an internal source and is combined with a realistic goal and circumstance, the odds of a good outcome are greatly increased.

Employability/Career Development

One of the keys to success in today's world of work is career self-reliance — the ability to actively manage worklife in a rapidly changing environment and the attitude of being self-employed whether inside or outside an organization. Acquiring the skills and knowledge to become career self-reliant will enable employees to survive and even thrive in times of great change.

Group Effectiveness

The move toward participative decision making and problem solving inevitably increases the potential for disagreement, particularly when the primary work unit is a peer team with no supervisor. This puts a premium on developing employees group effectiveness skills.

Interpersonal

Interpersonal skills training can help employees recognize and improve their ability to determine appropriate self-behaviour, cope with undesirable behaviour in others, absorb stress, deal with ambiguity, structure social interaction, share responsibility, and interact more easily with others. Teamwork skills are critical for improving individual task accomplishment because practical innovations and solutions are reached sooner through cooperative behaviour.

Negotiation and Teamwork

Negotiation skills are critical for the effective functioning of teams as well as for individual acceptance in an organization. Change strategies are usually dependent upon the ability of employees to pull together and refocus on the new common goal. Carnevale wrote in a previous book that there are two ways to increase productivity. "The first is by increasing the intensity with which we utilize (human) resources (working harder), and the second is by increasing the efficiency with which we mix and use available resources (working smarter)."

Influence

The new competitive standards affect organizational structures, requiring a move away from top-down systems and toward more flexible networks and work teams. Technical changes result in new work processes and procedures. These require constant updating of employer-specific technical knowledge. In a world of rapid change, obsolescence is an interminable danger. As technology replaces more of the hands-on work, more employees will be dedicated to service functions where they will spend more time face-to-face with co-workers and clients. Organizational formats in the New Economy require more general skills. Interpersonal skills, communications skills and effective leadership skills are required by more and more non-supervisory employees. Managers in the New Economy relinquish control of work processes to work teams and will need to provide integration through leadership and monitoring.

Organizational

To be effective, employees need a sense of how the organization works and how the actions of each individual affect organizational and strategic objectives. Skill in determining the forces and factors that interfere with the organizations ability to accomplish its tasks can help the worker become a master problem solver, an innovator, and a team builder. Organizational effectiveness skills are the building blocks for leadership. A proactive approach toward increasing organizational effectiveness skills through training reflects the commitment to shared leadership concepts operating in the organization.

Implementing shared leadership values has a positive impact on productivity. When leadership functions are dispersed, those who perform in leadership roles willingly take on the responsibility for creating and communicating the vision of the organization and what its work groups should accomplish. By their proximity, they are also better able to create and communicate the quality of the work environment necessary to realize that vision.

One approach is the superteam which is defined as a high performing team which produces outstanding achievements. Leaders of superteams spend as much time anticipating the future as they do managing the present by thinking forward to, and talking to others about their goal, for it is this that provides the team with its purpose and direction (Hastings, Bixby, and Chaudhry-Lawton, 1986). Deploying visionary leaders improves institutional response time to changing and increasingly complex external environment factors that affect the organization's ability to operate effectively.

Leadership

At its most elementary level, leadership means that one person influences another. An organization that supports the concepts of shared leadership encourages employees at all levels to assume this role where it is appropriate. The function of leadership include stating basic values, announcing goals, organizing resources, reducing tensions between individuals, creating coalitions, coalescing workers, and encouraging better performance. There is a direct correlation between the implementation of shared leadership practice and product improvement, higher morale, and innovative problem solving, which leads to a more hospitable environment for instituting change. Top management cannot make the system work without employees taking on shared leadership roles. A great many people must be in a state of psychological readiness to take leaderlike action to improve the functioning at their levels. Historically, the roots of business failure can often be traced to inadequate training in and attention to the importance of leadership as a basic workplace skill. Too frequently, companies designate leaders without providing proper evaluation and training to ensure that they are qualified to assume leadership roles.

Dreyfus Model of Skill Acquisition

In the fields of education and operations research, the Dreyfus model of skill acquisition is a model of how students acquire skills through formal instruction and practicing. Brothers Stuart and Hubert Dreyfus proposed the model in 1980 in an influential, 18-page report on their research at the University of California, Berkeley, Operations Research Centre for the United States Air Force Office of Scientific Research. The model proposes that a student passes through five distinct stages: novice, advanced beginner, competent, proficient, and expert.

Stages

In the novice stage, a person follows rules as given, without context, with no sense of responsibility beyond following the rules exactly. Competence develops when the individual develops organizing principles to quickly access the particular rules that are relevant to the specific task at hand; hence, competence is characterized by active decision making in choosing a course of action. Proficiency is shown by individuals who develop intuition to guide their decisions and devise their own rules to formulate plans. The progression is thus from rigid adherence to rules to an intuitive mode of reasoning based on tacit knowledge. Michael Eraut summarized the five stages of increasing skill as follows:

Novice;

- "rigid adherence to taught rules or plans"
- no exercise of "discretionary judgment".

Advanced beginner;

- limited "situational perception"
- all aspects of work treated separately with equal importance.

Competent;

- "coping with crowdedness" (multiple activities, accumulation of information)
- some perception of actions in relation to goals
- deliberate planning
- formulates routines.

Proficient;

- holistic view of situation
- prioritizes importance of aspects
- "perceives deviations from the normal pattern"
- employs maxims for guidance, with meanings that adapt to the situation at hand.

Expert;

- transcends reliance on rules, guidelines, and maxims
- "intuitive grasp of situations based on deep, tacit understanding"

- has "vision of what is possible"
- uses "analytical approaches" in new situations or in case of problems.

Verbal Learning

There was a time when many traditional educational theorists viewed students as blank slates waiting to be filled with new information and ideas. This assumption changed when Howard Gardner released the results of years of observation and research in 1983. His work, "Frames of Mind: The Theory of Multiple Intelligences," introduced people to the notion that students come to the classroom with learning styles and preferences in place, and that educators can capitalize on their innate intelligences by tailoring curriculum and activities to meet their needs and stimulate their minds. The verbal learning style was one of the easier intelligences to accommodate, because it was already widely integrated into school curricula.

Identification

Verbal learning styles, sometimes called linguistic intelligence, encompass both the written and spoken word. People with a verbal intelligence have an ear for words, vocabulary, sentence structure, foreign words and wordplay. Verbal learners feel comfortable in many traditional school settings that rely on lectures, readings, discussions and essays to impart knowledge and assess comprehension.

Features

Verbal-linguistic learners rely on descriptive language and definitions to take in new information. In settings in which words are minimal or absent, such as music or arithmetic, they may contrive words, rhymes, descriptions or other linguistic approaches to absorb information, solve problems and express themselves.

Function

In the classroom, students with verbal learning styles keep momentum going in discussions, debates and interviews. Verbal intelligence extends beyond the recitation of facts and information and into artistic forms of expression such as poetry readings, songs, raps, rhymes, jazz chants, theater and word games. Students with verbal-linguistic intelligence often become writers, translators, editors, poets, songwriters, lawyers and public speakers.

Considerations

People with verbal learning styles often perform well on authentic assessments such as essay exams, interviews and portfolio work. They can quickly express themselves through speech as well as writing, so they answer questions with nuanced observations. The may feel constrained by rote learning settings that expect more repetition and recitation than actual expression.

Misconceptions

Educators sometimes mistakenly label verbal learners as good in language arts and poor at math and science. However, students can possess multiple intelligences simultaneously. In addition, an integrated curriculum that features mathematical or scientific projects, reports, keeping journals, surveys, observation records and group work appeals to the strengths of verbal-linguistic learners.

Learning Styles

Learning styles are various approaches or ways of learning. They involve educating methods, particular to an individual, that are presumed to allow that individual to learn best. Most people prefer an identifiable method of interacting with, taking in, and processing stimuli or information. Based on this concept, the idea of individualized "learning styles" originated in the 1970s, and acquired "enormous popularity".

Proponents say that teachers should assess the learning styles of their students and adapt their classroom methods to best fit each student's learning style, which is called the '*meshing hypothesis*.

The alleged basis and efficacy for these proposals has been extensively criticized. Although children and adults express personal preferences, there is no evidence that identifying a student's learning style produces better outcomes, and there is significant evidence that the widespread "meshing hypothesis" (that a student will learn best if taught in a method deemed appropriate for the student's learning style) is invalid. Well-designed studies "flatly contradict the popular meshing hypothesis".

David Kolb's Model

The David A. Kolb styles model is based on the Experiential Learning Theory, as explained in his book *Experiential Learning: Experience as the source of learning and development* (1984). The ELT model outlines two related toward grasping experience: Concrete Experience and Abstract Conceptualization, as well as two related approaches toward transforming experience: Reflective Observation and Active Experimentation. According to Kolb's model, the ideal learning process engages all four of these modes in response to situational demands. In order for learning to be effective, all four of these approaches must be incorporated. As individuals attempt to use all four approaches, however, they tend to develop strengths in one experience-grasping approach and one experience-transforming approach. The resulting learning styles are combinations of the individual's preferred approaches. These learning styles are as follows:

1. Converger;
2. Diverger;
3. Assimilator;
4. Accommodator;.

Convergers are characterized by abstract conceptualization and active experimentation. They are good at making practical applications of ideas and using deductive reasoning to solve problems.

Divergers tend toward concrete experience and reflective observation. They are imaginative and are good at coming up with ideas and seeing things from different perspectives.

Assimilators are characterized by abstract conceptualization and reflective observation. They are capable of creating theoretical models by means of inductive reasoning. Accommodators use concrete experience and active experimentation. They are good at actively engaging with the world and actually doing things instead of merely reading about and studying them.

Kolb's model gave rise to the Learning Style Inventory, an assessment method used to determine an individual's learning style. An individual may exhibit a preference for one of the four styles – Accommodating, Converging, Diverging and Assimilating – depending on his approach to learning via the experiential learning theory model.

Honey and Mumford's Model

In the mid 1970's Peter Honey and Alan Mumford adapted David Kolb's model for use with a population of middle/senior managers in business. They published their version of the model in *The Manual of Learning Styles* (1982) and *Using Your Learning Styles* (1983).

Two adaptations were made to Kolb's experiential model. Firstly, the stages in the cycle were renamed to accord with managerial experiences of decision making/problem solving. The Honey & Mumford stages are:

1. Having an experience
2. Reviewing the experience
3. Concluding from the experience
4. Planning the next steps.

Secondly, the styles were directly aligned to the stages in the cycle and named Activist, Reflector, Theorist and Pragmatist. These are assumed to be acquired preferences that are adaptable, either at will or through changed circumstances, rather than being fixed personality characteristics. The Honey & Mumford *Learning Styles Questionnaire* (LSQ) is a self-development tool and differs from Kolb's Learning Style inventory by inviting managers to complete a checklist of work-related behaviours without directly asking managers how they learn. Having completed the self-assessment, managers are encouraged to focus on strengthening underutilised styles in order to become better equipped to learn from a wide range of everyday experiences. A MORI survey commissioned by *[The Campaign for Learning]* in 1999 found the Honey & Mumford

LSQ to be the most widely used system for assessing preferred learning styles in the local government sector in the UK.

Anthony Gregorc's Model

Dennis W. Mills, Ph.D., discusses the work of Anthony F. Gregorc and Kathleen A. Butler in his article entitled "Applying What We Know: Student Learning Styles". Gregorc and Butler worked to organize a model describing how the mind works. This model is based on the existence of perceptions—our evaluation of the world by means of an approach that makes sense to us. These perceptions in turn are the foundation of our specific learning strengths, or learning styles.

In this model, there are two perceptual qualities 1) concrete and 2) abstract; and two ordering abilities 1) random and 2) sequential.

Concrete perceptions involve registering information through the five senses, while abstract perceptions involve the understanding of ideas, qualities, and concepts which cannot be seen.

In regard to the two ordering abilities, sequential involves the organization of information in a linear, logical way and random involves the organization of information in chunks and in no specific order.

Both of the perceptual qualities and both of the ordering abilities are present in each individual, but some qualities and ordering abilities are more dominant within certain individuals.

There are four combinations of perceptual qualities and ordering abilities based on dominance: 1) Concrete Sequential; 2) Abstract Random; 3) Abstract Sequential; 4) Concrete Random. Individuals with different combinations learn in a different ways—they have different strengths, different things make sense to them, different things are difficult for them, and they ask different questions throughout the learning process.

Sudbury Model of Democratic Education

Some critics (Mazza) of today's schools, of the concept of learning disabilities, of special education, and of response to intervention, take the position that every child has a different learning style and pace and that each child is unique, not only capable of learning but also capable of succeeding.

Sudbury Model democratic schools assert that there are many ways to study and learn. They argue that learning is a process you do, not a process that is done to you. That is true of everyone; it's basic. The experience of *Sudbury model democratic schools* shows that there are many ways to learn without the intervention of teaching, to say, without the intervention of a teacher being imperative. In the case of reading for instance in the Sudbury model democratic schools, some children learn from being read to, memorizing the stories and then ultimately reading them.

Others learn from cereal boxes, others from games instructions, others from street signs. Some teach themselves letter sounds, others syllables, others whole words. Sudbury model democratic schools adduce that in their schools no one child has ever been forced, pushed, urged, cajoled, or bribed into learning how to read or write; and they have had no dyslexia. None of their graduates are real or functional illiterates, and no one who meets their older students could ever guess the age at which they first learned to read or write. In a similar form students learn all the subjects, techniques, and skills in these schools.

Describing current instructional methods as homogenization and lockstep standardization, alternative approaches are proposed, such as the *Sudbury Model of Democratic Education schools*, an alternative approach in which children, by enjoying personal freedom thus encouraged to exercise personal responsibility for their actions, learn at their own pace and style rather than following a compulsory and chronologically-based curriculum. Proponents of unschooling have also claimed that children raised in this method learn at their own pace and style, and do not suffer from learning disabilities.

Gerald Coles asserts that there are partisan agendas behind the educational policy-makers and that the scientific research that they use to support their arguments regarding the teaching of literacy are flawed. These include the idea that there are neurological explanations for learning disabilities.

Fleming's VAK/VARK Model

One of the most common and widely-used categorizations of the various types of learning styles is Fleming's VARK model (sometimes VAK) which expanded upon earlier Neuro-linguistic programming (VARK) models :

1. visual learners;
2. auditory learners;
3. reading/writing-preference learners;
4. kinesthetic learners or tactile learners.

Fleming claimed that visual learners have a preference for seeing (think in pictures; visual aids such as overhead slides, diagrams, handouts, etc.). Auditory learners best learn through listening (lectures, discussions, tapes, etc.). Tactile/kinesthetic learners prefer to learn via experience—moving, touching, and doing (active exploration of the world; science projects; experiments, etc.). Its use in pedagogy allows teachers to prepare classes that address each of these areas. Students can also use the model to identify their preferred learning style and maximize their educational experience by focusing on what benefits them the most.

Other Models

Aiming to explain why aptitude tests, school grades, and classroom performance often fail to identify real ability, Robert J. Sternberg listed various cognitive dimensions in his book *Thinking Styles* (1997). Several other models are also often used when researching learning styles. This includes the Myers Briggs Type Indicator (MBTI) and the DISC assessment.

A more Recent Evidence based Model of Learning

Chris J Jackson's neuropsychological hybrid model of learning in personality argues Sensation Seeking provides a core biological drive of curiosity, learning and exploration. A high drive to explore leads to dysfunctional learning consequences unless cognitions such as goal orientation, conscientiousness, deep learning and emotional intelligence re-express it in more complex ways to achieve functional outcomes such as high work performance. Latest research is summarized here. Evidence for this model is allegedly impressive. Siadaty & Taghiyareh (2007) report that training based on Conscientious Achievement increases performance but that training based on Sensation Seeking does not. These results strongly support Jackson's model since the model proposes that Conscientious Achievement will respond to intervention whereas Sensation Seeking (with its biological basis) will not. Jackson's papers can be downloaded here.

Assessment Methods

Learning Style Inventory

The Learning Style Inventory (LSI) is connected with Kolb's model and is used to determine a student's learning style. The LSI assesses an individual's preferences and needs regarding the learning process. It does the following: (1) allows students to designate how they like to learn and indicates how consistent their responses are, (2) provides computerized results which show the student's preferred learning style, (3) provides a foundation upon which teachers can build in interacting with students, (4) provides possible strategies for accommodating learning styles, (5) provides for student involvement in the learning process; 6) provides a class summary so students with similar learning styles can be grouped together.

Other Methods

Other methods (usually questionnaires) used to identify learning styles include Fleming's VARK Learning Style Test, Jackson's Learning Styles Profiler (LSP), and the NLP meta programs based iWAM questionnaire. Many other tests have gathered popularity and various levels of credibility among students and teachers.

Criticism

Learning-style theories have been criticized by many.

Some psychologists and neuroscientists have questioned the scientific basis for and the theories on which they are based. According to Susan Greenfield the practice is "nonsense" from a neuroscientific point of view: "Humans have evolved to build a picture of the world through our senses working in unison, exploiting the immense interconnectivity that exists in the brain."

Many educational psychologists believe that there is little evidence for the efficacy of most learning style models, and furthermore, that the models often rest on dubious theoretical grounds. According to Stahl, there has been an "utter failure to find that assessing children's learning styles and matching to instructional methods has any effect on their learning." Guy Claxton has questioned the extent that learning styles such as VARK are helpful, particularly as they can have a tendency to label children and therefore restrict learning.

The Critique Made by Coffield, et al.

A non-peer-reviewed literature review by authors from the University of Newcastle upon Tyne identified 71 different theories of learning style. This report, published in 2004, criticized most of the main instruments used to identify an individual's learning style. In conducting the review, Coffield and his colleagues selected 13 of the most influential models for closer study, including most of the models cited on this page. They examined the theoretical origins and terms of each model, and the instrument that was purported to assess types of learning style defined by the model.

They analysed the claims made by the author(s), external studies of these claims, and independent empirical evidence of the relationship between the 'learning style' identified by the instrument and students' actual learning. Coffield's team found that none of the most popular learning style theories had been adequately validated through independent research, leading to the conclusion that the idea of a learning cycle, the consistency of visual, auditory and kinesthetic preferences and the value of matching teaching and learning styles were all "highly questionable."

One of the most widely-known theories assessed by Coffield's team was the learning styles model of Dunn and Dunn, a VAK model. This model is widely used in schools in the United States, and 177 articles have been published in peer-reviewed journals referring to this model. The conclusion of Coffield et al. was as follows:

Despite a large and evolving research programme, forceful claims made for impact are questionable because of limitations in many of the supporting studies and the lack of independent research on the model.

Coffield's Critique of Gregorc's Style Delineator

Coffield's team claimed that another model, Gregorc's Style Delineator (GSD), was "theoretically and psychometrically flawed" and "not suitable for the assessment of individuals."

The Critique Regarding Kolb's Model

Mark K. Smith compiled and reviewed some critiques of Kolb's model in his article, "David A. Kolb on Experiential Learning". According to Smith's research, there are six key issues regarding the model.

They are as follows: 1) the model doesn't adequately address the process of reflection; 2) the claims it makes about the four learning styles are extravagant; 3) it doesn't sufficiently address the fact of different cultural conditions and experiences; 4) the idea of stages/steps doesn't necessarily match reality; 5) it has only weak empirical evidence; 6) the relationship between learning processes and knowledge is more complex than Kolb draws it.

Other Critiques

Coffield and his colleagues and Mark Smith are not alone in their judgements. Demos, a UK think tank, published a report on learning styles prepared by a group chaired by David Hargreaves that included Usha Goswami from Cambridge University and David Wood from the University of Nottingham. The Demos report said that the evidence for learning styles was "highly variable", and that practitioners were "not by any means frank about the evidence for their work."

Cautioning against interpreting neuropsychological research as supporting the applicability of learning style theory, John Geake, Professor of Education at the UK's Oxford Brookes University, and a research collabourator with Oxford University's Centre for Functional Magnetic Resonance Imaging of the Brain, commented that

We need to take extreme care when moving from the lab to the classroom. We do remember things visually and aurally, but information isn't defined by how it was received.

The 2009 APS Critique

The Association for Psychological Science (APS) commissions panels of leading psychologists and cognitive scientists to evaluate topics of public interest, and publishes their reports in Psychological Science in the Public Interest. As one commentator described it, the journal "has an interesting premise. The editor recruits three or four top researchers to review the scientific literature on a complex topic of public import. The researchers must be knowledgeable, but not directly involved in prior research on the topic, so that they will be impartial."

In late 2009, Psychological Science in the Public Interest published a report on the scientific validity of learning styles practices (Pashler et al., 2009). The panel was chaired by Hal Pashler (University of California, San Diego); the other members were Mark McDaniel (Washington University), Doug Rohrer (University of South Florida), and Robert Bjork (University of California, Los Angeles). The panel concluded that an adequate evaluation of the learning styles hypothesis – the idea that optimal learning demands that students receive instruction tailored to their learning styles – requires a particular kind of study. Specifically, students should be grouped into the learning style categories that are being evaluated (e.g., visual learners vs. verbal learners), and then students in each group must be randomly assigned to one of the learning methods (e.g., visual learning or verbal learning), so that some students will be "matched" and others will be "mismatched." At the end of the experiment, all students must sit for the same test. If the learning style hypothesis is correct, then, for example, visual learners should learn better with the visual method, whereas auditory learners should learn better with auditory method. Notably, other authors have reached the same conclusion.

As disclosed in the report, the panel found that studies utilizing this essential research design were virtually absent from the learning styles literature. In fact, the panel was able to find only a few studies with this research design, and all but one of these studies were negative findings-that is, they found that the same learning method was superior for all kinds of students.

Furthermore, the panel noted that, even if the requisite finding were obtained, the benefits would need to be large, and not just statistically significant, before learning style interventions could be recommended as cost-effective. That is, the cost of evaluating and classifying students by their learning style, and then providing customized instruction would need to be more beneficial than other interventions (e.g., one-on-one tutoring, after school remediation programs, etc.).

As a consequence, the panel concluded, "at present, there is no adequate evidence base to justify incorporating learning styles assessments into general educational practice. Thus, limited education resources would better be devoted to adopting other educational practices that have strong evidence base, of which there are an increasing number."

The article incited critical comments from some defenders of learning styles. The Chronicle of Higher Education reported that Robert Sternberg from Tufts University spoke out against the paper: "Several of the most-cited researchers on learning styles, Mr. Sternberg points out, do not appear in the paper's bibliography." This charge was also discussed by Science Magazine, which reported that Pashler said, "Just so...most of [the evidence] is 'weak.'"

Applications: Learning Styles in the Classroom

Various researchers have attempted to provide ways in which learning style theory can take effect in the classroom. Two such scholars are Dr. Rita Dunn and Dr. Kenneth Dunn.

In their book, Teaching Students Through Their Individual Learning Styles: A Practical Approach, they give a background of how learners are affected by elements of the classroom and follow it with recommendations of how to accommodate students' learning strengths. Dunn and Dunn write that "learners are affected by their: (1) immediate environment (sound, light, temperature, and design); (2) own emotionality (motivation, persistence, responsibility, and need for structure or flexibility);

(3) sociological needs (self, pair, peers, team, adult, or varied); and (4) physical needs (perceptual strengths, intake, time, and mobility)".

They analyse other research and make the claim that not only can students identify their preferred learning styles, but that students also score higher on tests, have better attitudes, and are more efficient if they are taught in ways to which they can more easily relate. Therefore, it is to the educator's advantage to teach and test students in their preferred styles.

Although learning styles will inevitably differ among students in the classroom, Dunn and Dunn say that teachers should try to make changes in their classroom that will be beneficial to every learning style. Some of these changes include room redesign, the development of small-group techniques, and the development of Contract Activity Packages. Redesigning the classroom involves locating dividers that can be used to arrange the room creatively (such as having different learning stations and instructional areas), clearing the floor area, and incorporating student thoughts and ideas into the design of the classroom.

Small-group techniques often include a "circle of knowledge" in which students sit in a circle and discuss a subject collaboratively as well as other techniques such as team learning and brainstorming. Contract Activity Packages are educational plans that facilitate learning by using the following elements: 1) clear statement of what the students needs to learn; 2) multisensory resources (auditory, visual, tactile, kinesthetic) that teach the required information; 3) activities through which the newly-mastered information can be used creatively; 4) the sharing of creative projects within small groups of classmates; 5) at least 3 small-group techniques; 6) a pre-test, a self-test, and a post-test. Another scholar who believes that learning styles should have an effect on the classroom is Marilee Sprenger, as evidenced by her book, Differentiation through Learning Styles and Memory.

Sprenger bases her recommendations for classroom learning on three premises: 1) Teachers can be learners, and learners can be teachers. We are all both. 2) Everyone can learn under the right circumstances. 3) Learning is fun! Make it appealing.

She details various ways in which teachers can teach so that students will remember. She categorizes these teaching methods according to which learning style they fit—visual, auditory, or tactile/kinesthetic.

Methods for visual learners include ensuring that students can see words written down, using pictures when describing things, drawing time lines for events in history, writing assignments on the board, using overhead transparencies/ handouts, and writing down instructions.

Methods for auditory learners include repeating difficult words and concepts aloud, incorporating small-group discussion, organizing debates, listening to books on tape, writing oral reports, and encouraging oral interpretation.

Methods for tactile/kinesthetic learners include providing hands-on activities (experiments, etc.), assigning projects, having frequent breaks to allow movement, using visual aids and objects in the lesson, using role play, and having field trips.

By using a variety of teaching methods from each of these categories, teachers are able to accommodate different learning styles. They are also able to challenge students to learn in different ways. Just as Kolb suggested that students who use all 4 approaches of his learning cycle learn more effectively, students who are able to learn through a variety of ways are more effective learners.

Research evaluating the high, intermediate, and moderate levels of teacher-centred versus learner-centred learning styles have found the congruent groups have no significant differences in achievement than incongruent groups (Spoon & Schell, 1998). Furthermore, learning style was significantly different on demographic variables, specifically age, suggesting a change in learning style as one gets older and acquires more experience. While significant age differences did occur, as well as no experimental manipulation of classroom assignment, the findings do call into question the aim of congruent teaching-learning styles in the classroom.

4

Transfer of Learning

Transfer of learning is the study of the dependency of human conduct, learning, or performance on prior experience. The notion was originally introduced as *transfer of practice* by Edward Thorndike and Robert S. Woodworth. They explored how individuals would transfer learning in one context to another context that shared similar characteristics – or more formally how "improvement in one mental function" could influence another related one.

Their theory implied that transfer of learning depends on the proportion to which the learning task and the transfer task are similar, or where "identical elements are concerned in the influencing and influenced function", now known as *identical element theory*. Transfer research has since attracted much attention in numerous domains, producing a wealth of empirical findings and theoretical interpretations. However, there remains considerable controversy about how transfer of learning should be conceptualized and explained, what its probability occurrence is, what its relation is to learning in general, or whether it may be said to exist at all.

Most discussions of transfer to date can be developed from a common operational definition, describing it as the process and the effective extent to which past experiences (also referred to as the transfer source) affect learning and performance in a current novel situation (the transfer target). This, however, is usually where the general consensus between various research approaches ends.

There are a wide variety of viewpoints and theoretical frameworks apparent in the literature. For review purposes, these are categorized as follows:

- a taxonomical approach to transfer research that usually intends to categorize transfer into different types;
- an application domain-driven approach by focusing on developments and contributions of different disciplines that have traditionally been interested in transfer;
- the examination of the psychological scope of transfer models with respect to the psychological functions or faculties that are being regarded; and
- a concept-driven evaluation, which reveals underlying relationships and differences between theoretical and empirical traditions.

Transfer Taxonomies

Of the various attempts to delineate transfer, typological and taxonomic approaches belong to the more common ones. Taxonomies are concerned with distinguishing different types of transfer, and therefore less involved with labelling the actual vehicle of transfer, i.e., what is the explanatory mental unit of transfer that is carried over. Hence, a key problem with many transfer taxonomies is that they offer an excessive number of labels for different types of transfer without engaging in a discussion of the underlying concepts that would justify their distinction; i.e., similarity and the nature of transferred information. This makes it very difficult to appreciate the internal validity of the models.

The Effect-perspective: Positive vs. Negative Transfer

Starting by looking at the effect side of transfer – in terms of the common performance criteria, speed and accuracy – transfer theories distinguish between two broad classes that underlie all other classifications: *negative* and *positive* transfer. Negative transfer refers to the impairment of current learning and performance due to the application of non-adaptive or inappropriate information or behaviour. Therefore, negative transfer is a type of interference effect of prior experience causing a slow-down in learning, completion or solving of a new task when compared to the performance of a hypothetical control group with no respective prior experience. Positive transfer, in contrast, emphasizes the beneficial effects of prior experience on current thinking and action. It is important to understand that the positive and negative effects of transfer are not mutually exclusive, and therefore real-life transfer effects are probably mostly a mixture of both.

The Situation Perspective: Specific vs. General, Near vs. far Transfer

The situation-driven perspective on transfer taxonomies is concerned with describing the relation between transfer source (i.e., the prior experience) and transfer target (i.e., the novel situation). In other words, the notion of novelty of the target situation per se is worthless without specifying the degree of novelty in relation to something that existed before. Butterfield and Nelson (1991), for example, distinguish between *within-task*, *across-task*, and *inventive* transfer. A similar classification approach reappears in many situation-driven transfer taxonomies (e.g., *similar* vs. *different* situations, *example-to-principle* and vice versa, *simple-to-complex* and vice versa) and can be noted as distinctions made along the *specific vs. general* dimension. Mayer and Wittrock discuss transfer under the labels of general "transfer of general skill", "specific transfer of specific skill", "specific transfer of general skill", and "meta-cognitive control of general and specific skills" as a sort of combination of the previous three views.

Haskell's (2001) taxonomy proposes a more gradual scheme of similarity between tasks and situations. It distinguishes between non-specific transfer (i.e., the constructivist idea that all learning builds on present knowledge), application transfer (i.e., the retrieval and use of knowledge on a previously learned task), context transfer (actually meaning context-free transfer between similar tasks), near vs. far transfer, and finally displacement or creative transfer (i.e., an inventive or analytic type of transfer that refers to the creation of a new solution during problem solving as a result of a synthesis of past and current learning experiences). Both near and far transfer are widely used terms in the literature. The former refers to transfer of learning when task and/or context change slightly but remain largely similar, the latter to the application of learning experiences to related but largely dissimilar problems.

The Process Perspective

The *specific vs. general* dimension applies not just to the focus on the relation between source and target, i.e., from where to where is transferred, but also to the question about the transfer process itself, i.e., what is transferred and how. *Reproductive* vs. *productive* transfer are good examples of this type of distinction, whereas reproductive transfer refers to the simple application of knowledge to a novel task, productive transfer implies adaptation; i.e. mutation and enhancement of retained information.

A similar dichotomous distinction is the one between *knowledge* transfer and *problem-solving* transfer. Knowledge transfer takes place when knowing something after learning task *A* facilitates or interferes with the learning process or performance in task *B*. Knowledge used is referred to by many different terms, such as declarative or procedural types (Anderson, 1976), but it means that there are representational elements that suit *A* and *B*. Problem solving transfer, on the other hand, is described as somewhat more "fluid knowledge" transfer, so that experience in solving a problem *A* helps finding a solution to problem *B*. This can mean that the two problems share little in terms of specific declarative knowledge entities or procedures, but call for a similar approach, or solution search strategies (e.g., heuristics and problem solving methods).

The issues discussed in problem-solving transfer literature are also closely related to the concepts of *strategic* and *theoretic* transfer, and cognitive research on analogical reasoning, rule-based thinking and meta-cognition. Indeed, far transfer can be considered as the prototypical type of transfer, and it is closely related to the study of analogical reasoning. Within the problem-solving literature the distinction between specific and general methods is made mostly with reference to Newell and Simon's (1972) strong vs. weak problem solving methods.

Another concern that is frequently addressed in transfer taxonomies is the question of conscious effort. *High-road* vs. *low-road* transfer expresses a distinction between such instances of transfer where active retrieval, mapping, and inference processes take place, as opposed to those instances that occur rather spontaneously or automatically. Hence, low-road transfer concerns frequently employed mental representations and automated, proceduralized knowledge, and occurs preferably in near transfer settings. In contrast, high-road transfer is more conception-driven, and requires cognitive and meta-cognitive effort.

Traditional Fields of Transfer Research

There are a nearly unlimited number of research fields that share some applied interest into the study of transfer, as it pertains to learning in general. Three fields that contributed in most substantial ways to the progress of transfer research, both from a conception and empirical point of view, are the fields of education science, linguistics, and human-computer interaction (HCI). In fact, most transfer research has been conducted in reference to one of these applied settings, rather than in basic cognitive psychological laboratory conditions.

Education Science: Teaching for Transfer

Due to their core concern with learning, educational science and practice are the classic fields of interest regarding transfer research, and probably the prime target for the application of theories. Transfer of learning represents much of the very basis of the educational purpose itself. What is learned inside one classroom about a certain subject should aid in the attainment of related goals in other classroom settings, and beyond that it should be applicable to the student's developmental tasks outside the school; the need for transfer becomes more accentuated. This is because the world educators teach in today is different from the world they themselves experienced as students, and differs equally from the one their students will have to cope with in the future.

By nature of their applied interest, educationalists' main concern has been less with the question of how transfer takes place, and much more with under what conditions, or, that it happens at all. The basic conviction that student's learning and achievement levels depend primarily on learning and achievement prerequisites, has constituted a central part in educational learning theories for quite some time. The major focus in educational transfer studies has, therefore, been on what kind of initial learning enables subsequent transfer: *teaching for transfer*. Research on learning and transfer has identified key characteristics with implications for educational practice.

From Formal Discipline to Meta-cognition

Educational transfer paradigms have been changing quite radically over the last one hundred years. According to the doctrinaire beliefs of the Formal Discipline (Binet, 1899) transfer was initially viewed as a kind of global spread of capabilities accomplished by training basic mental faculties (e.g., logic, attention, memory) in the exercise of suitable subjects, such as Latin or geometry. With the turn of the 20th century, learning, and therefore transfer of learning, was increasingly captured in behavioural and empiricist terms, as in the Connectionist and Associationist theories of Thorndike (e.g., 1932), Guthrie (e.g., 1935), Hull, and Skinner.

Thorndike attacked the Formal Discipline empirically and theoretically and introduced the theory of "identical elements", which is probably still today the most influential conception about transfer. Thorndike's belief that transfer of learning occurs when learning source and learning target share common stimulus-response elements prompted calls for a hierarchical curricular structure in education. "Lower" and specific skills should be learned before more complex skills, which were presumed to consist largely of configuration of basic skills. This small-to-large learning, also referred to as part-to-whole or vertical transfer, has been popular with theories of learning hierarchies (Gagné, 1968).

It has later been challenged from conceptualistic point of views, which argue that learning is not just an accumulation of pieces of knowledge (i.e., rote memorization), but rather a process and product of active construction of cognitive knowledge structures. Knowledge, from a constructivist perspective, was no more believed to be a simple transfer by generalization to all kinds of situations and tasks that contain similar components.

The critical issue was the identification of similarities in general principles and concepts behind the facades of two dissimilar problems; i.e., transfer by insight. This idea became popular in the Gestaltists' view on transfer, and, in combination with growing interest in learners as self activated problem-solvers (Bruner, 1986), encouraged the search for abstract problem-solving methods and mental schemata, which serve as analogy-enhancing transfer-bridges between different task situations.

Emerging from these developments, a new theme started to dominate educationalists' research in transfer: meta-cognition. In contrast to classical knowledge forms like declarative and procedural knowledge, different types of meta-knowledge and meta-cognitive skills such as strategic knowledge, heuristics, self-monitoring skills, and self-regulation quickly became the road to learning and transfer. Characterized as self-conscious management and organization of acquired knowledge (Brown, 1987) it is evident that meta-cognitive awareness of task features, problem structures, and solution methods makes relations between different situations cognitively salient: only an individual who learns from learning, learns for future learning. Soini (1999) developed on the same core ideas an examination of the preconditions for active transfer. Her emphasis is on the active and self-reflected management of knowledge to increase its accessibility. To some researchers, meta-cognition and transfer have become so entangled that the argument was generated that only the measurement of positive transfer effects truly supports inferences that meta-cognitive learning has taken place.

The Generality Predicament: Return to the Specificity View

Ever since the introduction of the meta-knowledge theme in education science, transfer discussions have been oscillating between the position taken by those representing the meta-cognitive view and those who stress that generic knowledge forms alone do not allow an effective transfer of learning. When knowledge stays "on the tip of the tongue", just knowing that one knows a solution to a problem, without being able to transfer specific declarative knowledge (i.e., know-what) or automated procedural knowledge (i.e., know-how), does not suffice. Specific teaching of the cognitive and behavioural requisites for transfer marked in principle a return to the identical element view, and can be summarized with Dettermann's (1993) conclusion that transfer does not substantially go beyond the restricted boundaries of what has been specifically taught and learned. The basic transfer paradigms in educational psychology keep replicating themselves, and fundamental promotion of transfer itself is seen to be achievable through sensibilization of students by creating a general culture and "a spirit of transfer" inside the classroom on the one hand, and by allowing concrete learning from transfer models on the other (Haskell, 2001).

Learning and Transfer: Implications for Educational Practice

A modern view of transfer in the context of educational practice shows little need to distinguish between the general and specific paradigms, recognizing the role of both identical elements and metacognition. In this view, the work of Bransford, Brown and Cocking (1999) identified four key characteristics of learning as applied to transfer. They are:

1. The necessity of initial learning;
2. The importance of abstract and contextual knowledge;
3. The conception of learning as an active and dynamic process; and
4. The notion that all learning is transfer.

First, the necessity of initial learning for transfer specifies that mere exposure or memorization is not learning; there must be understanding. Learning as understanding takes time, such that expertise with deep, organized knowledge improves transfer. Teaching that emphasizes how to use knowledge or that improves motivation should enhance transfer.

Second, while knowledge anchored in context is important for initial learning, it is also inflexible without some level of abstraction that goes beyond the context. Practices to improve transfer include having students specify connections across multiple contexts or having them develop general solutions and strategies that would apply beyond a single-context case.

Third, learning should be considered an active and dynamic process, not a static product. Instead of one-shot tests that follow learning tasks, students can improve transfer by engaging in assessments that extend beyond current abilities. Improving transfer in this way requires instructor prompts to assist students – such as dynamic assessments – or student development of metacognitive skills without prompting.

Finally, the fourth characteristic defines all learning as transfer. New learning builds on previous learning, which implies that teachers can facilitate transfer by activating what students know and by making their thinking visible. This includes addressing student misconceptions and recognizing cultural behaviours that students bring to learning situations.

A student-learning centred view of transfer embodies these four characteristics. With this conception, teachers can help students transfer learning not just between contexts in academics, but also to common home, work, or community environments.

Inter-language Transfer

Another traditional field of applied research is inter-language transfer. Here, the central questions were: how does learning one language (L1) facilitate or interfere (Weinreich, 1953) with the acquisition of and proficiency in a second language (L2), and how does the training and use of L2, in turn, affect L1? Several variations of this conception of inter-language transfer can be found in the literature, also referred to as mother tongue influence or cross language interference. What makes inter-language transfer a complex and valuable research matter is the fact that language knowledge skills continuously develop.

This is so for L1, as well as for L2, when only bilingualism is considered, while alternately at least one of them is continuously in use. This has led to the development of very different models of how languages are mentally represented and managed, with L1 and L2 seen as two independent or autonomous mental systems, as being represented in a single unified system, and as rooting in a common underlying, multi-lingual conceptual base.

Human-Computer Interaction: Designing for Transfer

A third research area that has produced a variety of transfer models and empirical results can be located within the field of Human-Computer Interaction (HCI). With the start of the user age in the 1980s, HCI and all kinds of virtual environments have, in many ways, become something like psychological micro-worlds for cognitive research. This is naturally also reflected in the study of transfer.

Developments in favour of cognitive approaches to transfer research were especially accelerated by rapid changes in modern lifestyles, resulting in a virtual upsurge of cognitive demands in interaction with technology. Thus, the call was on clearly domain-focused cognitive models to study the way users learn and perform when interacting with information technological systems.

Transfer based on the user Complexity Theory

Thorough investigations of cognitive skills involved in HCI tasks have their origins with the research on text editing. The offspring of this type of research were computational cognitive models and architectures of various degrees of sophistication, suitable for all kinds of man-machine interaction studies, as well as studies outside of the HCI domain. The original examples for these have become Kieras and Polson's (1985) user complexity theory (later rephrased as cognitive complexity theory) and the GOMS family (i.e., Goals, Operators, Methods, Selection) rules based on the Model Human Processor framework. All of these models have their roots in the basic principles of production systems and can be comprehended with the help of ends-means-selections and If-Then-rules, combined with the necessary declarative and procedural knowledge.

The crucial perspective for transfer became that of technology design. By applying cognitive models, scientists and practitioners aimed at minimizing the amount and complexity of new knowledge necessary to understand and perform tasks on a device, without trading off too much utility value. A key responsibility was given to skill and knowledge transfer. Due to the fact that the cognitive complexity theory is a psychological theory of transfer applied to HCI, the central question was how these models, united under the GOMS umbrella, can be used to explain and predict transfer of learning.

The basic transfer-relevant assumptions of the emerging models were that production rules are cognitive units, they are all equally difficult to learn, and that learned rules can be transferred to a new task without any cost. Because learning time for any task is seen as a function of the number of new rules that the user must learn, total learning time is directly reduced by inclusion of productions the user is already familiar with. The basic message of the cognitive complexity theory is to conceptualize and induce transfer from one system to another by function of shared production rules, which is a new interpretation of Thorndike's identical element premise and eventually echoed in Singley and Anderson's (1989) theory of transfer.

A practical implication of the procedural communality principle has been formulated by Lewis and Rieman (1993), who suggest something like "transfer of design" on the side of the industry: "You should find existing interfaces that work for users and then build ideas from those interfaces into your systems as much as practically and legally possible."

Emergence of Holistic Views of Use

Discouraged by the confined character of the GOMS-related transfer models, many research groups began to import and advance new concepts, such as schemata principles and general methods; a general development encouraged by the emerging cognitive approach to transfer that was also witnessed by other applied fields. Bhavnani and John (2000) analysed different computer applications and strived to identify such user strategies (i.e., general methods to perform a certain task), which generalize across three distinct computer domains (word processor, spreadsheet, and CAD). Their conclusive argument is that "strategy-conducive systems could facilitate the transfer of knowledge". Other research groups' authors that assessed the questions about how people learn in interaction with information systems, evaluated the usefulness of metaphors and how these should be taken into consideration when designing for exploratory environments.

As researchers became increasingly interested in the quality of a user's knowledge representation, mental models and adaptive expertise, as knowledge and skills which generalizes across different contexts of complex problem-solving tasks, became of paramount concern.

In contrast to the knowledge of strategies, the accentuation shifted towards strategic knowledge (Gott et al., 1993). Gott et al. demonstrated that surface similarities between different technical domains alone did not essentially facilitate transfer of learning because they limited the user's flexibility in the adaptation process. In accordance with the ideas of schema-based and meta-cognitive transfer, the authors further formulated that "robust performance is one in which procedural steps are not just naked, rule-based actions, but instead are supported by explanations that perform like theories to enable adaptiveness".

Gott et al. (1993) finally noted that mental models might be powerful instruments to analyse similarities between tasks as represented within a formulated cognitive architecture. However, they do not explain what particular similarities and differences are sufficiently salient from the individual's mental point of view to affect transfer of learning, nor can they predict motivational or emotional conditions of transfer that are essential requisites for every learning process.

Psychological Scope of Transfer Research

As transfer pertains to the dependency of an individual's experience and behaviour on prior experience and behaviour, its research must involve all aspects of psychological functioning, ranging from physical activities, cognitive processes (e.g., thinking), emotion and connation, to its social and environmental dimensions. Although the cognitive connotation of skill has largely emerged as the dominant conception, is not truly possible to appreciate the real meaning of skill without linking it to its motor or behavioural origins, and without extending its scope to include socio-emotional dimensions.

Cognitive Transfer

The greatest bulk of theoretical and empirical research published in recent decades has been done with reference to transfer of cognitive skills and knowledge; for example with regard to problem-solving and analogical reasoning. The cognitive shift in psychology showed a great impact on the evolution of new and refined concepts, methods, theories, and empirical data in transfer research, and it put the investigation of the phenomenon back on the general research agenda after a clear decline in relevant scientific publications between 1960 and the 1980s.

Cognition-oriented theories reinforced a series of key research frameworks to the study of transfer, including production systems, analogical reasoning, mental models, schema, heuristics, and meta-cognition. Specifically, research on transfer has profited from three main drivers within the study of human cognition: these are analogy, the computational metaphor, and the intensified interests with the nature and quality of mental representations.

Metaphor and Analogy

Metaphor refers to the use of a word or phrase to denote an object or concept not in a literary sense, but rather by suggesting an enhancement or replacement of the understanding and interpretation of the targeted object with the metaphor. The object we are indicating by a metaphor is holistically mapped onto the metaphor – and essentials of the metaphor's content are therefore transferred to the representation of the denoted object. The term metaphor comes from the Greek word "metapherein", meaning "to transfer".

In contrast to metaphor, the concepts of similarity and analogy are actually less inherently linked to the mental nature of transfer because they refer only to the circumstance of the relation between two representations. Here, object P is "seen" to be like Q (according to the Latin word "similis", meaning "like") in certain aspects. By inferring that there might be other similar states between P and Q to be found, P can be used as an analogy for Q. Transfer by analogy is not understood in the holistic way as is the case with metaphorical substitution of meaning, but rather in a channeled fashion due to aspectual (perceived or inferred) resemblance between P and Q.

Nevertheless, research on analogy, in all its nuances, proved to be most influential to the conceptualization of cognitive transfer. Many cognitive scientists, as well as road leading philosophers, consider analogy to be one if not the core principle of human thinking and thought. According to these views transfer has to be placed within the framework of analogy, rather than the other way around. Although research into analogy frequently penetrates traditional cognitive boundaries, for instance by involving emotionality and social cognition, it is usually associated with analogical reasoning and problem solving, both of which are closely related to the issue of transfer (Robertson, 2001).

Computational Models

The nearly unifying cognitive metaphor is known as the information-processing approach, and with the understanding of the learning individual inspired by the General Problem Solver. Cognitive research brought forth a variety of computational models and methods to study and simulate knowledge acquisition, retention, and use. This also provided a new framework for transfer theory development, particularly Singley and Anderson's (1985, 1989) cognitive account of Thorndike's identical element theory. Emphasis is put on the classic knowledge form distinction between declarative and procedural knowledge as well as between weak problem-solving methods (i.e., generalized, domain-independent knowledge and skills) and strong problem-solving methods.

Anderson (1995) criticized preceding research on analogical transfer for its dominant focus on traits of the source and target in terms of declarative knowledge, instead of performance orientated processing aspects. He points out for skill acquisition that declarative memory plays only initially a significant role and is in the course of practice quickly replaced by procedural memory; encoded and strengthened in the form use specific production rules (also called the effect of Einstellung; Luchins, 1942). The performance benefits from already compiled production rules are believed to be automatic, errorless, independent of each other, and largely independent of contextual variations of tasks within the same knowledge domain. The transfer distance between the performances in two tasks, or the solutions to two problems, is assumed to decrease proportionally to the number of share specific procedures. This procedural "proportionality-relationship" (Allport, 1937) is in effect the most straightforward interpretation of the Greek term of analogy, meaning proportion, and has in ideal cases of procedure-to-procedure transfer settings, been shown to make relatively good predictions. Anderson's assessment echoed the fact that research on human learning and problem-solving started to put increasing emphasis on issues like cognitive skills and mental operators, which found implementations in a variety of cognitive architectures such as Soar, CE+, and the development of several versions of Anderson's ACT theory.

In recent decades, cognitive scientists have developed numerous computational models of analogy such as the Structure Mapping Engine (SME) and the "model of similarity-based retrieval", Analogical Coherence Models Learning and Inference with Schemas and Analogies to name just a few. Within LISA's cognitive architecture, for instance, analogical mapping and retrieval functions are based on the premise that structural units in long-term memory (i.e., propositions, sub-propositions, objects and predicates) of source and target are represented by a collection of shared activated semantic units.

Motor Transfer

Senso-motor skills are an essential ingredient in learning and performance in most tasks and can be categorized into continuous (e.g., tracking), discrete, or procedural movements. Proceduralized motor skills have recently become the most referred to because they are consistent with the models of cognitive architectures and because they are seen as relevant to nearly all physical interactions with the environment, as is the case in transfer situations.

Open-loop and Closed-loop Processes

Before the birth of the proceduralization concept, theories of motor learning have been influenced by the open-loop vs.

closed loop system distinction. The original formulation of the closed-loop view on motor performance and learning build on the momentum of internal feedback from executed movements, which allow for error detection and adjustment of actions through the process of contrasting perceptual traces against memory representations (Adams, 1971). Motor learning was accordingly seen as dependent on repetition, accuracy, refinement, and synchronization of a series of called-up movement units (i.e., open-loop structures) that are regulated by closed-loop structures.

In response to this view, a different open-loop perspective emerged, namely the one of motor programs (Schmidt, 1975). The learning of motor skills was hereby seen in terms of the build-up, modification, and strengthening of schematic relations among movement parameters and outcomes. This learning results in the construction "generalized motor programs" (i.e., a sequence or class of automated actions) that are triggered by associative stimuli, habit strengths, and re-enforcers, and can be executed without delay.

Both theories have their origin with Thorndike's "Law of Effect", because the formation of motor behaviour is essentially dependent on knowledge of the outcome of the action taken. This is regardless of whether the essence of motor skills is seen with specific movements or parameters in a schematic motor program.

Another classic theme that was revived in the literature on transfer of motor skill is the part-to-whole transfer of training. It emerged because it is nearly inconceivable to learn a highly complex motor task as a complete entity. Much like in curriculum research, positive generalization of skill units into coherent task situations has been very limited. Particularly, it was found that initial whole-task performances after part-task training remains seriously impaired due to difficulties in the time-sharing of the activities. Whole task training remains generally superior to the part-task-whole-task transfer approach of learning.

Finally, motor research provided some evidence for context- and task-independent savings in learning effort on a new task that seems to be explainable by heightened plasticity and functional reorganisation in the senso-motor neural network system. This is naturally in line with the formal discipline argument.

Socio-emotional Dimensions of Transfer

Motor and cognitive transfer are, in many respects, inseparable from issues of emotion and motivation, just as cognitive research in general must embrace affective dimensions of experience and behaviour. This basic awareness has a long tradition in psychology and in the philosophical works of Aristoteles, Descartes, and Hume, but has to date not been sufficiently regarded in cognitive research.

Naturally, emotions and especially motivation have always been closely linked to learning in educational psychology, but their role was generally conceptualized as more of an assistant or moderating nature, i.e., in facilitating vs. hindering cognition. Approaches that focus on the same kind of relation between affect and transfer belong to the group that study main effects of affective beliefs on cognition in general, and in particular on transfer-relevant moderation and mediation effects of "will" on "skill". In short: "Knowing how to solve problems and believing that you know how to solve problems are often dissonant".

In a review of research on motivation and transfer, Pugh and Bergin (2006) concluded that motivational factors can influence transfer, although the research is limited and not wholly consistent. They found that mastery goals were more consistently linked to transfer success than were performance goals. They also found that interest was related to transfer success when this interest was associated with the learning content. However, when the interest was related to peripheral things, such as seductive details in text, it inhibited transfer success.

In addition, they found evidence that transfer success was positively related to self-efficacy. Finally, the reviewers proposed that the transfer process is affected by the presence of an explicit goal of achieving transfer. Pugh and Bergin (2006) predicted that motivational factors influence transfer in three ways. First, they can influence the quality of initial learning in ways that support transfer. Second, they can influence the initiation of transfer attempts, particularly in situations where individuals have an opportunity to apply learning but are not required to. Third, motivational factors can influence individuals' persistence when engaged in transfer tasks.

Transfer of Emotions

Emotional transfer must, however, be regarded as a distinct aspect or type of transfer itself, i.e., one where the experiential relation between two situations is of affective nature (e.g., affective connotations and skills). It occurs wherever previously experienced feelings and attitudes toward a situation, object, or task are re-evoked in a current confrontation with related "symbols".

The preferred emotional transfer model to date has been the one of analogical inference, e.g., if you like product X, and product Y is similar to X, then you will probably like Y. Thagard and Shelley (2001) criticized the simplicity of analogical inference based on mere comparison of objects and properties and proposed a more complex model that accounts for structures of analogies, e.g., by including relations and causality structures. Their emotional coherence theory implemented this idea in the form of the HOTCO model (standing for "hot coherence") by drawing on assumptions made in preceding models, including explanatory coherence (ECHO), conceptual coherence (IMP), analogical coherence (ACME), and deliberative coherence (DECO).

Conceptual Foundation of Transfer Research

The cognitive shift in psychology encouraged the research of mental forms and processes engaged in learning and transfer rather than the simple modification of overt reproductional behaviour; a change in viewpoint that the early Gestalt psychologists and constructivists such as Köhler, Wertheimer, or Piaget had already propagated for a couple of decades. The investigation of cognitive dimensions in transfer quickly became the major driver of research across applied domains and cognitive transfer emerged in many ways as the quintessential view of transfer in general.

Mental Representations and Transfer: Common Element-based vs. Schema-based Approaches

The majority of mental processes studied in research on human cognition have one thing in common: they all pertain in one way or another to the construction of mental representations. This is true, for instance, for perceiving, learning, problem-solving, reasoning and thinking, and recalling, as much as it is true for the phenomenon of transfer.

Although research on mental representation has been utterly manifold, two main traditions can be discerned. Some researchers have regarded mental representations in terms of abstract schemata, frames, patterns or mental models, while others have paid attention to semantic information and propositional nature of mental representations. These differential conceptualizations have, in general, been driven by distinct psychological paradigms adopted, such as Associationism and Connectionism, Behaviourism, Gestaltism, and Cognitivism.

GOMS and ACT-based procedural transfer theses are a good example of modern explanations fitting the atomistic and mechanistic nature of the Connectionist paradigm, i.e., by seeing transfer as an effect of commonality in semantic conditions-action-goal structures, mainly instantiated as If-Then production rule associations overlap. This view on transfer clearly replaced Behaviourist explanatory concepts of stimuli and response with more sophisticated mental concepts that serve as units of transfer. The cognitive architecture background also added important processing capabilities and some degree of flexibility concerning the identicality constraint (e.g., declarative-to-procedural, and declarative-to-declarative transfer). It did not, however, essentially defy the common underlying common element-based thought model of transfer.

Both the original habitual response-based idea of common element transfer as well as the modern production rule compilation and knowledge encapsulation account are in their core assumptions refuted by Gestaltists' theories. Koffka's (1925) scrutiny of Thorndike's (1911, 1913) and Köhler's (1917) arguments and findings revealed that explanations of learning and transfer based on the notions of association and automation fall short of explicating the nature of mental activity even for simple problem-solving tasks. Novel explanatory concepts were needed to account for "learning by understanding" (Katona, 1940) and problem-solving transfer. These were found with reference to the organization and structure of knowledge, abstraction and general principle inferences, the goal-and meaning-directedness of thinking and its holistic nature, and functional relations. Because this tradition of investigating transfer is based on Gestaltist ideas, they could be summarized under the header of schema-based theories of transfer.

In accord with the traditions regarding research on mental representation, two mainstream explanatory models for transfer can be concluded to date. One is the model of *common element-based* transfer, rooting in Thorndikean ideas, which explains transfer as confined to elementary correspondences between a primary and a secondary learning situation, such as procedures and their automated effect. The other model emerging from the Gestalt tradition can be labeled *schema-based* or analogical transfer, emphasizing elementary loosened structural or principle/rule-based coherence between transfer source and target. They continued Judd's (1908) line of work, resulting in further accentuation of "insightful" transfer, using terms like knowledge structures and schemata, solution principles, and functionality.

The problem is that as far as *transfer of learning* in both traditions refers to one and the same phenomenon, there can not be a situation with two incompatible theoretical frameworks standing side-by-side. Conceptual resolution in some form is clearly imperative. Several efforts have been made in recent years to review and revive transfer research, and to resolve controversies, but empirical justification is still in early stages.

The Similarity Predicament

The notion of similarity has been particularly problematic for transfer research for a number of reasons. The main problem is that *similarity* implies *dissimilarity*, i.e., although two instances may in parts be identical, they are after all also different.

First, similarity has been the cause for debate about how to distinguish transfer of learning from learning or problem-solving. The distinction of transfer of learning from learning is usually done with reference to a cut-off point on the similarity dimensions, by which the relation between a current and a past situation is estimated. The more similar two situations are rated, the more probable it becomes that any witnessed improvement in performance is due to learning rather than to transfer. The same logic is true in the other direction of the transfer-learning dimension. The discussion on the dissimilarity-similarity distinction has the ambivalent character of being conducted in reference to a dimensional or polar conception and dichotomous model interchangeably. Learning is usually implicitly awarded its own place at the periphery of transfer taxonomies that are based on near-far distinctions, and this raises the question whether it would not be sounder to concentrate more intensively on the common cognitive bases of learning and transfer than on some conceptual distinction between them.

For instance, while Butterfield and Nelson's (1991) categorization is intuitively appealing, it also conveys some typical problems and challenges. For instance, if transfer is to a task or situation which is so similar to a previously experienced one that it actually can be considered as the same task (i.e., within-task transfer), then how do we distinguish transfer from learning in general? The corresponding deliberation is that learning refers to mental processes involved in the course of a repeated confrontation with a certain type of task or situation, of which the single accounts can never be identical. Butterfield and Nelson have themselves not been blind to this argument, but they still refrain from equating learning and transfer as proposed by Salomon and Perkins. Across-task transfer, according to Butterfield and Nelson's (1991) model, refers to the application of a learned principle in a new task situation which is superficially different, yet functionally equivalent to the prior one. Inventive transfer, finally, is used to describe incidences where learners cannot make use of the same solution principles previously learned, but have to develop a new solution on the grounds of similarities and critical differences of source and target task. Understandably, Butterfield and Nelson pose the question to whether this should be rather characterized as problem-solving than transfer.

Second, transfer theories are built on the premise of identical constituents between transfer source and target, while differences are usually seen as cause of transfer failure. In spite of the manifold attempts to dissociate from one-to-one similarity concepts, the identicality constraint continued to produce most of the headaches to cognitive scientists, especially in the area of analogy research. Considering the diversity of transfer conditions, application domains, and contextual dependency of analogical thought, it is not surprising that few psychologists have conclusively put their fingers on what seems as the essence of analogical relations. While the talk of "sameness" and "transpositional similarity" appeals to common sense, much about what similarity means precisely, how it is established mentally, and, therefore, what justifies analogical reasoning remains unclear.

Overall, similarity constraint factors have been identified with respect to predicates, objects and propositions, relational and structural isomorphism, procedural matches, in relation to purpose or goals of tasks or episodes under analogical consideration, as well as in relation to the level or type of mental engagement. As noted, analogical transfer and analogical memory recall has been demonstrated with respect to similarity in superficial traits rather than in respect to relational analogy or structural correspondence, and has been best attained in within-domain and near-transfer settings. In spite of the claim that similarity between analogs fundamentally refers to the qualitative "alikeness" in the relations that hold within one common structure of mental objects, and not simply to the quantitative surface similarity of properties or features from which analogy is then inferred.

Nevertheless, if transfer by analogy is not to stumble over the boundaries of identical matches – be these superficial attributes between target and retrieved source, elements of declarative knowledge, procedural memory content, relational aspects, or otherwise – then the question what similarity means in the context of dissimilarity should be resolved. The focus should be on explicating the sameness in mental representations and assessing their impact on transfer, and not so much on the question "how similar is similar enough to be considered as an analog?"

Programmed Learning

Programmed Learning or Programmed Instruction is a learning methodology or technique first proposed by the behaviourist B. F. Skinner in 1958. According to Skinner, the purpose of programmed learning is to "manage human learning under controlled conditions". Programmed learning has three elements: (1) it delivers information in small bites, (2) it is self-paced by the learner, and (3) it provides immediate feedback, both positive and negative, to the learner. It was popular in the late 1960s and through the 1970s, but pedagogical interest was lost in the early 1980s as it was difficult to implement and its limitations were not well understood by practitioners. It was revived in the 1990s in the computerized Integrated Learning System (ILS) approach, primarily in the business and managerial context. Programmed learning remains popular in self-teaching textbooks.

The methodology involves self-administered and self-paced learning, in which the student is presented with information in small steps often referred to as "frames". Each frame contains a small segment of the information to be learned, and a question which the student must answer. After each frame the student uncovers, or is directed to, additional information based on an incorrect answer, or positive feedback for a correct answer.

Programmed Instruction

It typically consists of self-teaching with the aid of a specialized textbook or teaching machine that presents material structured in a logical and empirically developed sequence or sequences. Programmed instruction may be presented by a teacher as well, and it has been argued that the principles of Programmed Instruction can improve classic lectures and textbooks. Programmed instruction allows students to progress through a unit of study at their own rate, checking their own answers and advancing only after answering correctly. In one simplified form of PI, after each step, they are presented with a question to test their comprehension, then are immediately shown the correct answer or given additional information. However the objective of the instructional programming is to present the material in very small increments. The more sophisticated forms of programmed instruction may have the questions or tasks programmed well enough that the presentation and test model—an extropolation from traditional and classical instruction is not necessarily utilized.

Personalized System of Instruction

Personalized System of Instruction or (PSI), developed by Fred S. Keller, was another idea for how to incorporate programmed learning into the classroom.

Errorless Discrimination

Programmed instruction resulted from early efforts to implement Skinner's basic research findings on learning at Harvard that led to "errorless discrimination" techniques being developed. Programmed instruction had some early success in aphasia rehabilation.

Programmed Instruction Today

While not popular, programmed instruction continues to be used today. Recently, the application of programmed instruction principles was applied to training in computer programs and combined with Benjamin Bloom's taxonomy to teach college students. Some have argued that there is a resurgence of research on programmed instruction due to use of computers and the internet.

5

Learning in Children

A young child is a human being who, unlike his elders, is still engaged in the fundamental process of developing the major portion of his mental capacity. At least eighty percent of his intellectual aptitude (not his rote knowledge) is acquired during the first six years of his life. During this critical period, his brain grows and develops in accordance with his exercise of his mind and the intellectual stimulation provided by his environment. Denying a child's developing mind the proper stimulation, by postponing his education until the age of six, is analogous to denying his growing body the proper diet, by postponing his consumption of nutritional food until the age of eighteen!

A child of average genetic endowment, in an average environment, tends to achieve what are commonly called "a normal academic aptitude" and "a normal psychological profile" (assuming that culturally unbiased statistical parameters are employed). However, this same child, in an environment carefully prepared to satisfy fundamental intellectual and psychological requirements of his developing mind, tends to achieve what are commonly called "an abnormally superior academic aptitude" and "a psychological profile abnormally high in independence, empathy, and creativity".

A child, who has volitional consciousness, develops his intellectual capacity through a process of *self-programming* (not training) and acquires his factual knowledge through a process of *discovery* (not indoctrination). Through perception, identification, and integration of the data provided by his senses, he *can* exercise his own free will to come to *know facts of reality*. In an environment systematically ordered and enriched in varied sensory stimuli, if adults refrain from trammeling ("for his own good") his natural, childlike curiosity and self-confidence, he probably *will*.

Several theories of child development and learning have influenced discussions of school readiness. Three have had profound impact on kindergarten readiness practices. These three theories include the maturationist, environmentalist, and constructivist perspectives of development (Powell, 1991).

Maturationist Theory

The maturationist theory was advanced by the work of Arnold Gessell. Maturationists believe that development is a biological process that occurs automatically in predictable, sequential stages over time (Hunt, 1969). This perspective leads many educators and families to assume that young children will acquire knowledge naturally and automatically as they grow physically and become older, provided that they are healthy.

School readiness, according to maturationists, is a state at which all healthy young children arrive when they can perform tasks such as reciting the alphabet and counting; these tasks are required for learning more complex tasks such as reading and arithmetic.

Because development and school readiness occur naturally and automatically, maturationists believe the best practices are for parents to teach young children to recite the alphabet and count while being patient and waiting for children to become ready for kindergarten.

If a child is developmentally unready for school, maturationists might suggest referrals to transitional kindergartens, retention, or holding children out of school for an additional year (DeCos, 1997). These practices are sometimes used by schools, educators, and parents when a young child developmentally lags behind his or her peers. The young child's underperformance is interpreted as the child needing more time to acquire the knowledge and skills needed to perform at the level of his or her peers.

Environmentalist Theory

Theorists such as John Watson, B.F. Skinner, and Albert Bandura contributed greatly to the environmentalist perspective of development. Environmentalists believe the child's environment shapes learning and behaviour; in fact, human behaviour, development, and learning are thought of as reactions to the environment. This perspective leads many families, schools, and educators to assume that young children develop and acquire new knowledge by reacting to their surroundings.

Kindergarten readiness, according to the environmentalists, is the age or stage when young children can respond appropriately to the environment of the school and the classroom (e.g., rules and regulations, curriculum activities, positive behaviour in group settings, and directions and instructions from teachers and other adults in the school). The ability to respond appropriately to this environment is necessary for young children to participate in teacher-initiated learning activities. Success is dependent on the child following instructions from the teacher or the adult in the classroom. Many environmentalist-influenced educators and parents believe that young children learn best by rote activities, such as reciting the alphabet over and over, copying letters, and tracing numbers. This viewpoint is evident in kindergarten classrooms where young children are expected to sit at desks arranged in rows and listen attentively to their teachers. At home, parents may provide their young children with workbooks containing such activities as coloring or tracing letters and numbers—activities that require little interaction between parent and child. When young children are unable to respond appropriately to the classroom and school environment, they often are labeled as having some form of learning disabilities and are tracked in classrooms with curriculum designed to control their behaviours and responses.

Constructivist Theory

The constructivist perspective of readiness and development was advanced by theorists such as Jean Piaget, Maria Montessori, and Lev Vygotsky. Although their work varies greatly, each articulates a similar context of learning and development. They are consistent in their belief that learning and development occur when young children interact with the environment and people around them (Hunt, 1969). Constructivists view young children as active participants in the learning process. In addition, constructivists believe young children initiate most of the activities required for learning and development. Because active interaction with the environment and people are necessary for learning and development, constructivists believe that children are ready for school when they can initiate many of the interactions they have with the environment and people around them.

Constructivist-influenced schools and educators pay a lot of attention to the physical environment and the curriculum of the early childhood classroom. Kindergarten classrooms often are divided into different learning centers and are equipped with developmentally appropriate materials for young children to play with and manipulate. Teachers and adults have direct conversations with children, children move actively from centre to another, and daily activities are made meaningful through the incorporation of children's experiences into the curriculum. At home, parents engage their young children in reading and storytelling activities and encourage children's participation in daily household activities in a way that introduces such concepts as counting and language use. In addition, parents may provide young children with picture books containing very large print, and toys that stimulate interaction (such as building blocks and large puzzles). When a young child encounters difficulties in the learning process, the constructivist approach is neither to label the child nor to retain him or her; instead, constructivists give the child some individualized attention and customize the classroom curriculum to help the child address his or her difficulties.

Today, most researchers have come to understand child development and the learning process as articulated by the constructivists. However, this view has not been widely translated into practice. Many kindergarten teachers and parents still believe that young children are not ready for school unless they can recite the alphabet, count, and have the ability to follow instructions from adults.

Learning by Teaching

In professional education, learning by teaching (German: Lernen durch Lehren, short *LdL*) designates currently the method by Jean-Pol Martin that allows pupils and students to prepare and to teach lessons, or parts of lessons. Learning by teaching should not be confused with presentations or lectures by students, as students not only convey a certain content, but also choose their own methods and didactic approaches in teaching classmates that subject. Neither should it be confused with tutoring, because the teacher has intensive control of, and gives support for, the learning process in learning by teaching as against other methods.

History

Seneca the Younger told in his letters to Lucilius that we are learning if we teach (epistulae morales I, 7, 8): *docendo discimus* (lat.: "by teaching we are learning"). At all times in the history of schooling there have been phases where students were mobilized to teach their peers. Frequently, this was to reduce the number of teachers needed, so one teacher could instruct 200 students. However, since the end of the 19th century, a number of didactic-pedagogic reasons for student teaching have been put forward.

Students as Teachers in order to Spare Teachers

In 1795 the Scotsman Andrew Bell wrote a book about the mutual teaching method that he observed and used himself in Madras. The Londoner Joseph Lancaster picked up this idea and implemented it in his schools. This method was introduced 1815 in France in the "écoles mutuelles", because of the increasing number of students who had to be trained and the lack of teachers. After the French revolution of 1830, 2,000 "écoles mutuelles" were registered in France. Due to a political change in the French administration, the number of écoles mutuelles shrank rapidly and these schools were marginalized. It is important to stress that the learning level in the Bell-Lancaster-schools was very low. In hindsight, the low level can probably be attributed to the fact that the teaching-process was delegated entirely to the tutors and that the teachers did not supervise and support the teaching process.

Students as Teachers in order to Improve the Learning-process

The first attempts using the learning by teaching method in order to improve learning were started at the end of the 19th century.

Selective Descriptions and Researches

Systematic research – though initially only descriptive – began in the middle of the 20th century. For instance Gartner 1971 in the US, in Germany Krüger 1975, Wolfgang Steining 1985, Udo Kettwig 1986, Theodor F. Klassen 1988, Ursula Drews 1997 and A. Renkl 1997

LdL as a Comprehensive Method

The method received broader recognition starting in the early eighties, when Jean-Pol Martin developed the concept systematically for the teaching of French as a foreign language and gave it a theoretical background in numerous publications. 1987 he founded a network of more than a thousand teachers that employed learning by teaching (the specifical name: LdL = "Lernen durch Lehren") in many different subjects, documented its successes and approaches and presented their findings in various teacher training sessions. From 2001 on LdL has gained more and more supporters as a result of educational reform movements started throughout Germany.

Learning by Teaching by Martin (LdL)

LdL by Martin consists of two components: a general anthropological one and a subject-related one.

- The anthropological basis of LdL is related to the pyramid or hierarchy of needs introduced by Abraham Maslow, which consists, from base to peak, of 1) physiological needs, 2) safety/security, 3) social/love/ belonging, 4) esteem/self-confidence and 5) being/growth through self-actualization and self-transcendence. Personal growth moves upward through hierarchy, whereas regressive forces tend to push downward. The act of successful learning, preparation and teaching of others contributes to items 3 through 5 above. Facing the problems of our world today and in the future, it is essential to mobilize as many intellectual resources as possible, which happens in LdL lessons in a special way. Democratic skills are promoted through the communication and socialization necessary for this shared discovery and construction of knowledge.

- The subject related component (in foreign language teaching) of LdL aims to negate the alleged contradiction between the three main components: automatization of speech-related behaviour, teaching of cognitively internalized contents and authentic interaction/ communication.

The LdL Approach

After intensive preparation by the teacher, students become responsible for their own learning and teaching. The new material is divided into small units and student groups of not more than three people are formed. Each group familiarizes itself with a strictly defined area of new material and gets the assignment to teach the whole group in this area. One important aspect is that LdL should not be confused with a student-as-teacher-centred method. The material should be worked on didactically and methodologically (impulses, social forms, summarizing phases etc.). The teaching students have to make sure their audience has understood their message/topic/ grammar points and therefore use different means to do so (e.g. short phases of group or partner exercises, comprehension questions, quizzes etc.). An important effect from LdL is to develop the students' "websensibility," defined as "a cognitive and emotional sensibility for interdependence."

Advantages and Disadvantages

Most teachers using the method do not apply it in all their classes or all the time. They state the following advantages and disadvantages:

Advantages

- Student work is more motivated, efficient, active and intensive due to lowered inhibitions and an increased sense of purpose

- By eliminating the class division of authoritative teacher and passive audience, an emotive solidarity is obtained.
- Students may perform many routine tasks, otherwise unnecessarily carried out by the instructor
- Next to subject-related knowledge students gain important key qualifications like
  - o teamwork
  - o planning abilities
  - o reliability
  - o presentation and moderation skills
  - o self-confidence.

Disadvantages

- The introduction of the method requires a lot of time.
- Students and teachers have to work more than usual.
- There is a danger of simple duplication, repetition or monotony if the teacher does not provide periodic didactic impetus.

Reception of Martin's Methods

Martin's work has been well received in teacher training and by practicing teachers: since 1985 more than 100 teacher students in all subjects wrote their ending thesis about LdL. Also the education administration received both the theory and the practice of LdL. In didactics handbooks LdL has been described as an "*extreme form of learner centred teaching*"). On the university level, LdL has been disseminated by Joachim Grzega in Germany, Guido Oebel in Japan and Alina Rachimova in Russia.

Learning by Teaching Outside the LdL-context

Sudbury Schools

Sudbury schools, since 1968, do not segregate students by age, so that students of any age are free to interact with students in other age groups. One effect of this age mixing is that a great deal of the teaching in the school is done by students. Here are some statements about Learning by teaching in the Sudbury Schools: "*Kids love to learn from other kids. First of all, it's often easier. The child teacher is closer than the adult to the students' difficulties, having gone through them somewhat more recently. The explanations are usually simpler, better. There's less pressure, less judgment. And there's a huge incentive to learn fast and well, to catch up with the mentor.*

Kids also love to teach. It gives them a sense of value, of accomplishment. More important, it helps them get a better handle on the material as they teach; they have to sort it out, get it straight. So they struggle with the material until it's crystal clear in their own heads, until it's clear enough for their pupils to understand."

Pupil-Team Learning: The Durrell Studies

In the 1950s Dr. Donald D. Durrell and his colleagues at Boston University pursued similar methods which they named Pupil-Team Learning. A year-long efficacy study in the schools of Dedham, Massachusetts, was published in the Boston University Journal of Education, Vol. 142, December, 1959, entitled "Adapting Instruction to the Learning Needs of Children in the Intermediate Grades" in which one of the authors, Walter J. McHugh, reported significant learning gains from the use of pupil teams.

The Vygotsky Connection

In the 1930s Lev Vygotsky wrote extensively, in Russian, on the profound connection between language and cognition, and in particular oral language (speech) and learning. The implication of Vygotsky's observations for Learning by Teaching would appear to be direct and apt. "The one who does the talking, does the learning" may best summarize the point: students learn by teaching their peers.

Education

Education in the largest sense is any act or experience that has a formative effect on the mind, character or physical ability of an individual. In its technical sense, education is the process by which society deliberately transmits its accumulated knowledge, skills and values from one generation to another.

Etymologically, the word education is derived from *educare* (Latin) "bring up", which is related to *educere* "bring out", "bring forth what is within", "bring out potential" and *ducere*, "to lead".

Teachers in educational institutions direct the education of students and might draw on many subjects, including reading, writing, mathematics, science and history. This process is sometimes called schooling when referring to the education of teaching only a certain subject, usually as professors at institutions of higher learning. There is also education in fields for those who want specific vocational skills, such as those required to be a pilot. In addition there is an array of education possible at the informal level, such as in museums and libraries, with the Internet and in life experience. Many non-traditional education options are now available and continue to evolve.

Systems of Formal Education

Education is a concept, referring to the process in which students can learn something:

- Instruction refers to the facilitating of learning toward identified objectives, delivered either by an instructor or other forms.
- Teaching refers to the actions of a real live instructor designed to impart learning to the student.
- Learning refers to learning with a view toward preparing learners with specific knowledge, skills, or abilities that can be applied immediately upon completion.

Preschool Education

Preschool education or Infant education is the provision of education for children before the commencement of statutory and obligatory education, usually between the ages of zero or three and five, depending on the jurisdiction.

In British English, nursery school or simply "nursery" or playgroup is the usual term for preschool education. In the United States preschool and Pre-K are used, while "nursery school" is an older term. Preschool work is organized within a framework that professional educators create. The framework includes structural (administration, class size, teacher-child ratio, services, etc.), process (quality of classroom environments, teacher-child interactions, etc.), and alignment (standards, curriculum, assessments) components that are associated with each individual unique child that has both social and academic outcomes. Arguably the first pre-school institution was opened in 1816 by Robert Owen in New Lanark, Scotland. The Hungarian countess Theresa Brunszvik followed in 1828. In 1837, Friedrich Fröbel opened one in Germany, coining the term "kindergarten".

Developmental Areas

The areas of development which preschool education covers varies from country to country. However, the following main themes are represented in the majority of systems.

- Personal, social, economical, and emotional development
- Communication, including sign language, talking and listening
- Knowledge and understanding of the world
- Creative and aesthetic development
- Educational software
- Mathematical awareness and development
- Physical development
- Playing
- Self-help skills
- Social skills.

Allowing preschool aged children to discover and explore freely within each of these areas of development is the foundation for developmental learning. While the National Association for the Education of Young Children (NAEYC) and the National Association of Child Care Professionals (NACCP) have made tremendous strides in publicizing and promoting the idea of developmentally appropriate practice, there is still much work to be done. It is widely recognized that although many preschool educators are aware of the guidelines for developmentally appropriate practice, putting this practice to work effectively in the classroom is more challenging. The

NAEYC published that although 80% of Kindergarten classrooms claim to be developmentally appropriate, only 20% actually are.

Age and Importance

Preschool is generally considered appropriate for children between zero or three and five years of age, between the baby or toddler and school stages. During this stage of development, children learn and assimilate information rapidly, and express interest and fascination in each new discovery.

It is well established that the most important years of learning are begun at birth. A child's brain at this age is making connections that will last the rest of their life. During these early years, a human being is capable of absorbing more information at a time than they will ever be able to again. The environment of the young child influences the development of cognitive skills and emotional skills due to the rapid brain growth that occurs in the early years. Studies have shown that high quality preschools have a short and long term effect in improving the outcomes of a child, especially a disadvantaged child. However, some more recent studies dispute the accuracy of the earlier results which cited benefits to preschool education, and actually point at preschool being detrimental to a child's cognitive and social development. A study by UC Berkeley and Stanford University on 14,000 Kindergarteners revealed that while there is a temporary cognitive boost in pre-reading and math, preschool holds detrimental effects on social development and cooperation.

The Universal Preschool movement is an international effort to make access to preschool available to families in a similar way to compulsory primary education. Various jurisdictions and advocates have differing priorities for access, availability and funding sources. There has been a shift from preschools that operated primarily as controlled play groups to educational settings in which children learn specific, if basic, skills. It examines several different perspectives on teaching in kindergarten, including those of the developmentally appropriate practice, the academic approach, the child-centred approach, and the Montessori approach to the curriculum.

Gratuity

The gratuity of infant education has been established in some countries, as Spain, beginning in the second cycle (from three to six years), but extending to the first cycle (from birth to three years).

History of Preschool in the United States

Head Start, the first publicly funded preschool program, was created in 1965 by President Johnson. The federal government helped create this half-day program for preschool children from low-income families. Head Start began as a summer pilot program that included an education component, nutrition and health screenings for children, and support services for families (CPE, 2007). In the 1960s only ten percent of the nations three and four year olds were enrolled in a classroom setting.

Due to a large amount of people interested, and a lack of funding for Head Start, during the 1980s a handful of states started their own version of a program for students from low-income families. The positive success and effects of preschool meant many state leaders were showing interest in educational reform of these young students (CPE, 2007). By 2005 sixty-nine percent, or over 800,000, four year-old children nationwide participated in some type of state preschool program (CPE, 2007). The yearly increase in enrollment of preschool programs throughout the years is due to an increase of higher maternal employment rates, national anti-poverty initiatives, and research showing the link between early childhood experiences and the brain development of young children. These factors have caused the rate of attendance in preschool programs to grow each year (CPE, 2007).

In most states, there are multiple preschool or Pre-K options for young children. Parents have the choice of sending their child to a federally funded Head Start program, if their income is at the poverty level, state-funded preschool, government-funded special education programs, and for-profit and not-for-profit providers, including those that accept government subsidies that help low income parents pay. Currently, in the United States, Georgia, Illinois, Florida, Oklahoma, West

Virginia, and New York are the only states with legislation underway or which already have universal preschool for all four year olds in the state, and Preschool For All in Illinois is the only universal preschool program that serves three year olds as well.

International Preschool Systems

Kindergarten

Kindergarten (German, literally means "children's garden") is a form of education for young children that serves as a transition from home to the commencement of more formal schooling. Another definition, which overlaps with early childhood education and preschool, is education for pre-and emergent-literate children before the age of 6 or 7. Children are taught to develop basic skills and knowledge through creative play and social interaction, as well as sometimes formal lessons.

In most countries kindergarten is part of the preschool system of early childhood education. Children usually attend kindergarten any time between the ages of two and seven years, depending on the local custom.

In the United States and anglophone Canada, as well as in parts of Australia (New South Wales, Tasmania and the Australian Capital Territory) *kindergarten* is the word often restricted in use to describe the first year of education, or primary school. In some of these countries it is compulsory, that is parents must send children to their kindergarten year (generally, at age 5). In the United States, many states widely offer a free kindergarten year to children of five to six years of age, but do not make it compulsory, while other states require all five-year-olds to enrol. The terms preschool or less often, "Pre-K," (formerly, nursery school) are used to refer to earlier age-group education in the U.S.

In British English, nursery or playgroup is the usual term for preschool education, and *kindergarten* is rarely used, except in the context of special approaches to education, such as Steiner-Waldorf education (the educational philosophy of which was founded by Rudolf Steiner).

Methods of Preschool Education

Some preschools have adopted specialized methods of teaching, such as Montessori, Waldorf, Head Start, HighReach Learning, High Scope, *The Creative Curriculum*, Reggio Emilia approach, Bank Street, Forest kindergartens, and various other pedagogies which contribute to the foundation of education.

Creative Curriculum has an interactive website where parents and teachers can work together in evaluating preschool age children. The website is very user friendly and prints off many reports that are helpful in evaluating children and the classroom itself. The web site has a variety of activities that are targeted to each of the fifty goals on the continuum.

The International Preschool Curriculum adopted a bilingual approach to teaching and offers a curriculum that embraces international standards and recognizes national requirements for preschool education.

In the United States most preschool advocates support the National Association for the Education of Young Children's Developmentally Appropriate Practices.

Family childcare can also be nationally accredited by the National Association of Family Childcare if the provider chooses to go through the process. National accreditation is only awarded to those programs who demonstrate the quality standards set forth by the NAFCC.

Funding for Preschool Programs

While a majority of American preschool programs remain tuition-based, support for some public funding of early childhood education has grown over the years. As of 2008, 38 states and the District of Columbia invested in at least some pre-kindergarten programs, and many school districts were providing preschool services on their own, using local and federal funds.

The benefits and challenges of a public preschool are closely tied to the amount of funding provided. Funding for a public preschool can come in a variety of sources. According to Levin and Schwartz (2007) funding can range from federal, state, local public allocations, private sources, and parental fees. The problem of funding a public preschool occurs not only from limited sources but from the cost per child. The average cost across the 48 states is $6,582. There are four categories that determine the costs of public preschools: personnel ratios, personnel qualifications, facilities and transportation, and health and nutrition services. According to Levin and Schwartz (2007) these structural elements depend heavily on the cost and quality of services provided. The main personnel factor related to cost is the qualifications each preschool require for a teacher. Another determinate of cost is the length of a preschool day. The longer the session, the more increase in cost. Therefore, the quality of program accounts presumably for a major component of cost.

Collaboration has been a solution for funding issues in several districts. Wilma Kaplan, principal, turned to collaborating with the area Head Start and other private preschool to fund a public preschool in her district. "We're very pleased with the interaction. It's really added a dimension to our program that's been very positive" (Reeves, 2000). The National Head Start Bureau has been looking for more opportunities to partner with public schools. Torn Schultz of the National Head Start Bureau states, "We're turning to partnership as much as possible, either in funds or facilities to make sure children get everything necessary to be ready for school". The goal for funding is to develop a variety of sources that provide for all children to benefit from early learning within a public preschool.

Special Education in Preschool

In the United States, students who may benefit from special education receive services in preschools. Since the inception of the Individuals with Disabilities Education Act (IDEA) Public Law 101-476 in 1975 and its amendments, PL 102-119 and PL 105-17 in 1997, the educational system has moved away from self-contained classrooms and progressed to inclusion. As a result, there has been a need for special education teachers to practice in various settings in order to assist children with special needs, particularly by working with regular classroom teachers when possible to strengthen the inclusion of children with special needs. As with other stages in the life of a child with special needs, the Individualized Education Plan (IEP) or an Individual Family Service Plan (IFSP) is an important way for special education teachers, regular classroom teachers, administrators and parents to set guidelines for a partnership to help the child succeed in preschool.

Primary Education

Primary (or elementary) education consists of the first 5–7 years of formal, structured education. In general, primary education consists of six or eight years of schooling starting at the age of five or six, although this varies between, and sometimes within, countries. Globally, around 89% of primary-age children are enrolled in primary education, and this proportion is rising. Under the Education for All programs driven by UNESCO, most countries have committed to achieving universal enrollment in primary education by 2015, and in many countries, it is compulsory for children to receive primary education. The division between primary and secondary education is somewhat arbitrary, but it generally occurs at about eleven or twelve years of age. Some education systems have separate middle schools, with the transition to the final stage of secondary education taking place at around the age of fourteen. Schools that provide primary education, are mostly referred to as *primary schools*. Primary schools in these countries are often subdivided into infant schools and junior school.

Secondary Education

In most contemporary educational systems of the world, secondary education comprises the formal education that occurs during adolescence. It is characterized by transition from the typically compulsory, comprehensive primary education for minors, to the optional, selective tertiary, "post-secondary", or "higher" education (e.g., university, vocational school for adults. Depending on the system, schools for this period, or a part of it, may be called secondary or high schools, gymnasiums, lyceums, middle schools, colleges or vocational schools. The exact meaning of any of these terms varies from one system to another. The exact boundary between primary and secondary education also varies from country to country and even within them, but is generally around the seventh to the tenth year of schooling. Secondary education occurs mainly during the teenage years. In the United States, Canada and Australia primary and secondary education together are sometimes referred to as K-12 education, and in New Zealand Year 1-13 is used. The purpose of secondary education can be to give common knowledge, to prepare for higher education or to train directly in a profession.

The emergence of secondary education in the United States did not happen until 1910, caused by the rise in big businesses and technological advances in factories (for instance, the emergence of electrification), that required skilled workers. In order to meet this new job demand, high schools were created and the curriculum focused on practical job skills that would better prepare students for white collar or skilled blue collar work. This proved to be beneficial for both the employer and the employee, because this improvement in human capital caused employees to become more efficient, which lowered costs for the employer, and skilled employees received a higher wage than employees with just primary educational attainment.

In Europe, the grammar school or academy existed from as early as the 16th century; public schools or fee paying schools, or charitable educational foundations have an even longer history.

Higher Education

Higher education, also called tertiary, third stage, or post secondary education, is the non-compulsory educational level that follows the completion of a school providing a secondary education, such as a high school, secondary school. Tertiary education is normally taken to include undergraduate and postgraduate education, as well as vocational education and training. Colleges and universities are the main institutions that provide tertiary education. Collectively, these are sometimes known as tertiary institutions. Tertiary education generally results in the receipt of certificates, diplomas, or academic degrees.

Higher education includes teaching, research and social services activities of universities, and within the realm of teaching, it includes both the *undergraduate* level (sometimes referred to as tertiary education) and the *graduate* (or *postgraduate*) level (sometimes referred to as graduate school). Higher education generally involves work towards a degree-level or foundation degree qualification. In most developed countries a high proportion of the population (up to 50%) now enter higher education at some time in their lives. Higher education is therefore very important to national economies, both as a significant industry in its own right, and as a source of trained and educated personnel for the rest of the economy.

Adult Education

Adult education has become common in many countries. It takes on many forms, ranging from formal class-based learning to self-directed learning and e-learning. A number of career specific courses such as veterinary assisting, medical billing and coding, real estate license, bookkeeping and many more are now available to students through the Internet.

Alternative Education

Alternative education, also known as *non-traditional education* or *educational alternative*, is a broad term that may be used to refer to all forms of education outside of traditional education (for all age groups and levels of education). This may include not only forms of education designed for students with special needs (ranging from teenage pregnancy to intellectual disability), but also forms of education designed for a general audience and employing alternative educational philosophies and methods.

Alternatives of the latter type are often the result of education reform and are rooted in various philosophies that are commonly fundamentally different from those of traditional compulsory education. While some have strong political, scholarly, or philosophical orientations, others are more informal associations of teachers and students dissatisfied with certain aspects of traditional education. These alternatives, which include charter schools, alternative schools, independent schools, and home-based learning vary widely, but often emphasize the value of small class size, close relationships between students and teachers, and a sense of community.

Indigenous Education

Indigenous education refers to the inclusion of indigenous knowledge, models, methods and content within formal and non-formal educational systems. Often in a post-colonial context, the growing recognition and use of indigenous education methods can be a response to the erosion and loss of indigenous knowledge and language through the processes of colonialism. Furthermore, it can enable indigenous communities to "reclaim and revalue their languages and cultures, and in so doing, improve the educational success of indigenous students."

Increasingly, there has been a global shift toward recognising indigenous models of education (methods and content) as a viable alternative within the scope of many different education systems. The inclusion of indigenous models of education has come to represent a significant factor contributing to the success of those members of indigenous communities who choose to access these systems, both as students/learners and as teachers/instructors.

As an educational method, the inclusion of indigenous ways of knowing, learning, instructing, teaching and training, has been viewed by many critical and postmodern scholars as important for ensuring that students/learners and teachers/instructors (whether indigenous or non-indigenous) are able to benefit from education in a culturally sensitive manner that draws upon, utilizes, promotes and enhances awareness of indigenous traditions.

Benefits

For indigenous students or learners, and teachers or instructors, the inclusion of these methods often enhances educational effectiveness, success and learning outcomes by providing education that adheres to their own inherent perspectives, experiences and worldview. For non-indigenous students and teachers, education using such methods often has the effect of raising awareness of the individual traditions and collective experience of surrounding indigenous communities and peoples, thereby promoting greater respect for and appreciation of the cultural realities of these communities and peoples.

In terms of educational content, the inclusion of indigenous knowledge, traditions, perspectives, worldviews and conceptions within curricula, instructional materials, textbooks and course books have largely the same effects as the inclusion of indigenous methods in education. Indigenous students and teachers benefit from enhanced academic effectiveness, success and learning outcomes, while non-indigenous students/learners and teachers often have greater awareness, respect, and appreciation for indigenous communities and peoples in consequence of the content that is shared during the course of educational pursuits.

Importance

The importance of indigenous knowledge to modern environmental management is particularly pertinent in today's world. Environmental and land management strategies traditionally used by indigenous peoples have continued relevance. Indigenous cultures usually live in a particular bioregion for many generations and have learned how to live there sustainably. This quality often puts truly indigenous cultures in a unique position in modern times to be aware of and knowledgeable about the interrelationships, needs, benefits and dangers of their bioregion. This is not true of indigenous cultures which have been eroded through processes of colonialism or genocide or indigenous peoples who have been displaced.

The promotion of indigenous methods of education and the inclusion of traditional knowledge also enables those in western and post-colonial societies, to re-evaluate the inherent hierarchy of knowledge systems. Indigenous knowledge systems were historically denigrated by western educators; however there is a current shift towards the valuing of these traditions. The inclusion of aspects of indigenous education requires us to acknowledge the existence of multiple 'knowledge's' rather than one, standard, benchmark system.

A prime example of how indigenous methods and content can be used to promote the above outcomes is demonstrated within higher education in Canada. Due to certain jurisdictions' focus on enhancing academic success for Aboriginal learners and promoting the values of multiculturalism in society, the inclusion of indigenous methods and content in education is often seen as an important obligation and duty of both governmental and educational authorities.

Many scholars in the field assert that indigenous education and knowledge has a "transformative power," which can be applied in the fostering of "empowerment and justice," for indigenous communities. The shift to recognising indigenous models of education as legitimate forms is therefore important in the ongoing effort for indigenous rights, on a global scale.

Challenges

There are numerous practical challenges surrounding the implementation of indigenous education. Incorporating indigenous knowledge into formal western education models can prove challenging. However the discourse surrounding Indigenous education and knowledge suggests that including indigenous methods in traditional modes of schooling is an "ongoing process of 'cultural negotiation', rather than a simple return to, or retrenchment of past practices."

Associated Organisations

There are many organisations concerned with the promotion of Indigenous methods of education. The United Nations Declaration of the Rights of Indigenous Peoples makes particular reference to the educational rights of indigenous peoples in Article 14. It emphasises the responsibility of States to adequately provide access to education for indigenous people, particularly children, and when possible for education to take place within their own culture and to be delivered in their own language.

There are also many organisations founded by and actively run by Indigenous peoples. On a global scale, many of these organisations engage in active knowledge transfer in an effort to protect and promote Indigenous knowledge and education modes. One such organisation, the Indigenous Education Institute (IEI) aims to apply Indigenous knowledge and tradition to a contemporary context, with a particular focus on astronomy and other science disciplines. Another such organisation is the World Indigenous Nations Higher Education Consortium

(WINHEC). Launched during the World Indigenous Peoples Conference on Education (WIPCE) at Delta Lodge, Kananakis Calgary in Alberta, Canada in August 2002, the founding state/country members were Australia, the states of Hawai'i and Alaska and the American Indian Higher Education Consortium of the United States, Canada, the Wänanga of Aotearoa (New Zealand) and Saamiland (North Norway). The stated aims of WINHEC include the provision of an international forum for Indigenous Peoples to pursue common goals through higher education.

Process

Curriculum

In formal education, a curriculum is the set of courses, and their content, offered at a school or university. As an idea, curriculum stems from the Latin word for *race course*, referring to the course of deeds and experiences through which children grow to become mature adults. A curriculum is prescriptive, and is based on a more general syllabus which merely specifies what topics must be understood and to what level to achieve a particular grade or standard.

Historical Conception

In *The Curriculum*, the first textbook published on the subject, in 1918, John Franklin Bobbitt said that curriculum, as an idea, has its roots in the Latin word for *race-course*, explaining the curriculum as the course of deeds and experiences through which children become the adults they should be, *for success in adult society*. Furthermore, the curriculum encompasses the entire scope of formative deed and experience occurring in and out of school, and not only experiences occurring in school; experiences that are unplanned and undirected, and experiences intentionally directed for the purposeful formation of adult members of society.

To Bobbitt, the curriculum is a social engineering arena. Per his cultural presumptions and social definitions, his curricular formulation has two notable features: (i) that scientific experts would best be qualified to and justified in designing curricula based upon their expert knowledge of what qualities are desirable in adult members of society, and which experiences would generate said qualities; and (ii) curriculum defined as the deeds-experiences the student *ought to have* to become the adult he or she *ought to become*.

Hence, he defined the curriculum as an ideal, rather than as the concrete reality of the deeds and experiences that form people to who and what they are.

Contemporary views of curriculum reject these features of Bobbitt's postulates, but retain the basis of curriculum as the course of experience(s) that forms human beings into persons. Personal formation via curricula is studied at the personal level and at the group level, i.e. cultures and societies (e.g. professional formation, academic discipline via historical experience). The formation of a group is reciprocal, with the formation of its individual participants. Although it formally appeared in Bobbitt's definition, curriculum as a course of formative experience also pervades John Dewey's work (who disagreed with Bobbitt on important matters). Although Bobbitt's and Dewey's idealistic understanding of "curriculum" is different from current, restricted uses of the word, curriculum writers and researchers generally share it as common, substantive understanding of curriculum.

Curriculum in Formal Schooling

In formal education or schooling, a curriculum is the set of courses, course work, and content offered at a school or university. A curriculum may be partly or entirely determined by an external, authoritative body (i.e. the National Curriculum for England in English schools). In the U.S., each state, with the individual school districts, establishes the curricula taught. Each state, however, builds its curriculum with great participation of national academic subject groups selected by the United States Department of Education, e.g. National Council of Teachers of Mathematics (NCTM) for mathematical instruction. In Australia each state's Education Department establishes curricula with plans for a National Curriculum in 2011. UNESCO's International Bureau of Education has the primary mission of studying curricula and their implementation worldwide.

Curriculum means two things: (i) the range of courses from which students choose what subject matters to study, and (ii) a specific learning program. In the latter case, the curriculum collectively describes the teaching, learning, and assessment materials available for a given course of study.

Currently, a *spiral curriculum* is promoted as allowing students to revisit a subject matter's content at the different levels of development of the subject matter being studied. The constructivist approach, of the *tycoil curriculum*, proposes that children learn best via active engagement with the educational environment, i.e. discovery learning. Crucial to the curriculum is the definition of the course objectives that usually are expressed as *learning outcomes'* and normally include the program's assessment strategy. These outcomes and assessments are grouped as units (or modules), and, therefore, the curriculum comprises a collection of such units, each, in turn, comprising a specialised, specific part of the curriculum. So, a typical curriculum includes communications, numeracy, information technology, and social skills units, with specific, specialized teaching of each.

Curriculum Types in the United States

Many educational institutions are currently trying to balance two opposing forces. On the one hand, some believe students should have a common knowledge foundation, often in the form of a core curriculum; on the other hand, others want students to be able to pursue their own educational interests, often through early specialty in a major, however, other times through the free choice of courses. This tension has received a large amount of coverage due to Harvard University's reorganization of its core requirements.

An essential feature of curriculum design, seen in every college catalog and at every other level of schooling, is the identification of prerequisites for each course. These prerequisites can be satisfied by taking particular courses, and in some cases by examination, or by other means, such as work experience. In general, more advanced courses in any subject require some foundation in basic courses, but some coursework requires study in other departments, as in the sequence of math classes required for a physics major, or the language requirements for students preparing in literature, music, or scientific research. A more detailed curriculum design must deal with prerequisites within a course for each topic taken up. This in turn leads to the problems of course organization and scheduling once the dependencies between topics are known.

Core Curriculum

"Core curriculum" redirects here. For information about specific core curricula, use the links in the text below.

In education, a core curriculum is a curriculum, or course of study, which is deemed central and usually made mandatory for all students of a school or school system. However, this is not always the case. For example, a school might mandate a music appreciation class, but students may opt out if they take a performing musical class, such as orchestra, band, chorus, etc. Core curricula are often instituted, at the primary and secondary levels, by school boards, Departments of Education, or other administrative agencies charged with overseeing education.

In Primary and Secondary Education

In the United States, the Common Core State Standards Initiative promulgates a core curriculum for states to adopt and optionally expand upon. This coordination is intended to make it possible to use more of the same textbooks across states, and to move toward a more uniform minimum level of educational attainment. In 2009-10, states were given the incentive to adopt the standards with the possibility of competitive funds from the federal Race to the Top program.

In Higher Education

At the undergraduate level, individual college and university administrations and faculties sometimes mandate core curricula, especially in the liberal arts. But because of increasing specialization and depth in the student's major field of study, a typical core curriculum in higher education mandates a far smaller proportion of a student's course work than a high school or elementary school core curriculum prescribes. Amongst the best known and most expansive core curricula programs at leading American colleges are that of Columbia College at Columbia University, as well as the University of Chicago's. Both can take up to two years to complete without advanced standing, and are designed to foster critical skills in a broad range of academic disciplines, including: the social sciences, humanities, physical and biological sciences, mathematics, writing and foreign languages.

In 1999, the University of Chicago announced plans to reduce and modify the content of its core curriculum, including lowering the number of required courses from 21 to 15 and offering a wider range of content. When *The New York Times*, *The Economist*, and other major news outlets picked up this story, the University became the focal point of a national debate on education. The National Association of Scholars released a statement saying, "*It is truly depressing to observe a steady abandonment of the University of Chicago's once imposing undergraduate core curriculum, which for so long stood as the benchmark of content and rigor among American academic institutions.*" Simultaneously, however, a set of university administrators, notably then-President Hugo Sonnenschein, argued that reducing the core curriculum had become both a financial and educational imperative, as the university was struggling to attract a commensurate volume of applicants to its undergraduate division compared to peer schools as a result of what was perceived by the pro-change camp as a reaction by "the average eighteen year old" to the expanse of the collegiate core.

Further, as core curricula began to be diminished over the course of the twentieth century at many American schools, several smaller institutions became famous for embracing a core curriculum that covers nearly the student's entire undergraduate education, often utilizing classic texts of the western canon to teach all subjects including science. St. John's College in the United States is one example of this approach.

Distribution Requirements

Some colleges opt for the middle ground of the continuum between specified and unspecified curricula by using a system of distribution requirements. In such a system, students are required to take courses in particular categories, but are free to choose within these categories.

Open Curriculum

Other institutions have largely done away with core requirements in their entirety, as in the student-driven course selections of Brown University and Cornell University. Amherst College requires that students take one of a list of first-year seminars, but has no required classes or distribution requirements.

An academic discipline is a branch of knowledge which is formally taught, either at the university, or via some other such method. Each discipline usually has several sub-disciplines or branches, and distinguishing lines are often both arbitrary and ambiguous. Examples of broad areas of academic disciplines include the natural sciences, mathematics, computer science, social sciences, humanities and applied sciences.

Learning Modalities

There has been work on learning styles over the last two decades. Dunn and Dunn focused on identifying relevant stimuli that may influence learning and manipulating the school environment, at about the same time as Joseph Renzulli recommended varying teaching strategies. Howard Gardner identified individual talents or aptitudes in his Multiple Intelligences theories. Based on the works of Jung, the Myers-Briggs Type Indicator and Keirsey Temperament Sorter focused on understanding how people's personality affects the way they interact personally, and how this affects the way individuals respond to each other within the learning environment. The work of David Kolb and Anthony Gregorc's Type Delineator follows a similar but more simplified approach.

It is currently fashionable to divide education into different learning "modes". The learning modalities are probably the most common:

- Visual: learning based on observation and seeing what is being learned.
- Auditory: learning based on listening to instructions/ information.

- Kinesthetic: learning based on hands-on work and engaging in activities.

Although it is claimed that, depending on their preferred learning modality, different teaching techniques have different levels of effectiveness, recent research has argued "there is no adequate evidence base to justify incorporating learning styles assessments into general educational practice."

A consequence of this theory is that effective teaching should present a variety of teaching methods which cover all three learning modalities so that different students have equal opportunities to learn in a way that is effective for them. Guy Claxton has questioned the extent that learning styles such as VAK are helpful, particularly as they can have a tendency to label children and therefore restrict learning.

Teaching

Teachers need to understand a subject enough to convey its essence to students. While traditionally this has involved lecturing on the part of the teacher, new instructional strategies put the teacher more into the role of course designer, discussion facilitator, and coach and the student more into the role of active learner, discovering the subject of the course. In any case, the goal is to establish a sound knowledge base and skill set on which students will be able to build as they are exposed to different life experiences. Good teachers can translate information, good judgment, experience and wisdom into relevant knowledge that a student can understand, retain and pass to others. Studies from the US suggest that the quality of teachers is the single most important factor affecting student performance, and that countries which score highly on international tests have multiple policies in place to ensure that the teachers they employ are as effective as possible. With the passing of NCLB in the United States (No Child Left Behind), teachers must be highly qualified.

Technology

Technology is an increasingly influential factor in education. Computers and mobile phones are used in developed countries both to complement established education practices and develop new ways of learning such as online education (a type of distance education). This gives students the opportunity to choose what they are interested in learning. The proliferation of computers also means the increase of programming and blogging. Technology offers powerful learning tools that demand new skills and understandings of students, including Multimedia, and provides new ways to engage students, such as Virtual learning environments.

One such tool are virtual manipulatives, which are an "interactive, Web-based visual representation of a dynamic object that presents opportunities for constructing mathematical knowledge". In short, virtual manipulatives are dynamic visual/pictorial replicas of physical mathematical manipulatives, which have long been used to demonstrate and teach various mathematical concepts. Virtual manipulatives can be easily accessed on the Internet as stand-alone applets, allowing for easy access and use in a variety of educational settings. Emerging research into the effectiveness of virtual manipulatives as a teaching tool have yielded promising results, suggesting comparable, and in many cases superior overall concept-teaching effectiveness compared to standard teaching methods.

Technology is being used more not only in administrative duties in education but also in the instruction of students. The use of technologies such as PowerPoint and interactive whiteboard is capturing the attention of students in the classroom. Technology is also being used in the assessment of students. One example is the Audience Response System (ARS), which allows immediate feedback tests and classroom discussions.

Information and communication technologies (ICTs) are a "diverse set of tools and resources used to communicate, create, disseminate, store, and manage information." These technologies include computers, the Internet, broadcasting technologies (radio and television), and telephony. There is increasing interest in how computers and the Internet can improve education at all levels, in both formal and non-formal settings. Older ICT technologies, such as radio and television, have for over forty years been used for open and distance learning, although print remains the cheapest, most accessible and therefore most dominant delivery mechanism in both developed and developing countries. In addition to classroom application and growth of e-learning opportunities for knowledge attainment, educators involved in student affairs programming have recognized the increasing importance of computer usage with data generation for and about students. Motivation and retention counsellors, along with faculty and administrators, can impact the potential academic success of students by provision of technology based experiences in the University setting.

The use of computers and the Internet is in its infancy in developing countries, if these are used at all, due to limited infrastructure and the attendant high costs of access. Usually, various technologies are used in combination rather than as the sole delivery mechanism. For example, the Kothmale Community Radio Internet uses both radio broadcasts and computer and Internet technologies to facilitate the sharing of information and provide educational opportunities in a rural community in Sri Lanka. The Open University of the United Kingdom (UKOU), established in 1969 as the first educational institution in the world wholly dedicated to open and distance learning, still relies heavily on print-based materials supplemented by radio, television and, in recent years, online programming. Similarly, the Indira Gandhi National Open University in India combines the use of print, recorded audio and video, broadcast radio and television, and audio conferencing technologies.

The term "computer-assisted learning" (CAL) has been increasingly used to describe the use of technology in teaching.

Educational Theory

Education theory is the theory of the purpose, application and interpretation of education and learning. Its history begins with classical Greek educationalists and sophists and includes, since the 18th century, pedagogy and andragogy. In the 20th century, "theory" has become an umbrella term for a variety of scholarly approaches to teaching, assessment and education law, most of which are informed by various academic fields, which can be seen in the below sections.

Economics

It has been argued that high rates of education are essential for countries to be able to achieve high levels of economic growth. Empirical analyses tend to support the theoretical prediction that poor countries should grow faster than rich countries because they can adopt cutting edge technologies already tried and tested by rich countries. However, technology transfer requires knowledgeable managers and engineers who are able to operate new machines or production practices borrowed from the leader in order to close the gap through imitation. Therefore, a country's ability to learn from the leader is a function of its stock of "human capital". Recent study of the determinants of aggregate economic growth have stressed the importance of fundamental economic institutions and the role of cognitive skills.

At the individual level, there is a large literature, generally related back to the work of Jacob Mincer, on how earnings are related to the schooling and other human capital of the individual. This work has motivated a large number of studies, but is also controversial. The chief controversies revolve around how to interpret the impact of schooling.

Economists Samuel Bowles and Herbert Gintis famously argued in 1976 that there was a fundamental conflict in American schooling between the egalitarian goal of democratic participation and the inequalities implied by the continued profitability of capitalist production on the other.

History

The history of education according to Dieter Lenzen, president of the Freie Universität Berlin 1994, "began either millions of years ago or at the end of 1770". Education as a science cannot be separated from the educational traditions that existed before. Adults trained the young of their society in the knowledge and skills they would need to master and eventually pass on. The evolution of culture, and human beings as a species depended on this practice of transmitting knowledge. In pre-literate societies this was achieved orally and through imitation. Story-telling continued from one generation to the next. Oral language developed into written symbols and letters.

The depth and breadth of knowledge that could be preserved and passed soon increased exponentially. When cultures began to extend their knowledge beyond the basic skills of communicating, trading, gathering food, religious practices, etc., formal education, and schooling, eventually followed. Schooling in this sense was already in place in Egypt between 3000 and 500BC. Nowadays some kind of education is compulsory to all people in most countries. Due to population growth and the proliferation of compulsory education, UNESCO has calculated that in the next 30 years more people will receive formal education than in all of human history thus far.

Philosophy

Philosophy of education is the philosophical study of the purpose, process, nature and ideals of education. Philosophy of education can naturally be considered a branch of both philosophy and education. Philosophy of education is commonly housed in colleges and departments of education, yet it is applied philosophy, drawing from the traditional fields of philosophy (ontology, ethics, epistemology, etc.) and approaches (speculative, prescriptive, and/or analytic) to address questions regarding education policy, human development, education research methodology, and curriculum theory, to name a few.

Psychology

Educational psychology is the study of how humans learn in educational settings, the effectiveness of educational interventions, the psychology of teaching, and the social psychology of schools as organizations. Although the terms "educational psychology" and "school psychology" are often used interchangeably, researchers and theorists are likely to be identified as educational psychologists, whereas practitioners in schools or school-related settings are identified as school psychologists. Educational psychology is concerned with the processes of educational attainment in the general population and in sub-populations such as gifted children and those with specific disabilities.

Educational psychology can in part be understood through its relationship with other disciplines. It is informed primarily by psychology, bearing a relationship to that discipline analogous to the relationship between medicine and biology. Educational psychology in turn informs a wide range of specialities within educational studies, including instructional design, educational technology, curriculum development, organizational learning, special education and classroom management. Educational psychology both draws from and contributes to cognitive science and the learning sciences. In universities, departments of educational psychology are usually housed within faculties of education, possibly accounting for the lack of representation of educational psychology content in introductory psychology textbooks.

Sociology

The sociology of education is the study of how social institutions and forces affect educational processes and outcomes, and vice versa. By many, education is understood to be a means of overcoming handicaps, achieving greater equality and acquiring wealth and status for all (Sargent 1994). Learners may be motivated by aspirations for progress and betterment. Education is perceived as a place where children can develop according to their unique needs and potentialities. The purpose of education can be to develop every individual to their full potential. The understanding of the goals and means of educational socialization processes differs according to the sociological paradigm used.

6

Nature of Psychology and Learners

Educational psychology is the study of how humans learn in educational settings, the effectiveness of educational interventions, the psychology of teaching, and the social psychology of schools as organizations. Educational psychology is concerned with how students learn and develop, often focusing on subgroups such as gifted children and those subject to specific disabilities. Although the terms "educational psychology" and "school psychology" are often used interchangeably, researchers and theorists are likely to be identified in the US and Canada as educational psychologists, whereas practitioners in schools or school-related settings are identified as school psychologists. This distinction is however not made in the UK, where the generic term for practitioners is "educational psychologist".

Educational psychology can in part be understood through its relationship with other disciplines. It is informed primarily by psychology, bearing a relationship to that discipline analogous to the relationship between medicine and biology. Educational psychology in turn informs a wide range of specialities within educational studies, including instructional design, educational technology, curriculum development, organizational learning, special education and classroom management. Educational psychology both draws from and contributes to cognitive science and the learning sciences. In universities, departments of educational psychology are usually housed within faculties of education, possibly accounting for the lack of representation of educational psychology content in introductory psychology textbooks.

Social, Moral and Cognitive Development

To understand the characteristics of learners in childhood, adolescence, adulthood, and old age, educational psychology develops and applies theories of human development. Often represented as stages through which people pass as they mature, developmental theories describe changes in mental abilities (cognition), social roles, moral reasoning, and beliefs about the nature of knowledge.

For example, educational psychologists have researched the instructional applicability of Jean Piaget's theory of development, according to which children mature through four stages of cognitive capability. Piaget hypothesized that children are not capable of abstract logical thought until they are older than about 11 years, and therefore younger children need to be taught using concrete objects and examples. Researchers have found that transitions, such as from concrete to abstract logical thought, do not occur at the same time in all domains. A child may be able to think abstractly about mathematics, but remain limited to concrete thought when reasoning about human relationships. Perhaps Piaget's most enduring contribution is his insight that people actively construct their understanding through a self-regulatory process.

Piaget proposed a developmental theory of moral reasoning in which children progress from a naïve understanding of morality based on behaviour and outcomes to a more advanced understanding based on intentions. Piaget's views of moral development were elabourated by Kohlberg into a stage theory of moral development. There is evidence that the moral reasoning described in stage theories is not sufficient to account for moral behaviour. For example, other factors such as modeling (as described by the social cognitive theory of morality) are required to explain bullying.

Rudolf Steiner's model of child development interrelates physical, emotional, cognitive, and moral development in developmental stages similar to those later described by Piaget.

Developmental theories are sometimes presented not as shifts between qualitatively different stages, but as gradual increments on separate dimensions. Development of epistemological beliefs (beliefs about knowledge) have been described in terms of gradual changes in people's belief in: certainty and permanence of knowledge, fixedness of ability, and credibility of authorities such as teachers and experts. People develop more sophisticated beliefs about knowledge as they gain in education and maturity.

Individual Differences and Disabilities

Each person has an individual profile of characteristics, abilities and challenges that result from predisposition, learning and development. These manifest as individual differences in intelligence, creativity, cognitive style, motivation and the capacity to process information, communicate, and relate to others.

The most prevalent disabilities found among school age children are attention-deficit hyperactivity disorder (ADHD), learning disability, dyslexia, and speech disorder. Less common disabilities include mental retardation, hearing impairment, cerebral palsy, epilepsy, and blindness.

Although theories of intelligence have been discussed by philosophers since Plato, intelligence testing is an invention of educational psychology, and is coincident with the development of that discipline. Continuing debates about the nature of intelligence revolve on whether intelligence can be characterized by a single factor known as general intelligence, multiple factors (e.g., Gardner's theory of multiple intelligences), or whether it can be measured at all.

In practice, standardized instruments such as the Stanford-Binet IQ test and the WISC are widely used in economically developed countries to identify children in need of individualized educational treatment. Children classified as gifted are often provided with accelerated or enriched programs. Children with identified deficits may be provided with enhanced education in specific skills such as phonological awareness. In addition to basic abilities, the individual's personality traits are also important, with people higher in conscientiousness and hope attaining superior academic achievements, even after controlling for intelligence and past performance.

Learning and Cognition

Two fundamental assumptions that underlie formal education systems are that students (a) retain knowledge and skills they acquire in school, and (b) can apply them in situations outside the classroom. But are these assumptions accurate? Research has found that, even when students report not using the knowledge acquired in school, a considerable portion is retained for many years and long term retention is strongly dependent on the initial level of mastery. One study found that university students who took a child development course and attained high grades showed, when tested 10 years later, average retention scores of about 30%, whereas those who obtained moderate or lower grades showed average retention scores of about 20%. There is much less consensus on the crucial question of how much knowledge acquired in school transfers to tasks encountered outside formal educational settings, and how such transfer occurs. Some psychologists claim that research evidence for this type of *far transfer* is scarce, while others claim there is abundant evidence of far transfer in specific domains. Several perspectives have been established within which the theories of learning used in educational psychology are formed and contested. These include behaviourism, cognitivism, social cognitive theory, and constructivism. This section summarizes how educational psychology has researched and applied theories within each of these perspectives.

Behavioural Perspective

Applied behaviour analysis, a set of techniques based on the behavioural principles of operant conditioning, is effective in a range of educational settings. For example, teachers can alter student behaviour by systematically rewarding students who follow classroom rules with praise, stars, or tokens exchangeable for sundry items. Despite the demonstrated efficacy of awards in changing behaviour, their use in education has been criticized by proponents of self-determination theory, who claim that praise and other rewards undermine intrinsic motivation. There is evidence that tangible rewards decrease intrinsic motivation in specific situations, such as when the student already has a high level of intrinsic motivation to perform the goal behaviour. But the results showing detrimental effects are counterbalanced by evidence that, in other situations, such as when rewards are given for attaining a gradually increasing standard of performance, rewards enhance intrinsic motivation. Many effective therapies have been based on the principles of applied behaviour analysis, including pivotal response therapy which is used to treat autism spectrum disorders.

Cognitive Perspective

Among current educational psychologists, the cognitive perspective is more widely held than the behavioural perspective, perhaps because it admits causally related mental constructs such as traits, beliefs, memories, motivations and emotions. Cognitive theories claim that memory structures determine how information is perceived, processed, stored, retrieved and forgotten. Among the memory structures theorized by cognitive psychologists are separate but linked visual and verbal systems described by Allan Paivio's dual coding theory. Educational psychologists have used dual coding theory and cognitive load theory to explain how people learn from multimedia presentations.

The spaced learning effect, a cognitive phenomenon strongly supported by psychological research, has broad applicability within education. For example, students have been found to perform better on a test of knowledge about a text passage when a second reading of the passage is delayed rather than immediate. Educational psychology research has confirmed the applicability to education of other findings from cognitive psychology, such as the benefits of using mnemonics for immediate and delayed retention of information.

Problem solving, regarded by many cognitive psychologists as fundamental to learning, is an important research topic in educational psychology. A student is thought to interpret a problem by assigning it to a schema retrieved from long term memory. When the problem is assigned to the wrong schema, the student's attention is subsequently directed away from features of the problem that are inconsistent with the assigned schema. The critical step of finding a mapping between the problem and a pre-existing schema is often cited as supporting the centrality of analogical thinking to problem solving.

Developmental Perspective

Developmental psychology, and especially the psychology of cognitive development, opens a special perspective for educational psychology. This is so because education and the psychology of cognitive development converge on a number of crucial assumptions. First, the psychology of cognitive development defines human cognitive competence at successive phases of development. Education aims to help students acquire knowledge and develop skills which are compatible with their understanding and problem-solving capabilities at different ages. Thus, knowing the students' level on a developmental sequence provides information on the kind and level of knowledge they can assimilate, which, in turn, can be used as a frame for organizing the subject matter to be taught at different school grades. This is the reason why Piaget's theory of cognitive development was so influential for education, especially mathematics and science education. In the same direction, the neo-Piagetian theories of cognitive development suggest that in addition to the concerns above, sequencing of concepts and skills in teaching must take account of the processing and working memory capacities that characterize successive age levels.

Second, the psychology of cognitive development involves understanding how cognitive change takes place and recognizing the factors and processes which enable cognitive competence to develop. Education also capitalizes on cognitive change, because the construction of knowledge presupposes effective teaching methods that would move the student from a lower to a higher level of understanding. Mechanisms such as reflection on actual or mental actions vis-à-vis alternative solutions to problems, tagging new concepts or solutions to symbols that help one recall and mentally manipulate them are just a few examples of how mechanisms of cognitive development may be used to facilitate learning.

Finally, the psychology of cognitive development is concerned with individual differences in the organization of cognitive processes and abilities, in their rate of change, and in their mechanisms of change. The principles underlying intra- and inter-individual differences could be educationally useful, because knowing how students differ in regard to the various dimensions of cognitive development, such as processing and representational capacity, self-understanding and self-regulation, and the various domains of understanding, such as mathematical, scientific, or verbal abilities, would enable the teacher to cater for the needs of the different students so that no one is left behind.

Social Cognitive Perspective

Social cognitive theory is a highly influential fusion of behavioural, cognitive and social elements that was initially developed by educational psychologist Albert Bandura. In its earlier, neo-behavioural incarnation called *social learning theory*, Bandura emphasized the process of observational learning in which a learner's behaviour changes as a result of observing others' behaviour and its consequences. The theory identified several factors that determine whether observing a model will affect behavioural or cognitive change. These factors include the learner's developmental status, the perceived prestige and competence of the model, the consequences received by the model, the relevance of the model's behaviours and consequences to the learner's goals, and the learner's self-efficacy. The concept of self-efficacy, which played an important role in later developments of the theory, refers to the learner's belief in his or her ability to perform the modeled behaviour.

An experiment by Schunk and Hanson, that studied grade 2 students who had previously experienced difficulty in learning subtraction, illustrates the type of research stimulated by social learning theory. One group of students observed a subtraction demonstration by a teacher and then participated in an instructional program on subtraction. A second group observed other grade 2 students performing the same subtraction procedures and then participated in the same instructional program. The students who observed peer models scored higher on a subtraction post-test and also reported greater confidence in their subtraction ability. The results were interpreted as supporting the hypothesis that perceived similarity of the model to the learner increases self-efficacy, leading to more effective learning of modeled behaviour. It is supposed that peer modeling is particularly effective for students who have low self-efficacy.

Over the last decade, much research activity in educational psychology has focused on developing theories of self-regulated learning (SRL) and metacognition. These theories work from the central premise that effective learners are active agents who construct knowledge by setting goals, analysing tasks, planning strategies and monitoring their understanding. Research has indicated that learners who are better at goal setting and self-monitoring tend to have greater intrinsic task interest and self-efficacy; and that teaching learning strategies can increase academic achievement.

Constructivist Perspective

Constructivism is a category of learning theory in which emphasis is placed on the agency and prior 'knowing' and experience of the learner, and often on the social and cultural determinants of the learning process. Educational psychologists distinguish individual (or psychological) constructivism, identified with Piaget's theory of cognitive development, from social constructivism. A dominant influence on the latter type is Lev Vygotsky's work on sociocultural learning, describing how interactions with adults, more capable peers, and cognitive tools are internalized to form mental constructs. Elabourating on Vygotsky's theory, Jerome Bruner and other educational psychologists developed the important concept of instructional scaffolding, in which the social or information environment offers supports for learning that are gradually withdrawn as they become internalized.

Motivation

Motivation is an internal state that activates, guides and sustains behaviour. Educational psychology research on motivation is concerned with the volition or will that students bring to a task, their level of interest and intrinsic motivation, the personally held goals that guide their behaviour, and their belief about the causes of their success or failure.

A form of attribution theory developed by Bernard Weiner describes how students' beliefs about the causes of academic success or failure affect their emotions and motivations. For example, when students attribute failure to lack of ability, and ability is perceived as uncontrollable, they experience the emotions of shame and embarrassment and consequently decrease effort and show poorer performance. In contrast, when students attribute failure to lack of effort, and effort is perceived as controllable, they experience the emotion of guilt and consequently increase effort and show improved performance.

Motivational theories also explain how learners' goals affect the way they engage with academic tasks. Those who have *mastery goals* strive to increase their ability and knowledge. Those who have *performance approach goals* strive for high grades and seek opportunities to demonstrate their abilities. Those who have *performance avoidance* goals are driven by fear of failure and avoid situations where their abilities are exposed.

Research has found that mastery goals are associated with many positive outcomes such as persistence in the face of failure, preference for challenging tasks, creativity and intrinsic motivation. Performance avoidance goals are associated with negative outcomes such as poor concentration while studying, disorganized studying, less self-regulation, shallow information processing and test anxiety. Performance approach goals are associated with positive outcomes, and some negative outcomes such as an unwillingness to seek help and shallow information processing.

Locus of control is a salient factor in the successful academic performance of students. During the 1970s and 1980s, Cassandra B. Whyte did significant educational research studying locus of control as related to the academic achievement of students pursuing higher education coursework. Much of her educational research and publications focused upon the theories of Julian B. Rotter in regard to the importance of internal control and successful academic performance. Whyte reported that individuals who perceive and believe that their hard work may lead to more successful academic outcomes, instead of depending on luck or fate, persist and achieve academically at a higher level. Therefore, it is important to provide education and counselling in this regard.

Research Methodology

The research methods used in educational psychology tend to be drawn from psychology and other social sciences. There is also a history of significant methodological innovation by educational psychologists, and psychologists investigating educational problems. Research methods address problems in both research design and data analysis. Research design informs the planning of experiments and observational studies to ensure that their results have internal, external and ecological validity. Data analysis encompasses methods for processing both quantitive (numerical) and qualitative (non-numerical) research data. Although, historically, the use of quantitative methods was often considered an essential mark of scholarship, modern educational psychology research uses both quantitative and qualitative methods.

Quantitative Methods

Perhaps first among the important methodological innovations of educational psychology was the development and application of factor analysis by Charles Spearman. Factor analysis is mentioned here as one example of the many multivariate statistical methods used by educational psychologists. Factor analysis is used to summarize relationships among a large set of variables or test questions, develop theories about mental constructs such as self-efficacy or anxiety, and assess the reliability and validity of test scores. Over one hundred years after its introduction by Spearman, factor analysis has become a research staple figuring prominently in educational psychology journals.

Because educational assessment is fundamental to most quantitative research in the field, educational psychologists have made significant contributions to the field of psychometrics. For example, alpha, the widely used measure of test reliability was developed by educational psychologist Lee Cronbach. The reliability of assessments are routinely reported in quantitative educational research. Although, originally, educational measurement methods were built on classical test theory, item response theory and Rasch models are now used extensively in educational measurement worldwide. These models afford advantages over classical test theory, including the capacity to produce standard errors of measurement for each score or pattern of scores on assessments and the capacity to handle missing responses.

Meta-analysis, the combination of individual research results to produce a quantitative literature review, is another methodological innovation with a close association to educational psychology. In a meta-analysis, effect sizes that represent, for example, the differences between treatment groups in a set of similar experiments, are averaged to obtain a single aggregate value representing the best estimate of the effect of treatment. Several decades after Pearson's work with early versions of meta-analysis, Glass published the first application of modern meta-analytic techniques and triggered their broad application across the social and biomedical sciences. Today, meta-analysis is among the most common types of literature review found in educational psychology research.

Other quantitative research issues associated with educational psychology include the use of nested research designs (e.g., a student nested within a classroom, which is nested within a school, which is nested within a district, etc.) and the use of longitudinal statistical models to measure change.

Qualitative Methods

Qualitative methods are used in educational studies whose purpose is to describe events, processes and situations of theoretical significance. The qualitative methods used in educational psychology often derive from anthropology, sociology or sociolinguistics. For example, the anthropological method of ethnography has been used to describe teaching and learning in classrooms. In studies of this type, the researcher may gather detailed field notes as a participant observer or passive observer. Later, the notes and other data may be categorized and interpreted by methods such as grounded theory. Triangulation, the practice of cross-checking findings with multiple data sources, is highly valued in qualitative research.

Case studies are forms of qualitative research focusing on a single person, organization, event, or other entity. In one case study, researchers conducted a 150 minute, semi-structured interview with a 20-year old woman who had a history of suicidal thinking between the ages of 14 to 18. They analysed an audio-recording of the interview to understand the roles of cognitive development, identity formation and social attachment in ending her suicidal thinking.

Qualitative analysis is most often applied to verbal data from sources such as conversations, interviews, focus groups, and personal journals. Qualitative methods are thus, typically, approaches to gathering, processing and reporting verbal data. One of the most commonly used methods for qualitative research in educational psychology is protocol analysis. In this method the research participant is asked to *think aloud* while performing a task, such as solving a math problem. In protocol analysis the verbal data is thought to indicate which information the subject is attending to, but is explicitly not interpreted as an explanation or justification for behaviour. In contrast, the method of verbal analysis does admit learners' explanations as a way to reveal their mental model or misconceptions (e.g., of the laws of motion). The most fundamental operations in both protocol and verbal analysis are segmenting (isolating) and categorizing sections of verbal data. Conversation analysis and discourse analysis, sociolinguistic methods that focus more specifically on the structure of conversational interchange (e.g., between a teacher and student), have been used to assess the process of conceptual change in science learning. Qualitative methods are also used to analyse information in a variety of media, such as students' drawings and concept maps, video-recorded interactions, and computer log records.

Applications in Instructional Design and Technology

Instructional design, the systematic design of materials, activities and interactive environments for learning, is broadly informed by educational psychology theories and research. For example, in defining learning goals or objectives, instructional designers often use a taxonomy of educational objectives created by Benjamin Bloom and colleagues. Bloom also researched mastery learning, an instructional strategy in which learners only advance to a new learning objective after they have mastered its prerequisite objectives. Bloom discovered that a combination of mastery learning with one-to-one tutoring is highly effective, producing learning outcomes far exceeding those normally achieved in classroom instruction. Gagné, another psychologist, had earlier developed an influential method of task analysis in which a terminal learning goal is expanded into a hierarchy of learning objectives connected by prerequisite relations.

- Intelligent tutoring system
- Educational technology
- John R. Anderson
- Cognitive tutor
- Cooperative learning
- Collaborative learning
- problem-based learning
- Computer supported collaborative learning
- William Winn
- constructive alignment.

Applications in Teaching

Research on classroom management and pedagogy is conducted to guide teaching practice and form a foundation for teacher education programs. The goals of classroom management are to create an environment conducive to learning and to develop students' self-management skills. More specifically, classroom management strives to create positive teacher-student and peer relationships, manage student groups to sustain on-task behaviour, and use counselling and other psychological methods to aid students who present persistent psychosocial problems.

Introductory educational psychology is a commonly required area of study in most North American teacher education programs. When taught in that context, its content varies, but it typically emphasizes learning theories (especially cognitively oriented ones), issues about motivation, assessment of students' learning, and classroom management. A developing Wikibook about educational psychology gives more detail about the educational psychology topics that are typically presented in preservice teacher education.

Special Education

Special education is the education of students with special needs in a way that addresses the students' individual differences and needs. Ideally, this process involves the individually planned and systematically monitored arrangement of teaching procedures, adapted equipment and materials, accessible settings, and other interventions designed to help learners with special needs achieve a higher level of personal self-sufficiency and success in school and community than would be available if the student were only given access to a typical classroom education. Common special needs include challenges with learning, communication challenges, emotional and behavioural disorders, physical disabilities, and developmental disorders. Students with these kinds of special needs are likely to benefit from additional educational services such as different approaches to teaching, use of technology, a specifically adapted teaching area, or resource room. Intellectual giftedness is a difference in learning and can also benefit from specialized teaching techniques or different educational programs, but the term "special education" is generally used to specifically indicate instruction of students whose special needs reduce their ability to learn independently or in an ordinary classroom, and gifted education is handled separately.

In most developed countries, educators are modifying teaching methods and environments so that the maximum number of students are served in general education environments. Special education in developed countries is often regarded less as a "place" and more as "a range of services, available in every school." Integration can reduce social stigmas and improve academic achievement for many students.

The opposite of *special education* is *general education*. General education is the standard curriculum presented with standard teaching methods and without additional supports.

Individual Needs

A special education program should be customized to address each individual student's unique needs. Special educators provide a continuum of services, in which students with special needs receive services in varying degrees based on their individual needs. Special education programs need to be individualized so that they address the unique combination of needs in a given student.

Students with special needs are assessed to determine their specific strengths and weaknesses. Placement, resources, and goals are determined on the basis of the student's needs. Accommodations and Modifications to the regular program may include changes in curriculum, supplementary aides or equipment, and the provision of specialized physical adaptations that allow students to participate in the educational environment to the fullest extent possible.

Students may need this help to access subject matter, to physically gain access to the school, or to meet their emotional needs. For example, if the assessment determines that the student cannot write by hand because of a physical disability, then the school might provide a computer for typing assignments, or allow the student to answer questions orally instead.

If the school determines that the student is severely distracted by the normal activities in a large, busy classroom, then the student might be placed in a smaller classroom such as a resource room.

Methods of Provision

Education researchers, particularly in North America, have identified different kinds of provision in special education. They distinguish four types of provision:

- *Inclusion:* In this approach, students with special needs spend most or all of their time with students who do not have special educational needs. Implementation of this approach varies. Because inclusion can require substantial modification of the general curriculum, most schools use it only for selected students with mild to moderate special needs, for which is accepted as a best practice. In the United States, three out of five students with academic learning challenges spend the overwhelming majority of their time in the regular classroom. Students with special needs are educated in regular classes for nearly all of the day, or at least half of the day. Most specialized services are provided outside a regular classroom, particularly if these services require special equipment or might be disruptive to the rest of the class (such as speech therapy). In this case, the student occasionally leaves the regular classroom to attend smaller, more intensive instructional sessions in a resource room, or to receive other related services, such as speech and language therapy, occupational and/or physical therapy, and social work.

- *Mainstreaming* refers to the practice of educating students with special needs in regular classes during specific time periods based on their skills. Students are segregated in separate classes for the rest of the time.
- *Segregation* in a self-contained classroom or special school: Full-time placement in a special education classroom may be referred to as *segregation*. In this model, students with special needs spend no time in ordinary classes. Segregated students may attend the same school where regular classes are provided, but spend their time exclusively in a separate classroom for students with special needs. If their special class is located in an ordinary school, they may be provided opportunities for social integration. Alternatively, these students may attend a special school.
- *Exclusion:* A student who does not receive instruction in any school is said to be *excluded*. Such exclusion may occur where there is no legal mandate for special education services. It may also occur when a student is in hospital, homebound, or detained by the criminal justice system. These students may receive one-on-one instruction or group instruction. Students who have been suspended or expelled are not considered excluded in this sense.

Prerequisites for Inclusion

In an article in *British Journal of Special Education*, Professor Rita Jordan provided challenges to the idea of inclusion for young people with autistic spectrum disorders.

So, what would an effective inclusive educational system look like? Primarily, it would need to be flexible. It cannot rely on centrally-determined curricula and teaching methodologies, although there could, of course, be guidance. Who could manage such a system? Surely it could only be done by properly trained, and professional, teachers. I do not mean that all mainstream teachers must be 'experts' on ASD, but they must know about learning and teaching (and not just 'delivery' of packages) and about the diversity that exists in humankind in the way we learn and understand the world. If educators teach in a way that attains diversity (and modern Information Technology (IT) techniques will make this so much easier), then more children with different minds will be able to manage in mainstream settings, without needing to have special (and certainly not segregated) support. This will also benefit those disruptive boys currently disaffected by our female-and language-dominated educational system, and those with attention deficit hyperactivity disorder (ADHD), dyslexia and so on.

Related Services

Related services means developmental, corrective, and other supportive services as are required to assist a student with a disability and includes speech and language pathology, audiology, psychological services, physical therapy, occupational therapy, counselling services, including rehabilitation counselling, orientation and mobility services, medical services as defined by regulations, parent counselling and training, school health services, school social work, assistive technology services, other appropriate developmental or corrective support services, appropriate access to recreation and other appropriate support services.

In some countries, most related services are provided by the schools; in others, they are provided by the normal healthcare and social services systems.

Issues

At-risk students (those with educational needs that are not associated with a disability) are often placed in classes with students who have disabilities. Critics assert that placing at-risk students in the same classes as students with disabilities may impede the educational progress of people with disabilities. Special education classes under the mainstreaming model have been criticized for a watered-down curriculum. The practice of inclusion (in mainstream classrooms) has been criticized by advocates and some parents of children with special needs because some of these students require instructional methods that differ dramatically from typical classroom methods. Critics assert that it is not possible to deliver effectively two or more very different instructional methods in the same classroom. As a result, the educational progress of students who depend on different instructional methods to learn often fall even further behind their peers.

Parents of typically developing children sometimes fear that the special needs of a single "fully included" student will take critical levels of attention and energy away from the rest of the class and thereby impair the academic achievements of all students. Some parents, advocates, and students have concerns about the eligibility criteria and their application. In some cases, parents and students protest the students' placement into special education programs. For example, a student may be placed into the special education programs due to a mental health condition such as obsessive compulsive disorder, depression, anxiety, panic attacks or ADHD, while the student and his parents believe that the condition is adequately managed through medication and outside therapy. In other cases, students whose parents believe they require the additional support of special education services are denied participation in the program based on the eligibility criteria.

National Approaches

Asia

Japan

Training of disabled students, particularly at the upper-secondary level, emphasizes vocational education to enable students to be as independent as possible within society. Vocational training varies considerably depending on the student's disability, but the options are limited for some. It is clear that the government is aware of the necessity of broadening the range of possibilities for these students. Advancement to higher education is also a goal of the government, and it struggles to have institutions of higher learning accept more disabled students.

Australia

Australian Association of Special Education Inc (AASE)'s position is informed by the Disability Standards for Education 2005 which require that students with disabilities are treated on the same basis as other students in regards to enrolment and participation in education.

The characteristics of effective instruction are reported by educational researchers who study the critical teacher behaviours in classroom settings. it must be noted that effective instruction is not defined as a single method of teaching but rather as a series of characteristics which can be embedded into a range of teaching approaches. Effective instruction enables the efficient use of class time to maximise learning outcomes for students maximises on-task behaviour of students and minimises inappropriate behaviour.

Effective instruction involves implementing strategies in planning, managing, delivering and evaluating instruction. Meta-analyses of the research indicate that teaching approaches that combine direct instruction (explicit, teacher-directed instruction in basic skills and content) and strategy instruction (explicit instruction to teach cognitive and meta-cognitive strategies) are most successful. Effective teachers are competent with a wide array of instructional strategies, including teacher-directed, explicit instruction and are able to select the most appropriate strategies for individual students and specific content.

There is a danger of creating a self-fulfilling prophecy when teachers have low expectations of students with special educational needs. Teachers and school executive are able to create a positive school climate that values and accepts all students. With the advent of inclusive curriculum, collaborative partnerships between students, families, special educators, teachers, teacher aides and other relevant professional are imperative. Collaboration provides the vehicle for the pooling of knowledge about curriculum, current curriculum trends, and the knowledge of effective practices to meet the needs of the diverse range of students in any class.

Europe

Each country in Europe has its own special education support structures.

Denmark

In Denmark, 99% of students with specific learning difficulties like dyslexia are educated alongside students without any learning challenges.

Germany

Most students with special needs in Germany attend a special school that serves only children with special needs. These include:

- "Sonderschule für Lernbehinderte" (special school for learning disabilities)-for children who have challenges that impair learning
- "Schule mit dem Förderschwerpunkt Geistige Entwicklung" (school for cognitive development)-for children with very severe learning challenges
- "Förderschule Schwerpunkt emotionale und soziale Entwicklung" (school for emotional and social development)-for children who have special emotional needs

One in 21 German students attends a special school. Teachers at those schools are specially trained professionals who have specialized in special needs education while in college. Special schools often have a very favorable student-teacher ratio and facilities other schools do not have.

Some special needs children in Germany do not attend a special school, but are educated in a mainstream school such as a Hauptschule or Gesamtschule (comprehensive school).

The Netherlands

Norway

The National Support System for Special Needs Education (Statped) is managed by the Norwegian Directorate for Education and Training. The general objective for Statped is to give guidance and support to those in charge of the education in municipalities and county administrations to ensure that children, young people and adults with major and special educational needs are secured well-advised educational and developmental provisions. The institutions affiliated with Statped offer a broad spectrum of services. Statped consists of 13 resource centres owned by the State, and 4 units for special education, where Statped buys services. These centres offer special educational guidance and support for local authorities and county administrations.

United Kingdom

In England and Wales the acronym *SEN* for Special Educational Needs denotes the condition of having special educational needs, the services which provide the support and the programmes and staff which implement the education. In England *SEN PPS* refers to the Special Educational Needs Parent Partnership Service. *SENAS* is the special educational needs assessment service, which is part of the Local Authority. *SENCO* refers to a special educational needs coordinator, who usually works with schools and the children within schools who have special educational needs. The Special Educational Needs Parent Partnership Services help parents with the planning and delivery of their child's educational provision. The Department for Education oversees special education in England.

In Scotland the Additional Support Needs Act places an obligation on education authorities to meet the needs of all students in consultation with other agencies and parents. In Scotland the term Special Educational Needs (SEN), and its variants are not official terminology although the very recent implementation of the Additional Support for Learning Act means that both *SEN* and *ASN* (Additional Support Needs) are used interchangeably in current common practice.

North America

In North America, special education is commonly abbreviated as *special ed*, *SpecEd*, *SPED*, or *SpEd* in a professional context.

United States

All special-needs students receive an Individualized Education Program (IEP) that outlines how the school will meet the student's individual needs. The Individuals with Disabilities Education Act (IDEA) requires that students with special needs be provided with a Free Appropriate Public Education in the Least Restrictive Environment that is appropriate to the student's needs. Government-run schools provide special education in varying degrees from least restrictive to the most restrictive.

History

Beginning in 1952, Civitans were the first to provide widespread training for teachers of children with developmental disorders in the United States. During the 1960s, in some part due to the civil rights movement, some researchers began to focus on the disparity of education amongst people with disabilities.

However, students with substantial impairments were frequently not allowed to enrol in regular public schools until the passage of the federal Education for All Handicapped Children Act in 1975 (since renamed the Individuals with Disabilities Education Act (IDEA)). This law required schools to provide services to students previously denied access to an appropriate education. According to the Department of Education, approximately 6 million children (roughly 10 percent of all school-aged children) currently receive some type of special education services.

Lesson Plan

A lesson plan is a teacher's detailed description of the course of instruction for an individual lesson. Lesson plan is a plan or a frame work of how a topic is to be thought to the students in a class room. A daily lesson plan is developed by a teacher to guide class instruction. The detail of the plan will vary depending on the preference of the teacher, subject being covered, and the need and/or curiosity of children. There may be requirements mandated by the school system regarding the plan.

Developing a Lesson Plan

While there are many formats for a lesson plan, most lesson plans contain some or all of these elements, typically in this order:

- *Title* of the lesson
- *Time* required to complete the lesson
- List of required *materials*
- List of *objectives*, which may be *behavioural objectives* (what the student can *do* at lesson completion) or *knowledge objectives* (what the student *knows* at lesson completion)
- The *set* (or lead-in, or bridge-in) that focuses students on the lesson's skills or concepts—these include showing pictures or models, asking leading questions, or reviewing previous lessons
- An *instructional component* that describes the sequence of events that make up the lesson, including the teacher's instructional input and guided practice the students use to try new skills or work with new ideas
- *Independent practice* that allows students to extend skills or knowledge on their own
- A *summary*, where the teacher wraps up the discussion and answers questions
- An *evaluation* component, a test for mastery of the instructed skills or concepts—such as a set of questions to answer or a set of instructions to follow
- *Analysis* component the teacher uses to reflect on the lesson itself —such as what worked, what needs improving
- A *continuity* component reviews and reflects on content from the previous lesson.

A Well Developed Lesson Plan

A well developed lesson plan reflects interests and needs of students. It incorporates best practices for the educational field. The lesson plan correlates with the teacher's philosophy of education, which is what the teacher feels is the purpose of educating the students.

Secondary English program lesson plans, for example, usually centre around four topics. They are literary theme, elements of language and composition, literary history, and literary genre. A broad, thematic lesson plan is preferable, because it allows a teacher to create various research, writing, speaking, and reading assignments. It helps an instructor teach different literature genres and incorporate videotapes, films, and television programs. Also, it facilitates teaching literature and English together. School requirements and a teacher's personal tastes, in that order, determine the exact requirements for a lesson plan.

Unit plans follow much the same format as a lesson plan, but cover an entire unit of work, which may span several days or weeks. Modern constructivist teaching styles may not require individual lesson plans. The unit plan may include specific objectives and timelines, but lesson plans can be more fluid as they adapt to student needs and learning styles.

Setting an Objective

The first thing a teacher must do is decide on the lesson plan's focus. The teacher creates one idea or question they want the students to explore or answer. Next, the teacher creates classroom activities that correlate with the established idea or question. This includes individual and group activities. Having established these activities, the teacher identifies what language arts skills the lesson plan must cover. After the teacher completes these activities, they must ensure the lesson plan adheres to the best practices used in language arts. This includes conducting research on what teaching methods result in a high success rate for students. The teacher must ensure the lesson plan goals are compatible with the developmental level of the students. The teacher must also ensure their student achievement expectations are reasonable.

Selecting Lesson Plan Material

A lesson plan must correlate with the text book the class uses. The school usually selects the text books or provides teachers with a limited text book choice for a particular unit. The teacher must take great care and select the most appropriate book for the students.

Types of Assignments

The instructor must decide whether class assignments are whole-class, small groups, workshops, independent work, peer learning, or contractual:

- Whole-class—the teacher lectures to the class as a whole and has the class collectively participate in classroom discussions.
- Small groups—students work on assignments in groups of three or four.
- Workshops—students perform various tasks simultaneously. Workshop activities must be tailored to the lesson plan.
- Independent work—students complete assignments individually.
- Peer learning—students work together, face to face, so they can learn from one another.
- Contractual work—teacher and student establish an agreement that the student must perform a certain amount of work by a deadline.

These assignment categories (e.g. peer learning, independent, small groups) can also be used to guide the instructor's choice of assessment measures that can provide information about student and class comprehension of the material. As discussed by Biggs (1999), there are additional questions an instructor can consider when choosing which type of assignment would provide the most benefit to students. These include:

- What level of learning do the students need to attain before choosing assignments with varying difficulty levels?

- What is the amount of time the instructor wants the students to use to complete the assignment?
- How much time and effort does the instructor have to provide student grading and feedback?
- What is the purpose of the assignment? (e.g. to track student learning; to provide students with time to practice concepts; to practice incidental skills such as group process or independent research)
- How does the assignment fit with the rest of the lesson plan? Does the assignment test content knowledge or does it require application in a new context?

History

Modern educational psychologists are not the first to analyse educational processes. Philosophers of education such as Democritus, Quintilian, Vives and Comenius, had examined, classified and judged the methods of education centuries before the beginnings of psychology in the late 1800s. Instead, aspirations of the new discipline rested on the application of the scientific methods of observation and experimentation to educational problems. Even in the earliest years of the discipline, educational psychologists recognized the limitations of this new approach. In his famous series of lectures *Talks to Teachers on Psychology*, published in 1899 and now regarded as the first educational psychology textbook, the pioneering American psychologist William James commented that:

> *"Psychology is a science, and teaching is an art; and sciences never generate arts directly out of themselves. An intermediate inventive mind must make that application, by using its originality. "*

According to Berliner educational psychology theorists' attitude to the world of educational practice has shifted from initial interest to disdain, and eventually to respect.

Charles Hubbard Judd

In 1912, Thorndike, who developed the theory of instrumental conditioning, presaged later work on programmed instruction, mastery learning and computer-based learning:

"If, by a miracle of mechanical ingenuity, a book could be so arranged that only to him who had done what was directed on page one would page two become visible, and so on, much that now requires personal instruction could be managed by print."

Among the few works of educational psychology historiography is *Educational Psychology: A Century of Contributions* which presents chapter-length biographies of 16 eminent scholars whose work has significantly influenced the development of educational psychology.

Careers in Educational Psychology

Education and Training

A person may be considered an educational psychologist after completing a graduate degree in educational psychology or a closely related field. Universities establish educational psychology graduate programs in either psychology departments or, more commonly, faculties of education.

Educational psychologists work in a variety of settings. Some work in university settings where they carry out research on the cognitive and social processes of human development, learning and education. Educational psychologists may also work as consultants in designing and creating educational materials, classroom programs and online courses.

Educational psychologists who work in k-12 school settings (called school psychologists in the US and Canada) are trained at the masters and doctoral levels. In addition to conducting assessments, school psychologists provide services such as academic and behavioural intervention, counselling, teacher consultation, and crisis intervention. In the UK, status as a *Chartered Educational Psychologist* is gained by completing:

- an undergraduate degree in psychology permitting registration with the British Psychological Society
- two or three years experience working with children, young people and their families.
- a three-year professional doctorate in educational psychology.

The previous requirement to train and work for two years as a teacher has now been abandoned.

Employment Outlook

Employment for psychologists in the United States is expected to grow faster than most occupations through the year 2014, with anticipated growth of 18-26%. One in four psychologists are employed in educational settings. In the United States, the median salary for psychologists in primary and secondary schools is US$58,360 as of May 2004.

In recent decades the participation of women as professional researchers in North American educational psychology has risen dramatically. The percentage of female authors of peer-reviewed journal articles doubled from 1976 (24%) to 1995 (51%), and has since remained constant. Female membership on educational psychology journal editorial boards increased from 17% in 1976 to 47% in 2004. Over the same period, the proportion of chief editor positions held by women increased from 22% to 70%.

7

Stages of Human Development

Human development is the process of growing to maturity. In biological terms, this entails growth from a one-celled zygote to an adult human being.

Physical Stages of Human Life

There are no universal definitions for terms of age-related physical development stages, but following are some approximate age ranges:

- Prenatal (fertilization-birth)
    - o Embryo-(fertilization-8 weeks of gestational phase)
        - * Zygote, the point of conception, fertilization
        - * Blastocyst the period between conception and embryonic stages
        - * Embryo; the embryonic period starts at three weeks and continues until the end of the 8th week of pregnancy
    - o Fetus (8 weeks of gestational phase-birth)
- Child (birth-puberty)
    - o Neonate (newborn) (0-30 days)
    - o Infant (baby) (1 month-11 months)
    - o Toddler (1-2 years)
    - o Play age (3-5 years)
    - o Primary school age (also called prepubescence) (4-12)

    * Elementary school age (also called middle childhood) (4-9)
    * Preadolescence (preteen, or late childhood. The child in this and the previous phase are called *schoolchild* (*schoolboy* or *schoolgirl*), when still of primary school age.) (10-12 years)

- Adolescence and puberty (13-19 years)
    - o Peripuberty (8-10 until 15-17)
- Adult (20+ years)
    - o Early adulthood (20-39 years)
    - o Middle adulthood (40-59 years)
    - o Advanced adulthood/Senior citizen (60+ years)
- Death (occurs at various ages, depending on person)
    - o Decomposition (breakdown of the body after death).

Childhood

Childhood is the age span ranging from birth to adolescence. In developmental psychology, childhood is divided up into the developmental stages of toddlerhood (learning to walk), early childhood (play age), middle childhood (school age), and adolescence (post-puberty).

Age Ranges of Childhood

The term *childhood* is non-specific and can imply a varying range of years in human development. Developmentally, it refers to the period between infancy and adulthood. In common terms, childhood is considered to start from birth. Some consider that childhood, as a concept of play and innocence, ends at adolescence. In many countries, there is an age of majority when childhood officially ends and a person legally becomes an adult. The age ranges anywhere from 13 to 21, with 18 being the most common.

Developmental Stages of Childhood

Child development stages describe theoretical milestones of child development. Many stage models of development have been proposed, used as working concepts and in some cases asserted as nativist theories.

Specifications Sorted by Reached Age

1–4 Months

Physical

- Head and chest circumference are nearly equal to the part of the abdomen.
- Head circumference increases approximately 2 cm per month until two months, then increases 1.5 cm per month until four months. Increases are an important indication of continued brain growth.
- Continues to breathe using abdominal muscles.
- Posterior fontanel.
- Anterior fontanel.
- Skin remains sensitive and easily irritated.
- Legs.
- Gums are red.
- Has six to ten baby teeth.
- Cries with tears.
- Eyes begin moving together in unison (binocular vision).

Motor Development

- Rooting and sucking reflexes are well developed.
- Swallowing reflex and tongue movements are immature;inability to move food to the back of the mouth.
- Grasp reflex.
- *Landau reflex* appears near the middle of this period; when baby is held in a prone (face down) position, the head is held upright and legs are fully extended.
- Grasps with entire hand; strength insufficient to hold items. Holds hands in an open or semi-open position.
- Movements are large and jerky.
- Raises head and upper body on arms when in a prone position.
- Turns head side to side when in a supine (face up)

position; can not hold head up and in line with the body.

- Upper body parts are more active: clasps hands above face, waves arms about, reaches for objects.
- Is not a baby.

4–8 Months

Physical

- Head and chest circumferences are basically equal.
- Head circumference increases approximately 1 cm per month until six to seven months, then 0.5 cm per month; head circumference should continue to increase steadily, indicating healthy, ongoing brain growth.
- Breathing is abdominal; respiration rate depending on activity; rate and patterns vary from infant to infant.
- Teeth may begin to appear, with upper and lower incisors coming in first. Gums may become red and swollen, accompanied by increased drooling, chewing, biting, and mouthing of objects.
- Legs may appear bowed; bowing gradually disappears as infant grows older.
- Fat rolls ("Baby Fat") appear on thighs, upper arms and neck.
- True eye color is established.

Motor Development

- Reflexive behaviours are changing:
- Blinking reflex is well established
- Sucking reflex becomes voluntary
- Moro reflex disappears
- When lowered suddenly, infant throws out arms as a protective measure.
- Swallowing reflex appears and allows infant to move solid foods from front of mouth to the back for swallowing.
- Picks up objects using finger and thumb (pincer grip).

- Reaches for objects with both arms simultaneously; later reaches with one hand or the other.
- Transfers objects from one hand to the other; grasps object using entire hand (palmar grasp).
- Handles, shakes, and pounds objects; puts everything in mouth.
- Able to hold bottle.
- Sits alone without support, holding head erect, back straightened, and arms propped forward for support
- Pulls self into a crawling position by raising up on arms and drawing knees up beneath the body; rocks back and forth, but generally does not move forward.
- Lifts head when placed on back.
- Can roll over from back or stomach position.
- May accidentally begin scooting backwards when placed on stomach; soon will begin to crawl forward.
- Looks for fallen objects by 7 months
- Plays 'peek-a-boo' games
- Cannot understand "no" or "danger"

8–12 Months

Physical

- Respiration rates vary with activity
- Environmental conditions, weather, activity, and clothing still affect variations in body temperature.
- Head and chest circumference remain equal.
- Continues to use abdominal muscles for breathing.
- Anterior fontanel begins to close.
- More teeth appear, often in the order of two lower incisors then two upper incisors followed by four more incisors and two lower molars but some babies may still be waiting for their first.
- Arm and hands are more developed than feet and legs (cephalocaudal development); hands appear large in proportion to other body parts.

- Legs may continue to appear bowed.
- "Baby Fat" continues to appear on thighs, upper arms and neck.
- Feet appear flat as arch has not yet fully developed.
- Both eyes work in unison (true binocular coordination).
- Can see distant objects (4 to 6 m or 13 to 20 ft away) and points at them.

Motor Development

- Reaches with one hand leading to grasp an offered object or toy.
- Manipulates objects, transferring them from one hand to the other.
- Explores new objects by poking with one finger.
- Uses deliberate pincer grasp to pick up small objects, toys, and finger foods.
- Stacks objects; also places objects inside one another.
- Releases objects or toys by dropping or throwing; cannot intentionally put an object down.
- Beginning to pull self to a standing position.
- Beginning to stand alone, leaning on furniture for support; moves around obstacles by side-stepping.
- Has good balance when sitting; can shift positions without falling.
- Creeps on hands and knees; crawls up and down stairs.
- Walks with adult support, holding onto adult's hand; may begin to walk alone.
- Watches people, objects, and activities in the immediate environment.
- Shows awareness of distant objects (4 to 6 m or 13 to 20 ft away) by pointing at them.
- Responds to hearing tests (voice localization); however, loses interest quickly and, therefore, may be difficult to test informally.
- Follows simple instructions.

- Reaches for toys that are out of reach but visible
- Recognizes objects in reverse
- Drops thing intentionally and repeats and watches object
- Imitates activities like playing drum.

Toddlers (12–24 Months)

Physical

- Weight is now approximately 3 times the child's birth weight.
- Respiration rate varies with emotional state and activity.
- Rate of growth slows
- Head size increases slowly; grows approximately 1.3 cm every six months; anterior fontanelle is nearly closed at eighteen months as bones of the skull thicken.
- Chest circumference is larger than head circumference.
- Rapid eruption of teeth; six to ten new teeth will appear.
- Legs may still appear bowed.
- Toddler will begin to lose the "Baby Fat" once he/she begins walking.
- Body shape changes; takes on more adult-like appearance; still appears top-heavy; abdomen protrudes, back is swayed.

Motor Development

- Crawls skillfully and quickly.
- Stands alone with feet spread apart, legs stiffened, and arms extended for support.
- Gets to feet unaided.
- Most children walk unassisted near the end of this period; falls often; not always able to maneuver around obstacles, such as furniture or toys.
- Uses furniture to lower self to floor; collapses backwards into a sitting position or falls forward on hands and then sits.
- Enjoys pushing or pulling toys while walking.

- Repeatedly picks up objects and throws them; direction becomes more deliberate.
- Attempts to run; has difficulty stopping and usually just drops to the floor.
- Crawls up stairs on all fours; goes down stairs in same position.
- Sits in a small chair.
- Carries toys from place to place.
- Enjoys crayons and markers for scribbling; uses whole-arm movement.
- Helps feed self; enjoys holding spoon (often upside down) and drinking from a glass or cup; not always accurate in getting utensils into mouth; frequent spills should be expected.
- Helps turn pages in book.
- Stacks two to six objects per day.

Cognitive Development

- Enjoys object-hiding activities
- Early in this period, the child always searches in the same location for a hidden object (if the child has watched the hiding of an object). Later, the child will search in several locations.
- Passes toy to other hand when offered a second object (referred to as "crossing the midline"-an important neurological development).
- Manages three to four objects by setting an object aside (on lap or floor) when presented with a new toy.
- Puts toys in mouth less often.
- Enjoys looking at picture books.
- Demonstrates understanding of functional relationships (objects that belong together): Puts spoon in bowl and then uses spoon as if eating; places teacup on saucer and sips from cup; tries to make doll stand up.
- Shows or offers toy to another person to look at.
- Names many everyday objects.

- Shows increasing understanding of spatial and form discrimination: puts all pegs in a pegboard; places three geometric shapes in large formboard or puzzle.
- Places several small items (blocks, clothespins, cereal pieces) in a container or bottle and then dumps them out.
- Tries to make mechanical objects work after watching someone else do so.
- Responds with some facial movement, but cannot truly imitate facial expression.
- Most children with autism are diagnosed at this age.

Language

- Produces considerable "jargon": puts words and sounds together into speech-like (inflected) patterns.
- Holophrastic speech: uses one word to convey an entire thought; meaning depends on the inflection ("me" may be used to request more cookies or a desire to feed self). Later; produces two-word phrases to express a complete thought (telegraphic speech): "More cookie," "Daddy bye-bye."
- Follows simple directions, "Give Daddy the cup."
- When asked, will point to familiar persons, animals, and toys.
- Identifies three body parts if someone names them: "Show me your nose (toe, ear)."
- Indicates a few desired objects and activities by name: "Bye-bye," "cookie"; verbal request is often accompanied by an insistent gesture.
- Responds to simple questions with "yes" or "no" and appropriate head movement.
- Speech is 25 to 50 percent intelligible during this period.
- Locates familiar objects on request (if child knows location of objects).
- Acquires and uses five to fifty words; typically these are words that refer to animals, food, and toys.
- Uses gestures, such as pointing or pulling, to direct adult attention.

- Enjoys rhymes and songs; tries to join in.
- Seems aware of reciprocal (back and forth) aspects of conversational exchanges; some turn-taking in other kinds of vocal exchanges, such as making and imitating sounds.

Social

- less wary of strangers.
- Helps pick up and put away toys.
- Plays by themselves
- Enjoys being held and read to.
- Often imitates adult actions in play.
- Enjoys adult attention; likes to know that an adult is near; gives hugs and kisses.
- Recognizes self in mirror.
- Enjoys the companionship of other children, but does not play cooperatively.
- Beginning to assert independence; often refuses to cooperate with daily routines that once were enjoyable; resists getting dressed, putting on shoes, eating, taking a bath; wants to try doing things without help.
- May have a tantrum when things go wrong or if overly tired or frustrated.
- Exceedingly curious about people and surroundings; toddlers need to be watched carefully to prevent them from getting into unsafe situations.

Psychological

Autonomy vs. Shame and Doubt (will); (J. Chasse, 2008) Psychosocial stimulation is vital during the toddler years. Play begins to become interactive. Toddlers begin to learn and exhibit independence, but ironically they enjoy sharing this discovery with others. Another important advancement is active social play with adults including mirroring and repeating. Songs, rhymes, and finger plays (e.g. incy wincy spider, little teapot, etc.) are a great way to encourage and stimulate this area of development.

Two Year Old

Physical

- Posture is more erect; abdomen still large and protruding, back swayed, because abdominal muscles are not yet fully developed.
- Respirations are slow and regular
- Body temperature continues to fluctuate with activity, emotional state, and environment.
- Brain reaches about 80 percent of its adult size.
- 15 baby teeth almost finished growing out.

Motor Development

- Can walk around obstacles and walk more erect
- Squats for long periods while playing.
- Climbs stairs unassisted (but not with alternating feet).
- Balances on one foot (for a few moments), jumps up and down, but may fall.
- Often achieves toilet training during this year (depending on child's physical and neurological development) although accidents should still be expected; the child will indicate readiness for toilet training.
- Throws large ball underhand without losing balance. Holds cup or glass (be sure it is unbreakable) in one hand. Unbuttons large buttons; unzips large zippers.
- Opens doors by turning doorknobs.
- Grasps large crayon with fist; scribbles enthusiastically on large paper.
- Climbs up on chair, turns around and sits down.
- Enjoys pouring and filling activities-sand, water, styrofoam peanuts.
- Stacks four to six objects on top of one another.
- Uses feet to propel wheeled riding toys.

Cognitive

- Eye–hand movements better coordinated; can put objects together, take them apart; fit large pegs into pegboard.
- Begins to use objects for purposes other than intended (may push a block around as a boat).
- Does simple classification tasks based on one dimension (separates toy dinosaurs from toy cars).
- Stares for long moments; seems fascinated by, or engrossed in, figuring out a situation: where the tennis ball has rolled, where the dog has gone, what has caused a particular noise.
- Attends to self-selected activities for longer periods of time. Discovering cause and effect: squeezing the cat makes her scratch.
- Knows where familiar persons should be; notes their absence; finds a hidden object by looking in last hiding place first. (This is what Piaget termed object permanence, which usually occurs during the sensorimotor stage of Piaget's childhood theory of cognitive development)
- Names objects in picture books; may pretend to pick something off the page and taste or smell it.
- Recognizes and expresses pain and its location.
- Is expected to use magical thinking, such as believing that a toy bear is a real bear.
- Tells about objects and events not immediately present (this is both a cognitive and linguistic advance).

Language

- Enjoys being read to if allowed to participate by pointing, making relevant noises, turning pages.
- Realizes that language is effective for getting others to respond to needs and preferences.
- Uses fifty to three hundred different words; vocabulary continuously increasing.

- Has broken the linguistic code; in other words, much of a two-year-old's talk has meaning to him or her.
- Receptive language is more developed than expressive language; most two-year olds understand significantly more than they can talk about.
- Utters three-and four-word statements; uses conventional word order to form more complete sentences.
- Refers to self as "me" or sometimes "I" rather than by name: "Me go bye-bye"; has no trouble verbalizing "mine."
- Expresses negative statements by tacking on a negative word such as "no" or "not": "Not more milk."
- Repeatedly asks, "What's that?"
- Uses some plurals.
- Some stammering and other dysfluencies are common.
- Speech is as much as 65 to 70 percent intelligible.
- Is able to verbalize needs.

Social and Emotional

- Shows signs of empathy and caring: comforts another child if hurt or frightened; appears to sometimes be overly affectionate in offering hugs and kisses to children
- Continues to use physical aggression if frustrated or angry (for some children, this is more exaggerated than for others); Physical aggression usually lessens as verbal skills improve.
- Temper tantrums likely to peak during this year; cannot be reasoned with while tantrum is in progress.
- Impatient; finds it difficult to wait or take turns.
- Enjoys "helping" with household chores; imitates everyday activities: may try to toilet a stuffed animal, feed a doll.
- "Bossy" with parents and caregivers; orders them around, makes demands, expects immediate compliance from adults.

- Watches and imitates the play of other children, but seldom interacts directly, plays near others, often choosing similar toys and activities (parallel play); solitary play is often simple and repetitive.
- Offers toys to other children, but is usually possessive of playthings; still tends to hoard toys.
- Making choices is difficult; wants it both ways.
- Often defiant; shouting "no" becomes automatic.
- Ritualistic; wants everything "just so"; routines carried out exactly as before; belongings placed "where they belong."

Three Year Old

Physical

- Growth is steady though slower than in first two years.
- Adult height can be predicted from measurements of height at three years of age; males are approximately 53% of their adult height and females, 57%.
- Legs grow faster than arms,
- Circumference of head and chest is equal; head size is in better proportion to the body.
- "Baby fat" disappears as neck appears.
- Posture is more erect; abdomen no longer protrudes.
- Slightly knock-kneed.
- can jump from low step
- can stand up and walk around on tiptoes
- "baby" teeth stage over.
- Needs to consume approximately 6,300 J (1,500 calories) daily.

Motor Development

- Walks up and down stairs unassisted, using alternating feet; may jump from bottom step, landing on both feet.
- Can walk on one foot, balance momentarily.
- Can kick big ball-shaped objects.

- Needs minimal assistance eating.
- Jumps on the spot.
- Pedals a small tricycle.
- Throws a ball overhand; aim and distance are limited.
- Catches a large bounced ball with both arms extended.
- Enjoys swinging on a swing (not too high or too fast).
- Shows improved control of crayons or markers; uses vertical, horizontal and circular strokes.
- Holds crayon or marker between first two fingers and thumb (tripod grasp), not in a fist as earlier.
- Can turn pages of a book one at a time
- Enjoys building with blocks.
- Builds a tower of eight or more blocks.
- Enjoys playing with clay; pounds, rolls, and squeezes it.
- May begin to show hand dominance.
- Carries a container of liquid, such as a cup of milk or bowl of water, without much spilling; pours liquid from pitcher into another container.
- Manipulates large buttons and zippers on clothing.
- Washes and dries hands; brushes own teeth, but not thoroughly.
- Usually achieves complete bladder control during this time.

Cognitive Development

- Listens attentively to age-appropriate stories.
- Makes relevant comments during stories, especially those that relate to home and family events.
- Likes to look at books and may pretend to "read" to others or explain pictures.
- Enjoys stories with riddles, guessing, and "suspense."
- Speech is understandable most of the time.
- Produces expanded noun phrases: "big, brown dog."

- Produces verbs with "ing" endings; uses "-s" to indicate more than one; often puts "-s" on already pluralized forms: geeses, mices.
- Indicates negatives by inserting "no" or "not" before a simple noun or verb phrase: "Not baby."
- Answers "What are you doing?", "What is this?", and "Where?" questions dealing with familiar objects and events.

Four Year Old

Physical Development

- Head circumference is usually not measured after age three.
- Requires approximately 1,700 calories daily.
- Hearing acuity can be assessed by child's correct usage of sounds and *Language also, by the child's appropriate responses to questions and instructions.

Motor Development

- Walks a straight line (tape or chalk line on the floor).
- Hops on one foot.
- Pedals and steers a wheeled toy with confidence; turns corners, avoids obstacles and oncoming "traffic."
- Climbs ladders, trees, playground equipment.
- Jumps over objects 12 to 15 cm (5 to 6 in) high; lands with both feet together.
- Runs, starts, stops, and moves around obstacles with ease.
- Throws a ball overhand; distance and aim improving.
- Builds a tower with ten or more blocks.
- Forms shapes and objects out of clay: cookies, snakes, simple animals.
- Reproduces some shapes and letters.
- Holds a crayon or marker using a tripod grasp.
- Paints and draws with purpose; may have an idea in mind, but often has problems implementing it so calls the creation something else.

- Becomes more accurate at hitting nails and pegs with hammer.
- Threads small wooden beads on a string.
- Can run in a circle

Cognitive

- Can recognize that certain words sound similar
- Names eighteen to twenty uppercase letters. Writes several letters and sometimes their name.
- A few children are beginning to read simple books, such as alphabet books with only a few words per page and many pictures.
- Likes stories about how things grow and how things operate.
- Delights in wordplay, creating silly Language.
- Understands the concepts of "tallest," "biggest," "same," and "more"; selects the picture that has the "most houses" or the "biggest dogs."
- Rote counts to 20 or more.
- Understands the sequence of daily events: "When we get up in the morning, we get dressed, have breakfast, brush our teeth, and go to school."
- When looking at pictures, can recognize and identify missing puzzle parts (of person, car, animal).
- Very good storytellers.
- Counts 1 to 7 objects out loud, but not always in order
- follows two to three step directions given individually or in a group
- may put the "ed" on the end of words such as "I goed outside and I played."

Language

- Uses the prepositions "on," "in," and "under."
- Uses possessives consistently: "hers," "theirs," "baby's."
- Answers "Whose?", "Who?", "Why?", and "How many?"
- Produces elaborate sentence structures: "The cat ran under the house before I could see what color it was."

- Speech is almost entirely intelligible.
- Begins to correctly use the past tense of verbs: "Mommy closed the door," "Daddy went to work."
- Refers to activities, events, objects, and people that are not present.
- Changes tone of voice and sentence structure to adapt to listener's level of under-standing: To baby brother, "Milk gone?" To Mother, "Did the baby drink all of his milk?"
- States first and last name, gender, siblings' names, and sometimes own telephone number.
- Answers appropriately when asked what to do if tired, cold, or hungry. Recites and sings simple songs and rhymes.

Social Development

- Outgoing; friendly; overly enthusiastic at times.
- Moods change rapidly and unpredictably; laughing one minute, crying the next; may throw tantrum over minor frustrations (a block structure that will not balance); sulk over being left out.
- Imaginary playmates or companions are common; holds conversations and shares strong emotions with this invisible friend.
- Boasts, exaggerates, and "bends" the truth with made-up stories or claims of boldness; tests the limits with "bathroom" talk.
- Cooperates with others; participates in group activities.
- Shows pride in accomplishments; seeks frequent adult approval.
- Often appears selfish; not always able to take turns or to understand taking turns under some conditions; tattles on other children.
- Insists on trying to do things independently, but may get so frustrated as to verge on tantrums when problems arise: paint that drips, paper airplane that will not fold right.

- Enjoys role-playing and make-believe activities.
- Relies (most of the time) on verbal rather than Physical aggression; may yell angrily rather than hit to make a point; threatens: "You can't come to my birthday party"
- Name-calling and taunting are often used as ways of excluding other children.
- Establishes close relationships with playmates; beginning to have "best" friends.

Five Year Old

Physical

- Head size is approximately that of an adult's.
- May begin to lose "baby" (deciduous) teeth.
- Body is adult-like in proportion.
- Requires approximately 7,500 J (1,800 calories) daily
- Visual tracking and binocular vision are well developed.

Motor Development

- Walks backwards, toe to heel.
- Walks unassisted up and down stairs, alternating feet.
- May learn to turn somersaults (should be taught the right way in order to avoid injury).
- Can touch toes without flexing knees.
- Walks a balance beam.
- Learns to skip using alternative feet.
- Catches a ball thrown from 1 m (3.3 ft) away.
- Rides a tricycle or wheeled toy with speed and skilful steering; some children learning to ride bicycles, usually with training wheels.
- Jumps or hops forward ten times in a row without falling.
- Balances on either foot with good control for ten seconds.
- Builds three-dimensional structures with small cubes by copying from a picture or model.

- Reproduces many shapes and letters: square, triangle, A, I, O, U, C, H, L, T.
- Demonstrates fair control of pencil or marker; may begin to color within the lines.
- Cuts on the line with scissors (not perfectly).
- Hand dominance is fairly well established.

Cognitive

- Forms rectangle from two triangular cuts.
- Builds steps with set of small blocks.
- Understands concept of same shape, same size.
- Sorts objects on the basis of two dimensions, such as color and form.
- Sorts a variety of objects so that all things in the group have a single common feature (classification skill: all are food items or boats or animals).
- Understands the concepts of smallest and shortest; places objects in order from shortest to tallest, smallest to largest.
- Identifies objects with specified serial position: first, second, last.
- Rote counts to 20 and above; many children count to 100.
- Recognizes numerals from 1 to 10.
- Understands the concepts of less than: "Which bowl has less water?"
- Understands the terms dark, light, and early: "I got up early, before anyone else. It was still dark."
- Relates clock time to daily schedule: "Time to turn on TV when the little hand points to 5."
- Some children can tell time on the hour: five o'clock, two o'clock.
- Knows what a calendar is for.
- Recognizes and identifies coins; beginning to count and save money.

- Many children know the alphabet and names of upper- and lowercase letters.
- Understands the concept of half; can say how many pieces an object has when it's been cut in half.
- Asks innumerable questions: Why? What? Where? When?
- Eager to learn new things.

Language Development

- Vocabulary of 1,500 words plus.
- Tells a familiar story while looking at pictures in a book.
- Defines simple words by function: a ball is to bounce; a bed is to sleep in.
- Identifies and names four to eight colours.
- Recognizes the humour in simple jokes; makes up jokes and riddles.
- Produces sentences with five to seven words; much longer sentences are not unusual.
- States the name of own city or town, birthday, and parents' names.
- Answers telephone appropriately; calls person to phone or takes a brief message
- Speech is almost entirely intelligible.
- Uses "would" and "could" appropriately.
- Uses past tense of irregular verbs consistently: "went," "caught," "swam."
- Uses past-tense inflection (-ed) appropriately to mark regular verbs: "jumped," "rained," "washed."

Social Development

- Enjoys and often has one or two focus friendships.
- Plays cooperatively (can lapse), is generous, takes turns, shares toys.
- Participates in group play and shared activities with other children; suggests imaginative and elaborate play ideas.

- Shows affection and caring towards others especially those "below" them or in pain
- Generally subservient to parent or caregiver requests.
- Needs comfort and reassurance from adults but is less open to comfort.
- Has better self-control over swings of emotions.
- Likes entertaining people and making them laugh.
- Boasts about accomplishments.

Six Year Old

Physical

- Weight gains reflect significant increases in muscle mass.
- Heart rate and respiratory rates are close to adults.
- Body may appear lanky as through period of rapid growth.
- Baby teeth beginning to be replaced by permanent ones, starting with the two lower front teeth
- 20/20 eyesight; if below 20/40 should see a professional.
- The most common vision problem during middle childhood is myopia, or nearsightedness. (Berk, 2007).
- Uses 6,700 J to 7,100 J (1,600 to 1,700 calories) a day.

Motor Development

- Gains greater control over large and fine motor skills; movements are more precise and deliberate, though some clumsiness persists.
- Enjoys vigorous running, jumping, climbing, and throwing est.
- Has trouble staying still.
- Span of attention increases; works at tasks for longer periods of time, though
- Can concentrate effort but not always consistently.
- Understands time (today, tomorrow, yesterday) and simple motion (things go faster than others).

- Recognizes seasons and major activities done in the times.
- Has fun with problem solving and sorting activities like stacking, puzzles and mazes
- Enjoys the challenge of puzzles, counting and sorting activities, paper-and-pencil mazes, and games that involve matching letters and words with pictures.
- Recognizes some words by sight; attempts to sound out words
- In some cases the child may be reading well.
- functioning which facilitates learning to ride a bicycle, swim, swing a bat, or kick a ball.
- Making things is enjoyed.
- Reverses or confuse certain letters: b/d, p/g, g/q, t/f.
- Able to trace objects.
- Folds and cuts paper into simple shapes.
- Can Tie Laces, string (like shoes).

Language

- Can identify right and left hands fairly consistently.
- Holds onto positive beliefs involving the unexplainable (magic or fantasy)
- Arrives at some understanding about death and dying; expresses fear that parents may die.
- Talks a lot.
- Loves telling jokes and riddles; often, the humour is far from subtle.
- Experiments with slang and profanity and finds it funny.
- Enthusiastic and inquisitive about surroundings and everyday events.
- Able to carry on adult-like conversations; asks many questions.
- Learns 5 to 10 words a day; vocabulary of 10,000–14,000.
- Uses appropriate verb tenses, word order, and sentence structure.

Social and Emotional

- Uses language rather than tantrums or physical aggression to express displeasure: "That's mine! Give it back, you dummy."
- Talks self through steps required in simple problem-solving situations (though the "logic" may be unclear to adults).
- Has mood swings towards primary caregiver depending on the day
- Friendship with parent is less depended on but still needs closeness and nurturing.
- Anxious to please; needs and seeks adult approval, reassurance, and praise; may complain excessively about minor hurts to gain more attention.
- Often can't view the world from another's point of view
- Self-perceived failure can make the child easily disappointed and frustrated.
- Can't handle things not going their own way
- Does not understand ethical behaviour or moral standards especially when doing things that have not been given rules
- Understands when he or she has been thought to be "bad"; values are based on others enforced values.
- May be increasingly fearful of the unknown like things in the dark, noises, and animals.

Early Childhood

Early childhood follows the infancy stage, and begins with toddlerhood when the child begins speaking or taking steps independently.

While toddlerhood ends around age three when the child becomes less dependent on parental assistance for basic needs, early childhood continues approximately through years seven or eight. According to the National Association for the Education of Young Children, early childhood spans the human life from birth to age eight.

Middle Childhood

Middle childhood begins at around age seven or eight, approximating primary school age and ends around puberty, the beginning of adolescence.

Preadolescence

Preadolescence is a stage of human development through childhood that occurs prior to adolescence.

Span

The point at which a child becomes an adolescent is usually defined by the onset of puberty. However, in some individuals (particularly females), puberty begins in the preadolescence years, and adolescence may extend a few years beyond the teenage years in others (typically males).

In terms of age in years, dictionary definitions generally designate preadolescence as the years from 10 to 13 (ages 12–13 for girls and 11-13 for boys), although there is no exact agreement.

Psychological Development

Preadolescent children have a different view of the world from younger children in significant ways:

- May have a fear of kidnappings, rapes, and scary media events, as opposed to fantasy things (e.g., witches, monsters, ghosts).
- Have a more developed sense of looking into the future and seeing effects of their actions (as opposed to early childhood where children often do not worry about their future).
- Have more realistic job expectations ("I want to be an engineer when I grow up", as opposed to "I want to be a wizard").
- View human relationships differently (i.e. they may notice the flawed, human side of authority figures).
- Begin to develop a sense of self-identity.
- Have increased feelings of independence.

- Have a different view on morality.
- More mature, sensible, realistic thoughts and actions
- Are responsible for younger siblings and relatives, such as babysitting.
- Often beginning to experience limerence, Puppy Love, or love.
- May start caring about what they look like and what they are wearing.
- May become more exposed to popular culture than childhood and may have interests that are more based on internet trends, television shows, movies, fashion, technology, and music, but are very shallow and corporate compared to the means of more rebellious and open teenagers. Preadolescents generally prefer certain brands, and are a heavily targeted market of many advertisers. Their tendency to buy brand-name items may be due to a desire to fit in, although the desire is not as strong as it is with teenagers. Many of these brands include clothing and music.

Freud on Preadolescence

Sigmund Freud termed this the latency period, which he saw as a period of unparalleled repression of sexual desires and erogenous impulses. During the latency period, children direct this repressed libidal energy into asexual pursuits such as school, athletics, and same-sex friendships. He saw the latency period as a time of relative calm when there is little psychosexual conflict and unconscious conflicts and drives go underground and are therefore relatively inaccessible and unavailable. But soon puberty arrives, and the genitals once again become a central focus of libidal energy.

Adolescence

Adolescence, or late childhood, begins around the time of puberty. The end of adolescence and the beginning of adulthood varies by country and by function, and even within a single nation-state or culture there may be different ages at which an individual is considered to be (chronologically and legally) mature enough to be entrusted by society with certain tasks.

Adolescence (from Latin: *adolescere* meaning "to grow up") is a transitional stage of physical and mental human development generally occurring between puberty and legal adulthood (age of majority), but largely characterized as beginning and ending with the teenage stage. According to Erik Erikson's stages of human development, for example, a young adult is generally a person between the ages of 20 and 40, whereas an adolescent is a person between the ages of 13 and 19. Historically, puberty has been heavily associated with teenagers and the onset of adolescent development. However, the start of puberty has had somewhat of an increase in preadolescence (particularly females, as seen with early and precocious puberty), and adolescence has had an occasional extension beyond the teenage years (typically males) compared to previous generations. These changes have made it more difficult to rigidly define the time frame in which adolescence occurs.

The end of adolescence and the beginning of adulthood varies by country and by function, and furthermore even within a single nation-state or culture there can be different ages at which an individual is considered to be (chronologically and legally) mature enough to be entrusted by society with certain tasks. Such milestones include, but are not limited to, driving a vehicle, having legal sexual relations, serving in the armed forces or on a jury, purchasing and drinking alcohol, voting, entering into contracts, completing certain levels of education, and marrying.

Adolescence is usually accompanied by an increased independence allowed by the parents or legal guardians and less supervision, contrary to the preadolescence stage.

In many societies, adolescence was not recognized as a phase of life. Most societies simply distinguished between childhood and adulthood. Stanley Hall is generally credited with "discovering" adolescence with his 1904 study "Adolescence" in which he describes the developmental phase now recognized as adolescence. Hall attributed the new stage to social changes at the turn of the 20th century. Child labour laws kept individuals under 16 out of the work force, and universal education laws kept them in secondary school, thus prolonging the period of dependence — a dependence that allowed them to address psychological tasks they might have ignored when they took on adult roles straight out of childhood.

Puberty

Puberty is a period of several years in which rapid physical growth and psychological changes occur, culminating in sexual maturity. The average onset of puberty is at 10 for girls and age 12 for boys. Every person's individual timetable for puberty is influenced primarily by heredity, although environmental factors, such as diet and exercise, also exert some influence. These factors can also contribute to precocious puberty and delayed puberty.

Puberty begins with a surge in hormone production, which in turn causes a number of physical changes. It is also the stage of life in which a child develops secondary sex characteristics (for example, a deeper voice and larger adam's apple in boys, and development of breasts and more curved and prominent hips in girls) as his or her hormonal balance shifts strongly towards an adult state. This is triggered by the pituitary gland, which secretes a surge of hormonal agents into the blood stream, initiating a chain reaction. The male and female gonads are subsequently activated, which puts them into a state of rapid growth and development; the triggered gonads now commence the mass production of the necessary chemicals. The testes primarily release testosterone, and the ovaries predominantly dispense estrogen. The production of these hormones increases gradually until sexual maturation is met. Some boys may develop gynecomastia due to an imbalance of sex hormones, tissue responsiveness or obesity. Put simply, puberty is the time when a child's body starts changing into an adult's body.

Facial hair in males normally appears in a specific order during puberty: The first facial hair to appear tends to grow at the corners of the upper lip, typically between 14 to 16 years of age. It then spreads to form a moustache over the entire upper lip. This is followed by the appearance of hair on the upper part of the cheeks, and the area under the lower lip. The hair eventually spreads to the sides and lower border of the chin, and the rest of the lower face to form a full beard. As with most human biological processes, this specific order may vary among some individuals. Facial hair is often present in late adolescence, around ages 17 and 18, but may not appear until significantly later. Some men do not develop full facial hair for 10 years after puberty. Facial hair will continue to get coarser, darker and thicker for another 2–4 years after puberty.

The major landmark of puberty for males is the first ejaculation, which occurs, on average, at age 13. For females, it is menarche, the onset of menstruation, which occurs, on average, between ages 12 and 13. The age of menarche is influenced by heredity, but a girl's diet and lifestyle contribute as well. Regardless of genes, a girl must have certain proportion of body fat to attain menarche. Consequently, girls who have a high-fat diet and who are not physically active begin menstruating earlier, on average, than girls whose diet contains less fat and whose activities involve fat reducing exercise (e.g. ballet and gymnastics). Girls who experience malnutrition or are in societies in which children are expected to perform physical labour also begin menstruating at later ages.

The timing of puberty can have important psychological and social consequences. Early maturing boys are usually taller and stronger than their friends. They have the advantage in capturing the attention of potential partners and in becoming hand-picked for sports. Pubescent boys often tend to have a good body image, are more confident, secure, and more independent.

Late maturing boys can be less confident because of poor body image when comparing themselves to already developed friends and peers. However, early puberty is not always positive for boys; early sexual maturation in boys can be accompanied by increased aggressiveness due to the surge of hormones that affect them. Because they appear older than their peers, pubescent boys may face increased social pressure to conform to adult norms; society may view them as more emotionally advanced, despite the fact that their cognitive and social development may lag behind their appearance. Studies have shown that early maturing boys are more likely to be sexually active and are more likely to participate in risky behaviours.

For girls, early maturation can sometimes lead to increased self-consciousness, though a typical aspect in maturing females. Because of their bodies developing in advance, pubescent girls can become more insecure. Consequently, girls that reach sexual maturation early are more likely than their peers to develop eating disorders.

Nearly half of all American high school girls' diet is to lose weight. In addition, girls may have to deal with sexual advances from older boys before they are emotionally and mentally mature. In addition to having earlier sexual experiences and more unwanted pregnancies than late maturing girls, early maturing girls are more exposed to alcohol and drug abuse. Those who have had such experiences tend to perform less well in school than their "inexperienced" age peers.

Girls have usually reached full physical development by ages 15–17, while boys usually complete puberty by ages 16–18. Any increase in height beyond these ages is uncommon. Girls attain reproductive maturity about 4 years after the first physical changes of puberty appear. In contrast, boys accelerate more slowly but continue to grow for about 6 years after the first visible pubertal changes. Teenage and early adult males may continue to gain natural muscle growth even after puberty.

Psychology

Adolescence is characterized by a number of cognitive, emotional, physical and attitudinal changes, which can be a cause of conflict on one hand and positive personality development on the other.

The home environment and parents are still important for the behaviours and choices of adolescents. Adolescents who have a good relationship with their parents are less likely to engage in various risk behaviours, such as smoking, drinking, fighting, and/or sexual intercourse. In conflict with their parents, adolescents are more flexible than younger children, but more hostile and rigid compared to adults. The topics of conflicts between adolescents and their parents are often about the extent to which parents can control and supervise the adolescent, for instance conflicts about chores, schoolwork, curfew, and the adolescent's right to privacy.

For the first time in their lives adolescents may start to view their friends, their peer group, as more important and influential than their parents or guardians. Peer groups offer its members the opportunity to develop various social skills, such as empathy, sharing and leadership. Peer groups can have positive influences on an individual, for instance on academic motivation and performance, but they can also have negative influences and lead to an increase in experimentation with drugs, drinking, vandalism, and stealing. Susceptibility to peer pressure increases during early adolescence, peaks around age 14, and declines thereafter.

In the search for a unique social identity for themselves, adolescents are frequently confused about what is 'right' and what is 'wrong.' G. Stanley Hall denoted this period as one of "Storm and Stress" and, according to him, conflict at this developmental stage is normal and not unusual. Margaret Mead, on the other hand, attributed the behaviour of adolescents to their culture and upbringing.

Adolescence is also a time for rapid cognitive development. Piaget describes adolescence as the stage of life in which the individual's thoughts start taking more of an abstract form and the egocentric thoughts decrease. This allows the individual to think and reason in a wider perspective. A combination of behavioural and fMRI studies have demonstrated development of executive functions, that is, cognitive skills that enable the control and coordination of thoughts and behaviour, which are generally associated with the prefrontal cortex. The thoughts, ideas and concepts developed at this period of life greatly influence one's future life, playing a major role in character and personality formation.

Adolescent psychology is associated with notable changes in mood sometimes known as mood swings.

Positive psychology is sometimes brought up when addressing adolescent psychology as well. This approach towards adolescents refers to providing them with motivation to become socially acceptable and notable individuals, since many adolescents find themselves bored, indecisive and/or unmotivated.

Struggles with adolescent identity and depression usually set in when an adolescent experiences a loss. The most important loss in their lives is the changing relationship between the adolescent and their parents. Adolescents may also experience strife in their relationships with friends. This may be due to the activities their friends take part in, such as smoking, which causes adolescents to feel as though participating in such activities themselves is likely essential to maintaining these friendships. Teen depression can be extremely intense at times because of physical and hormonal changes but emotional instability is part of adolescence. Their changing mind, body and relationships often present themselves as stressful and that change, they assume, is something to be feared. Sleep deprivation has also been linked to adolescent depression, particularly in the teen years.

Views of family relationships during adolescence are changing. The old view of family relationships during adolescence put an emphasis on conflict and disengagement and thought storm and stress was normal and even inevitable. However, the new view puts emphasis on transformation or relationships and maintenance of connectedness.

Sexuality

Adolescent sexuality refers to sexual feelings, behaviour and development in adolescents and is a stage of human sexuality. Sexuality and sexual desire usually begins to intensify along with the onset of puberty. The expression of sexual desire among adolescents (or anyone, for that matter), might be influenced by family values and the culture and religion they have grown up in (or as a backlash to such), social engineering, social control, taboos, and other kinds of social mores.

In contemporary society, adolescents also face some risks as their sexuality begins to transform. Whilst some of these such as emotional distress (fear of abuse or exploitation) and sexually transmitted diseases (including HIV/AIDS) may not necessarily be inherent to adolescence, others such as pregnancy (through non-use or failure of contraceptives) are seen as social problems in most western societies. In terms of sexual identity, while all sexual orientations found in adults are also represented among adolescents, statistically the suicide rate amongst LGBT adolescents is up to four times higher than that of their heterosexual peers.

According to anthropologist Margaret Mead and psychologist Albert Bandura, the turmoil found in adolescence in Western society has a cultural rather than a physical cause; they reported that societies where young women engaged in free sexual activity had no such adolescent turmoil.

In a 2008 study conducted by YouGov for Channel 4, 20% of 14"17-year-olds surveyed revealed that they had their first sexual experience at 13 or under. Another study from 2002 found that those aged 15–44 reported that the average age of first sexual intercourse was 17.0 for males and 17.3 for females.

The age of consent to sexual activity varies widely between international jurisdictions, ranging from 12 to 21 years.

Culture

In commerce, this generation is seen as an important target. Mobile phones, contemporary popular music, movies, television programs, websites, sports, video games and clothes are heavily marketed and often popular amongst adolescents.

In the past (and still in some cultures) there were ceremonies that celebrated adulthood, typically occurring during adolescence. *Seijin shiki* (literally "adult ceremony") is a Japanese example of this. Upanayanam is a coming of age ceremony for males in the Hindu world. In Judaism, 13-year-old boys and 12-year-old girls become Bar or Bat Mitzvah, respectively, and often have a celebration to mark this coming of age. Among some denominations of Christianity, the rite or sacrament of Confirmation is received by adolescents and may be considered the time at which adolescents become members of the church in their own right (there is also a Confirmation ceremony in some Reform Jewish temples, although the bar or bat mitzvah ceremony appears to have precedence). In United States, girls will often have a "sweet sixteen" party to celebrate turning the aforementioned age, a tradition similar to the quinceañera in Latin culture. In modern western society, events such as getting your first driver's license, high school and later on college graduation and first career related job are thought of as being more significant markers in transition to adulthood. Adolescents have also been an important factor in many movements for positive social change around the world. The popular history of adolescents participating in these movements may perhaps start with Joan of Arc, and extend to present times with popular youth activism, student activism, and other efforts to make the youth voice heard.

Legal Issues, Rights and Privileges

Internationally, those who reach a certain age (often 18, though this varies) are legally considered to have reached the age of majority and are regarded as adults and are held to be responsible for their actions. People below this age are considered minors or children. A person below the age of majority may gain adult rights through legal emancipation.

Those who are under the age of consent, or legal responsibility, may be considered too young to be held accountable for criminal action. This is called *doli incapax* or the defence of infancy. The age of criminal responsibility varies from 7 in India to 18 in Belgium. After reaching the initial age, there may be levels of responsibility dictated by age and type of offense, and crimes committed by minors may be tried in a juvenile court.

The legal working age in Western countries is usually 14 to 16, depending on the number of hours and type of employment. In the United Kingdom and Canada, for example, young people between 14 and 16 can work at certain types of light work with some restrictions to allow for schooling; while youths over 16 can work full-time (excluding night work). Many countries also specify a minimum school leaving age, ranging from 10 to 18, at which a person is legally allowed to leave compulsory education.

The age of consent to sexual activity varies widely between jurisdictions, ranging from 13 to 21 years, the average age is 16. In a 2008 study of 14 to 17-year-olds conducted by YouGov for Channel 4, it was revealed that one in three 15-year-olds were sexually active.

Sexual intercourse with a person below the local age of consent is usually treated as the crime of statutory rape. Some jurisdictions allow an exemption where both partners are close in age; for example, a 16-year-old and an 18-year-old. The age at which people are allowed to marry also varies, from 17 in Yemen to 22 for males and 20 for females in China. In Western countries, people are typically allowed to marry at 18, although they are sometimes allowed to marry at a younger age with parental or court consent. In developing countries, the legal marriageable age does not always correspond with the age at which people actually marry; for example, the legal age for marriage in Ethiopia is 18 for both males and females, but in rural areas most girls are married by age 16.

In most democratic countries, a citizen is eligible to vote at 18. For example, in the United States, the Twenty-sixth amendment decreased the voting age from 21 to 18. In a minority of countries, the voting age is 17 (for example, Indonesia) or 16 (for example, Brazil). By contrast, some countries have a minimum voting age of 21 (for example, Singapore) whereas the minimum age in Uzbekistan is 25. Age of candidacy is the minimum age at which a person can legally qualify to hold certain elected government offices. In most countries, a person must be 18 or over to stand for elected office, but some countries such as the United States and Italy have further restrictions depending on the type of office.

The sale of selected items such as cigarettes, alcohol, and videos with violent or pornographic content is also restricted by age in most countries. In the U.S, the minimum age to buy an R-rated movie, M-rated game or an album with a parental advisory label is 17 (in some states 18 or even 21). In practice, it is common that young people engage in underage smoking or drinking, and in some cultures this is tolerated to a certain degree. In the United States, teenagers are allowed to drive between 14–18 (each state sets its own minimum driving age of which a curfew may be imposed), in the US, adolescents 17 years of age can serve in the military. In Europe it is more common for the driving age to be higher (usually 18) while the drinking age is lower than that of the US (usually 16 or 18). In Canada, the drinking age is 18 in some areas and 19 in other areas. In Australia, universally the minimum drinking age is 18, unless a person is in a private residence or is under parental supervision in a licensed premises. The driving age varies from state to state but the more common system is a graduated system of "L plates" (a learning license that requires supervision from a licensed driver) from age 16, red "P plates" (probationary license) at 17, green "P plates" at 18 and finally a full license, i.e. for most people around the age of 20.

The legal gambling age also depends on the jurisdiction, although it is typically 18. The minimum age for donating blood in the U.S is 17 although it may be 16 with parental permission in some states such as New York, New Jersey, and Pennsylvania.

Suitable age and discretion is a legal definition of maturity

A number of social scientists, including anthropologist Margaret Mead and sociologist Mike Males, have noted the contradictory treatment of laws affecting adolescents in the United States. As Males has noted, the US Supreme Court has, "explicitly ruled that policy-makers may impose adult responsibilities and punishments on individual youths as if they were adults at the same time laws and policies abrogate adolescents' rights en masse as if they were children."

The issue of youth activism affecting political, social, educational, and moral circumstances is of growing significance around the world. Youth-led organizations around the world have fought for social justice, the youth vote seeking to gain teenagers the right to vote, to secure more youth rights, and demanding better schools through student activism.

Geographies of Childhood

The geographies of childhood involves how (adult) society perceives the very idea of childhood and the many ways the attitudes and behaviours of adults affects children's lives. This includes ideas about the surrounding environment of children and its related implications. This is similar in some respects to children's geographies which examines the places and spaces in which children live.

Modern Concepts of Childhood

The concept of childhood appears to evolve and change shape as lifestyles change and adult expectations alter. Some believe that children should not have any worries and should not have to work; life should be happy and trouble-free. Childhood is usually a mixture of happiness, wonder, angst and resilience. It is generally a time of playing, learning, socializing, exploring, and worrying in a world without much adult interference, aside from parents. It is a time of learning about responsibilities without having to deal with adult responsibilities.

Childhood is often retrospectively viewed as a time of innocence, which is generally viewed as a positive term, connoting an optimistic view of the world, in particular one where the lack of knowledge stems from a lack of wrongdoing, whereas greater knowledge comes from doing wrong. A "loss of innocence" is a common concept, and is often seen as an integral part of coming of age. It is usually thought of as an experience or period in a child's life that widens their awareness of evil, pain or the world around them. This theme is demonstrated in the novels *To Kill a Mockingbird* and *Lord of the Flies*. The fictional character Peter Pan was the embodiment of a childhood that never ends.

Nature Deficit Disorder

Nature Deficit Disorder, a term coined by Richard Louv in his 2005 book *Last Child in the Woods,* refers to the alleged trend in the United States that children are spending less time outdoors, resulting in a wide range of behavioural problems. With the advent of the computer, video games and television, children have more reasons to stay inside rather than outdoors exploring. "The average American child spends 44 hours a week with electronic media". Parents are also keeping children indoors in order to protect them from their growing fear of "stranger danger". Recent research has drawn a further contrast between the declining number of National Park visits in the United States and increasing consumption of electronic media by children.

Childhood Play

Play is essential to the cognitive, physical, social, and emotional well-being of children. It offers children opportunities for physical (running, jumping, climbing, etc.), intellectual (social skills, community norms, ethics and general knowledge) and emotional development (empathy, compassion, and friendships). Unstructured play encourages creativity and imagination. Playing and interacting with other children, as well as some adults, provides opportunities for friendships, social interactions, conflicts and resolutions.

It is through play that children at a very early age engage and interact in the world around them. Play allows children to create and explore a world they can master, conquering their fears while practicing adult roles, sometimes in conjunction with other children or adult caregivers. Undirected play allows children to learn how to work in groups, to share, to negotiate, to resolve conflicts, and to learn self-advocacy skills. However when play is controlled by adults, children acquiesce to adult rules and concerns and lose some of the benefits play offers them, particularly in developing creativity, leadership, and group skills.

Play is considered to be so important to optimal child development that it has been recognized by the United Nations High Commission for Human Rights as a right of every child. Children who are being raised in a hurried and pressured style may limit the protective benefits they would gain from child-driven play.

Street Culture

Children's street culture refers to the cumulative culture created by young children and is sometimes referred to as their *secret world*. It is most common in children between the ages of seven and twelve. It is strongest in urban working class industrial districts where children are traditionally free to play out in the streets for long periods without supervision. It is invented and largely sustained by children themselves with little adult interference.

Young children's street culture usually takes place on quiet backstreets and pavements, and along routes that venture out into local parks, playgrounds, scrub and wasteland, and to local shops. It often imposes imaginative status on certain sections of the urban realm (local buildings, kerbs, street objects, etc.). Children designate specific areas that serve as informal meeting and relaxation places. An urban area that looks faceless or neglected to an adult may have deep 'spirit of place' meanings in to children. Since the advent of indoor distractions such as video games, and television, concerns have been expressed about the vitality-or even the survival-of children's street culture.

Human Cognitive Development Pattern

Cognitive development is a field of study in neuroscience and psychology focusing on a child's development in terms of information processing, conceptual resources, perceptual skill, language learning, and other aspects of brain development and cognitive psychology. A large portion of research has gone into understanding how a child conceptualizes the world. Jean Piaget was a major force in the founding of this field, forming his "theory of cognitive development". Many of his theoretical claims have since fallen out of favour. However, his description of the general tendencies of cognitive development (e.g., that it moves from being dependent on actions and perception in infancy to understanding of the more observable aspects of reality in childhood to capturing the underlying abstract rules and principles in adolescence is still generally acceptable. Moreover, many of the phenomena that he discovered, such as object permanence in infancy and the conservations in school age children, are real and still attract the interest of researchers. In the recent years alternative models have been advanced, including the neo-Piagetian theories of cognitive development, which aim to integrate Piaget's ideas which stood up well the test of time with more recent theorizing and methods in developmental and cognitive science.

A major controversy in cognitive development has been "nature vs. nurture", or nativism versus empiricism. However, it is now recognized by most experts that this is a false dichotomy: there is overwhelming evidence from biological and behavioural sciences that from the earliest points in development, gene activity interacts with events and experiences in the environment. Therefore the "vs." is false: there is no dichotomy. Another question is how culture and social experience relate to developmental changes in thinking. Another question is phylogenic convergence or homology with non-human animals. Most aspects of learning and cognition are similar in humans and non-human animals. These issues propagate to nearly every aspect of cognitive development.

Speculated Core Systems of Cognition

Nativists theorize that children are born with many innate cognitive systems designed to tackle problems that the human species have faced over a very long evolutionary time. Empiricists study how these skills may be learned in such a short time. The debate is over whether these systems are learned by general-purpose learning devices, or domain-specific cognition. Moreover, many modern cognitive developmental psychologists, recognizing that the term "innate" does not square with modern knowledge about epigenesis, neurobiological development, or learning, favour a non-nativist framework. Researchers who discuss "core systems" often speculate about differences in thinking and learning between proposed domains. The more modern framework questions how differences in processing different kinds of information (not necessarily called "domains") emerge with experience and brain development within general dynamic systems. This is sometimes called the "neuroconstructivist" approach.

Researchers who posit a set of so-called "core domains" suggest that children are innate sensitivity to specific kinds of patterns of information. Those commonly cited include:

Number

Infants appear to have two systems for dealing with numbers. One deals with small numbers, often called subitizing. Another deals with larger numbers in an approximate fashion.

Space

Very young children appear to have some skill in navigation. This basic ability to infer the direction and distance of unseen locations develops in ways that are not entirely clear. However, there is some evidence that it involves the development of complex language skills between 3 and 5 years. Also, there is evidence that this skill depends importantly on visual experience, because congenitally blind individuals have been found to have impaired abilities to infer new paths between familiar locations.

Later in life, adults can use language and symbols (e.g., maps) to reason about information. When adults' language processing is engaged in other tasks, they reason is different ways.

Visual Perception

One of the original nativist versus empiricist debates was over depth perception. There is some evidence that children less than 72 hours old can perceive such complex things as biological motion. However, it is unclear how visual experience in the first few days contributes to this perception. There are far more elaborate aspects of visual perception that develop during infancy and beyond.

Essentialism

Young children seem to be predisposed to think of biological entities (e.g., animals and plants) in an essentialistic way. This means that they expect such entities (as opposed to, e.g., artifacts) to have many traits such as internal properties that are caused by some "essence" (such as, in our modern Western conceptual framework, the genome).

Language Acquisition

A major, well-studied process and consequence of cognitive development is language acquisition. The traditional view was that this is the result of deterministic, human-specific genetic structures and processes. Other traditions, however, have emphasized the role of learning and social experience in language learning. However, the relation of gene activity, experience, and language development is now recognized as incredibly complex and difficult to specify. Language development is sometimes separated into learning of phonology, morphology, syntax, semantics, and discourse or pragmatics. However, all of these aspects of language knowledge—which were originally posited by the linguist Noam Chomsky to be autonomous or separate—are now recognized to interact in complex ways.

Organisation of Guidance and Counselling Services for Adolescents in Schools

Professional school counsellors ideally implement a counselling program that promotes and enhances student achievement..School counsellors, in most USA states, usually have a Master's degree in school counselling from a Counsellor Education graduate program. In Canada, they must be licensed teachers with additional school counselling training and focus on academic, career, and personal/social issues. China requires at least three years of college experience. In Japan, school counsellors were added in the mid-1990s, part-time basis and primarily focused on behavioural issues. In Taiwan, they are often teachers with recent legislation requiring school counselling licensure focused on individual and group counselling related to academic, career, and personal issues. In Korea, school counsellors are mandated in middle and high schools. They are employed in elementary, middle, and high schools and in district supervisory, counsellor education faculty positions (usually with an earned Ph.D. in Counsellor Education in the USA or related graduate doctorates abroad) and post-secondary settings doing academic, career, college readiness, and personal/social counselling, consultation, and program coordination. Their work is varied, with attention focused on developmental stages of student growth, including the needs, tasks, and student interests related to those stages.

Professional school counsellors meet the needs of student in three basic domains: academic development, career development, and personal/social development with an increasing emphasis on college access. Knowledge, understanding and skill in these domains are developed through classroom instruction, appraisal, consultation, counselling, coordination, and collaboration. For example, in appraisal, school counsellors may use a variety of personality and career assessment methods (such as the or (based on the) to help students explore career and college needs and interests.

The Responsive Services component of the Professional School Counsellor's role provides individual and/or small group counselling for students. For example, if a student's behaviour is interfering with his or her achievement, the school counsellor may observe that student in a class, provide consultation to teachers and other stakeholders to develop (with the student) a plan to address the behavioural issue(s), and then collaborate to implement and evaluate the plan. They also provide consultation services to family members such as college access, career development, parenting skills, study skills, child and adolescent development, and help with school-home transitions.

School counsellors may lead classroom lessons on a variety of topics within the three domains such as personal/social issues relative to student needs, or establish groups to address common issues among students, such as divorce or death. The topics of character education, diversity and multiculturalism (Portman, 2009), and school safety are important areas of focus for school counsellors. Often school counsellors will coordinate outside groups that wish to help with student needs such as academics, or coordinate a state program that teaches about child abuse or drugs, through on-stage drama (Schmidt, 2003)

The ASCA National Model has four main areas:

- Foundation-a written school counselling program mission statement, a beliefs and philosophy statement, and a focus on the ASCA standards and competencies and how they are implemented for every student;
- Delivery System-how lessons and individual and group counselling are delivered;
- Management System (use of calendars, time, building leader-school counsellor role agreements, creation of action plans); and * Accountability System-use of a School Counselling program audit, results reports, and school counsellor performance evaluations based on 13 key competencies. The model is implemented using key skills from the Education Trust's Transforming School Counselling Initiative: Advocacy, Leadership, Teaming and Collaboration, and Systemic Change

Elementary School Counselling

Elementary professional school counsellors following best practices provide developmental school counselling curriculum lessons on academic, career, college access, and personal and social competencies, advising and academic/career/college access planning to all students, and individual and group counselling for some students and their families to meet the developmental needs of young children K-6.

Increased emphasis is starting to be placed on college access counselling at the elementary school level as more school counselling programs move to evidence-based work with data and specific results. Research has shown that school counselling programs help to close achievement and opportunity gaps in terms of which students have access to school counselling programs and early college access activities and which students do not. To facilitate the school counselling process, school counsellors use a variety of theories and techniques including developmental, cognitive-behavioural, person-centred (Rogerian) listening and influencing skills, systemic, family, multicultural, narrative, and play therapy. released a research study showing the effectiveness of elementary school counselling programs in Washington state.

Middle School Counselling

In middle school counselling, professional school counsellors provide school counselling curriculum lessons on academic, career, college access, and personal and social competencies, advising and academic/career/college access planning to all students and individual and group counselling for some students and their families.

Middle School College Access curricula have been developed by The College Board that can be used to assist students and their families in this process. To facilitate the school counselling process, school counsellors use theories and techniques including developmental, cognitive-behavioural, person-centred (Rogerian) listening and influencing skills, sytemic, family, multicultural, narrative, and play therapy. Transitional issues to ensure successful transitions to high school are a key area including career exploration and assessment with seventh and eighth grade students. Sink, Akos, Turnbull, & Mvududu released a study in 2008 confirming the effectiveness of middle school comprehensive school counselling programs in Washington state.

High School Counselling

Emphasis is being placed on college access counselling at the early high school level as more school counselling programs move to evidence-based work with data and specific results that show how school counselling programs help to close achievement and opportunity gaps ensuring all students have access to school counselling programs and early college access activities. High School College Access curricula have been developed by The College Board to assist this process.

To facilitate school counselling, school counsellors use varied theories and techniques including developmental, cognitive-behavioural, person-centred (Rogerian) listening and influencing skills, systemic, family, multicultural, narrative, and play therapy. Transitional issues to ensure successful transitions to college, other post-secondary educational options, and careers are a key area. The high school counsellor helps students and their families prepare for post-secondary education and/or training options (e.g. college, trade school) by engaging students and their families in finding information on entrance requirements, financial aid, recommendation letters, test-preparation and so forth. School counsellors at the high school level spend much of their time helping students and their families monitor their progress toward graduation and being prepared for post-secondary options including college. Some students turn to private college admissions counsellors but the ethics of so doing is open to debate in terms of who has the funding and no research-based evidence of effectiveness on the part of outside parties.

8

Learning and Motivation

Motivation is the activation of goal-oriented behaviour. Motivation is said to be intrinsic or extrinsic. The term is generally used for humans but, theoretically, it can also be used to describe the causes for animal behaviour as well. This article refers to human motivation. According to various theories, motivation may be rooted in the basic need to minimize physical pain and maximize pleasure, or it may include specific needs such as eating and resting, or a desired object, goal, state of being, ideal, or it may be attributed to less-apparent reasons such as altruism selfishness, morality, or avoiding mortality. Conceptually, motivation should not be confused with either volition or optimism. Motivation is related to, but distinct from, emotion.

Motivation Concepts

Intrinsic and Extrinsic Motivation

Intrinsic motivation refers to motivation that is driven by an interest or enjoyment in the task itself, and exists within the individual rather than relying on any external pressure. Intrinsic motivation has been studied by social and educational psychologists since the early 1970s. Research has found that it is usually associated with high educational achievement and enjoyment by students. Explanations of intrinsic motivation have been given in the context of Fritz Heider's attribution theory, Bandura's work on self-efficacy, and Deci and Ryan's cognitive evaluation theory. Students are likely to be intrinsically motivated if they:

- attribute their educational results to internal factors that they can control (e.g. the amount of effort they put in),
- believe they can be effective agents in reaching desired goals (i.e. the results are not determined by luck),
- are interested in mastering a topic, rather than just rote-learning to achieve good grades.

Extrinsic motivation comes from outside of the individual. Common extrinsic motivations are rewards like money and grades, coercion and threat of punishment. Competition is in general extrinsic because it encourages the performer to win and beat others, not to enjoy the intrinsic rewards of the activity. A crowd cheering on the individual and trophies are also extrinsic incentives.

Social psychological research has indicated that extrinsic rewards can lead to overjustification and a subsequent reduction in intrinsic motivation. In one study demonstrating this effect, children who expected to be (and were) rewarded with a ribbon and a gold star for drawing pictures spent less time playing with the drawing materials in subsequent observations than children who were assigned to an unexpected reward condition and to children who received no extrinsic reward.

Self-determination theory proposes that extrinsic motivation can be internalised by the individual if the task fits with their values and beliefs and therefore helps to fulfil their basic psychological needs.

Self-control

The self-control of motivation is increasingly understood as a subset of emotional intelligence; a person may be highly intelligent according to a more conservative definition (as measured by many intelligence tests), yet unmotivated to dedicate this intelligence to certain tasks. Yale School of Management professor Victor Vroom's "expectancy theory" provides an account of when people will decide whether to exert self control to pursue a particular goal.

Drives and desires can be described as *a deficiency or need that activates behaviour that is aimed at a goal or an incentive.*

These are thought to originate within the individual and may not require external stimuli to encourage the behaviour. Basic drives could be sparked by deficiencies such as hunger, which motivates a person to seek food; whereas more subtle drives might be the desire for praise and approval, which motivates a person to behave in a manner pleasing to others.

By contrast, the role of extrinsic rewards and stimuli can be seen in the example of training animals by giving them treats when they perform a trick correctly. The treat motivates the animals to perform the trick consistently, even later when the treat is removed from the process.

Motivational Theories

Incentive Theory

A reward, tangible or intangible, is presented after the occurrence of an action (i.e. behaviour) with the intent to cause the behaviour to occur again. This is done by associating positive meaning to the behaviour. Studies show that if the person receives the reward immediately, the effect would be greater, and decreases as duration lengthens. Repetitive action-reward combination can cause the action to become habit. Motivation comes from two sources: oneself, and other people. These two sources are called intrinsic motivation and extrinsic motivation, respectively.

Applying proper motivational techniques can be much harder than it seems. Steven Kerr notes that when creating a reward system, it can be easy to reward A, while hoping for B, and in the process, reap harmful effects that can jeopardize your goals.

A reinforcer is different from reward, in that reinforcement is intended to create a measured increase in the rate of a desirable behaviour following the addition of something to the environment.

Incentive theory in psychology, treats motivation and behaviour of the individual, as they are influenced by beliefs, such as engaging in activities that are expected to be profitable. Incentive theory is promoted by behavioural psychologists, such as B.F. Skinner and literalized, by behaviourists, especially by

Skinner in his philosophy of Radical behaviourism, to mean that a person's actions always have social ramifications: and if actions are positively received people are more likely to act in this manner, or if negatively received people are less likely to act in this manner. Incentive theorists tend to distinguish between wanting and liking, where *liking* is a passive function evaluating a stimulus, but *wanting* adds an active process "attracting" the person towards the stimulus.

Incentive theory distinguishes itself from other motivation theories, such as drive theory, in the direction of the motivation. In incentive theory, stimuli "attract", to use the term above, a person towards them. As opposed to the body seeking to reestablish homeostasis pushing it towards the stimulus. In terms of behaviourism, *incentive theory* involves positive reinforcement: the stimulus has been conditioned to make the person happier. For instance, a person knows that eating food, drinking water, or gaining social capital will make them happier. As opposed to in *drive theory*, which involves negative reinforcement: a stimulus has been associated with the removal of the punishment— the lack of homeostasis in the body. For example, a person has come to know that if they eat when hungry, it will eliminate that negative feeling of hunger, or if they drink when thirsty, it will eliminate that negative feeling of thirst.

Drive-reduction Theories

There are a number of drive theories. The Drive Reduction Theory grows out of the concept that we have certain biological drives, such as hunger. As time passes the strength of the drive increases if it is not satisfied (in this case by eating). Upon satisfying a drive the drive's strength is reduced. The theory is based on diverse ideas from the theories of Freud to the ideas of feedback control systems, such as a thermostat.

Drive theory has some intuitive or folk validity. For instance when preparing food, the drive model appears to be compatible with sensations of rising hunger as the food is prepared, and, after the food has been consumed, a decrease in subjective hunger. There are several problems, however, that leave the validity of drive reduction open for debate. The first problem is that it does not explain how secondary reinforcers reduce drive. For example, money satisfies no biological or psychological needs, but a pay check appears to reduce drive through second-order conditioning. Secondly, a drive, such as hunger, is viewed as having a "desire" to eat, making the drive a homuncular being—a feature criticized as simply moving the fundamental problem behind this "small man" and his desires.

In addition, it is clear that drive reduction theory cannot be a complete theory of behaviour, or a hungry human could not prepare a meal without eating the food before he finished cooking it. The ability of drive theory to cope with all kinds of behaviour, from not satisfying a drive (by adding on other traits such as restraint), or adding additional drives for "tasty" food, which combine with drives for "food" in order to explain cooking render it hard to test.

Cognitive Dissonance Theory

Suggested by Leon Festinger, this occurs when an individual experiences some degree of discomfort resulting from an incompatibility between two cognitions. For example, a consumer may seek to reassure himself regarding a purchase, feeling, in retrospect, that another decision may have been preferable.

Another example of cognitive dissonance is when a belief and a behaviour are in conflict. A person may wish to be healthy, believes smoking is bad for one's health, and yet continues to smoke.

Need Theories

Need Hierarchy Theory

Abraham Maslow's theory is one of the most widely discussed theories of motivation.

The theory can be summarized as follows:

- Human beings have wants and desires which influence their behaviour. Only unsatisfied needs influence behaviour, satisfied needs do not.
- Since needs are many, they are arranged in order of importance, from the basic to the complex.

- The person advances to the next level of needs only after the lower level need is at least minimally satisfied.
- The further the progress up the hierarchy, the more individuality, humanness and psychological health a person will show.

The needs, listed from basic (lowest-earliest) to most complex (highest-latest) are as follows:

- Physiology (hunger, thirst, sleep, etc.)
- Safety/Security/Shelter/Health
- Belongingness/Love/Friendship
- Self-esteem/Recognition/Achievement
- Self actualization.

Herzberg's Two-factor Theory

Frederick Herzberg's two-factor theory, a.k.a. intrinsic/ extrinsic motivation, concludes that certain factors in the workplace result in job satisfaction, but if absent, they don't lead to dissatisfaction but no satisfaction. The factors that motivate people can change over their lifetime, but "respect for me as a person" is one of the top motivating factors at any stage of life.

He distinguished between:

- Motivators; (e.g. challenging work, recognition, responsibility) which give positive satisfaction, *and*
- Hygiene factors; (e.g. status, job security, salary and fringe benefits) that do not motivate if present, but, if absent, result in demotivation.

The name Hygiene factors is used because, like hygiene, the presence will not make you healthier, but absence can cause health deterioration. The theory is sometimes called the "Motivator-Hygiene Theory" and/or "The Dual Structure Theory." Herzberg's theory has found application in such occupational fields as information systems and in studies of user satisfaction.

Alderfer's ERG Theory

Alderfer, expanding on Maslow's hierarchy of needs, created

the ERG theory (existence, relatedness and growth). Physiological and safety, the lower order needs, are placed in the existence category, while love and self esteem needs are placed in the relatedness category. The growth category contains our self-actualization and self-esteem needs. Alderfer argues that there are three groups of core needs — existence, relatedness, and growth hence the label: ERG theory. The existence group is concerned with providing our basic material existence requirements. They include the items that Maslow considered to be physiological and safety needs. The second group of needs are those of relatedness-the desire we have for maintaining important interpersonal relationships. These social and status desires require interaction with others if they are to be satisfied, and they align with Maslow's social need and the external component of Maslow's esteem classification. Finally, Alderfer isolates growth needs' an intrinsic desire for personal development. These include the intrinsic component from Maslow's esteem category and the characteristics included under self-actualization.

Self-determination Theory

Self-determination theory, developed by Edward Deci and Richard Ryan, focuses on the importance of intrinsic motivation in driving human behaviour. Like Maslow's hierarchical theory and others that built on it, SDT posits a natural tendency toward growth and development. Unlike these other theories, however, SDT does not include any sort of "autopilot" for achievement, but instead requires active encouragement from the environment. The primary factors that encourage motivation and development are autonomy, competence feedback, and relatedness.

Broad Theories

The latest approach in Achievement Motivation is an integrative perspective as outlined in the "Onion-Ring-Model of Achievement Motivation" by Heinz Schuler, George C. Thornton III, Andreas Frintrup and Rose Mueller-Hanson. It is based on the premise that performance motivation results from the way broad components of personality are directed towards performance. As a result, it includes a range of dimensions that are relevant to success at work but which are not conventionally regarded as being part of performance motivation. Especially it integrates formerly separated approaches as Need for Achievement with e.g. social motives like dominance. The Achievement Motivation Inventory (AMI) (Schuler, Thornton, Frintrup & Mueller-Hanson, 2003) is based on this theory and assesses three factors (17 separated scales) relevant to vocational and professional success.

Cognitive Theories

Goal-setting Theory

Goal-setting theory is based on the notion that individuals sometimes have a drive to reach a clearly defined end state. Often, this end state is a reward in itself. A goal's efficiency is affected by three features: proximity, difficulty and specificity. An ideal goal should present a situation where the time between the initiation of behaviour and the end state is close. This explains why some children are more motivated to learn how to ride a bike than mastering algebra. A goal should be moderate, not too hard or too easy to complete. In both cases, most people are not optimally motivated, as many want a challenge (which assumes some kind of insecurity of success). At the same time people want to feel that there is a substantial probability that they will succeed. Specificity concerns the description of the goal in their class. The goal should be objectively defined and intelligible for the individual. A classic example of a poorly specified goal is to get the highest possible grade. Most children have no idea how much effort they need to reach that goal.

Models of Behaviour Change

Social-cognitive models of behaviour change include the constructs of motivation and volition. Motivation is seen as a process that leads to the forming of behavioural intentions. Volition is seen as a process that leads from intention to actual behaviour. In other words, motivation and volition refer to goal setting and goal pursuit, respectively. Both processes require self-regulatory efforts. Several self-regulatory constructs are needed to operate in orchestration to attain goals. An example of such a motivational and volitional construct is perceived self-efficacy. Self-efficacy is supposed to facilitate the forming of behavioural intentions, the development of action plans, and the initiation of action. It can support the translation of intentions into action.

Unconscious Motivation

Some psychologists believe that a significant portion of human behaviour is energized and directed by unconscious motives. According to Maslow, "Psychoanalysis has often demonstrated that the relationship between a conscious desire and the ultimate unconscious aim that underlies it need not be at all direct."

Intrinsic Motivation and the 16 Basic Desires Theory

Starting from studies involving more than 6,000 people, Professor Steven Reiss has proposed a theory that find 16 basic desires that guide nearly all human behaviour. The desires are:

- Acceptance, the need for approval
- Curiosity, the need to learn
- Eating, the need for food
- Family, the need to raise children
- Honor, the need to be loyal to the traditional values of one's clan/ethnic group
- Idealism, the need for social justice
- Independence, the need for individuality
- Order, the need for organized, stable, predictable environments
- Physical activity, the need for exercise
- Power, the need for influence of will
- Romance, the need for sex
- Saving, the need to collect
- Social contact, the need for friends (peer relationships)
- Status, the need for social standing/importance
- Tranquility, the need to be safe
- Vengeance, the need to strike back/to win.

In this model, people differ in these basic desires. These basic desires represent intrinsic desires that directly motivate a person's behaviour, and not aimed at indirectly satisfying other desires. People may also be motivated by non-basic desires, but in this case this does not relate to deep motivation, or only as a means to achieve other basic desires.

Other Theories

- Reversal theory
- Motivating operation.

Controlling Motivation

The control of motivation is only understood to a limited extent. There are many different approaches of *motivation training*, but many of these are considered pseudoscientific by critics. To understand how to control motivation it is first necessary to understand why many people lack motivation.

Drugs

Some authors, especially in the transhumanist movement, have suggested the use of "smart drugs", also known as nootropics, as "motivation-enhancers". The effects of many of these drugs on the brain are emphatically not well understood, and their legal status often makes open experimentation difficult.

Applications

Education

Motivation is of particular interest to educational psychologists because of the crucial role it plays in student learning. However, the specific kind of motivation that is studied in the specialized setting of education differs qualitatively from the more general forms of motivation studied by psychologists in other fields.

Motivation in education can have several effects on how students learn and how they behave towards subject matter. It can:

1. Direct behaviour toward particular goals

2. Lead to increased effort and energy
3. Increase initiation of, and persistence in, activities
4. Enhance cognitive processing
5. Determine what consequences are reinforcing
6. Lead to improved performance.

Because students are not always internally motivated, they sometimes need *situated motivation*, which is found in environmental conditions that the teacher creates.

The majority of new student orientation leaders at colleges and universities recognize that distinctive needs of students should be considered in regard to orientation information provided at the beginning of the higher education experience. Research done by Whyte in 1986 raised the awareness of counsellors and educators in this regard. In 2007, the National Orientation Directors Association reprinted Cassandra B. Whyte's research report allowing readers to ascertain improvements made in addressing specific needs of students over a quarter of a century later to help with academic success.

There are two kinds of motivation:

- Intrinsic motivation occurs when people are internally motivated to do something because it either brings them pleasure, they think it is important, or they feel that what they are learning is significant. It has been shown that intrinsic motivation for education drops from grades 3-9 though the exact cause cannot be ascertained. Also, in younger students it has been shown that contextualizing material that would otherwise be presented in an abstract manner increases the intrinsic motivation of these students.
- Extrinsic motivation comes into play when a student is compelled to do something or act a certain way because of factors external to him or her (like money or good grades).

Whyte researched and reported about the importance of locus of control and academic achievement. Students tending toward a more internal locus of control are more academically successful, thus encouraging curriculum and activity development with consideration of motivation theories. Motivation has been found to be an important element in the concept of Andragogy (what motivates the adult learner, and in treating Autism Spectrum Disorders, as in Pivotal Response Therapy.

Sudbury Model Schools' Approach to Motivation

Sudbury Model schools adduce that the cure to the problem of procrastination, of learning in general, and particularly of scientific illiteracy is to remove once and for all what they call the underlying disease: compulsion in schools.

They contend that human nature in a free society recoils from every attempt to force it into a mold; that the more requirements we pile onto children at school, the surer we are to drive them away from the material we are trying to force down their throats; that after all the drive and motivation of infants to master the world around them is legendary. They assert that schools must keep that drive alive by doing what some of them do: nurturing it on the freedom it needs to thrive.

Sudbury Model schools do not perform and do not offer evaluations, assessments, transcripts, or recommendations, asserting that they do not rate people, and that school is not a judge; comparing students to each other, or to some standard that has been set is for them a violation of the student's right to privacy and to self-determination. Students decide for themselves how to measure their progress as self-starting learners as a process of self-evaluation: real life-long learning and the proper educational evaluation for the 21st century, they adduce.

According to Sudbury Model schools, this policy does not cause harm to their students as they move on to life outside the school. However, they admit it makes the process more difficult, but that such hardship is part of the students learning to make their own way, set their own standards and meet their own goals. The no-grading and no-rating policy helps to create an atmosphere free of competition among students or battles for adult approval, and encourages a positive cooperative environment amongst the student body.

Factors of Learning: Personal and Environmental

Learning, as we know, can be considered as the process by which skills, attitudes, knowledge and concepts are acquired, understood, applied and extended. All human beings, whether grown ups or children engage in the process of learning, either consciously, sub-consciously or subliminally. It is through learning that their competence and ability to function in their environment get enhanced. It is important to understand that while we learn some ideas and concepts through instruction or teaching, we also learn through our feelings and experiences. Feelings and experiences are a tangible part of our lives and these greatly influence what we learn, how we learn and why we learn.

Learning has been considered partly a cognitive process and partly a social and affective one. It qualifies as a cognitive process because it involves the functions of attention, perception, reasoning, analysis, drawing of conclusions, making interpretations and giving meaning to the observed phenomena. All of these are mental processes which relate to the intellectual functions of the individual. Learning is a social and affective process, as the societal and cultural context in which we function and the feelings and experiences which we have, greatly influence our ideas, concepts, images and understanding of the world.

These constitute inner subjective interpretations and represent our own unique, personalized constructions of the specific universe of functioning. Our knowledge, ideas, concepts, attitudes, beliefs and the skills which we acquire are a consequence of these combined processes. You may be wondering why we are discussing the concept of learning, since our concern in this unit is with factors affecting learning.

We are doing this to enable you to appreciate the fact that the process of learning involves cognition, feeling, experience and a context. Individuals vary greatly with regard to their ability, capacity and interest in learning. You must have noticed such variations among your friends and students. In any family, children of the same parents differ with respect to what they can learn and how well they can learn. For example, a particular child may be very good at acquiring practical skills such as repairing electrical gadgets, shopping for the household etc., while his brother or sister may in contrast be very poor on these, and good at academic tasks, instead.

Even for yourself, you may be perplexed why you can do some tasks well, but not others given the same competence level. For example, learning the tunes of songs and even their lyrics is often found to be easier than learning a formula or a poem. Do4 you ever wonder why this is so? You may have observed that for some people,

learning driving or swimming or cooking is achieved easily, while for some others it is 1 a nightmare. Why this happens, what could be the underlying reasons and why individuals differ with respect to how and what they learn, are the key questions addressed in the present unit. To find some answers to these questions, we will try to identify and understand the various factors affecting learning.

There are some personal factors affecting learning that deal with the innate aspects of an individual and are unique to hirn/her. These are extremely significant as they influence what the individual can learn, how much time, effort and energy helshe is required to put in and how well helshe is likely to learn. The environmental factors are other factors which mediate the learning process. Research has shown that the following are the key factors that affect learning:

* Intelligence
* Aptitude
* Goals
* Interests
* Readiness & Maturation
* Motivation
* Self Concept
* Attitudes & Values
* Level of Aspiration
* Learning style
* Socio cultural determinants.

Each of these factors play a significant role in learning. We will now examine them one by one a little later, in terms of what they mean, how they vary across individuals and how they influence the process of learning. CLASSIFICATION OF FACTORS To understand how we categories the factors affecting learning, let us begin by considering the following examples:

1. Ravi is sixteen years old and wants to please his mother by getting good results in his board examinations. He is so eager to please her, that he spends long hours of concentrated time and energy on his studies. He consciously tries to control other sources of distraction in his life and reduces the time spent on watching television, playing games and chatting with his friends.
2. Rita Williams wants to be a famous tennis player. To achieve her goal, she practices tennis whenever she can, even though she gets no encouragement from her family. She makes it a point to watch tennis matches and maintain a good rapport with her sports teacher.
3. Yuvraj is a good student, but lately he has been scoring very low marks at school. He is not able to concentrate or pay attention and his class work and home assignments reflect a very poor quality. Sources revealed that his parents fight a lot with each other and are about to get divorced.
4. Arti and Kavita are two sisters. Arti is very good at art and craft and can sketch just about anything she sees. Kavita has a ear for music. She knows most songs and can sing them even if she has heard them only once. Both of them spend hours together pursuing their respective interest areas.
5. Sayeeda is tall, attractive and has a very good figure. She wants to be a model or an air-hostess and nurtures this secretly as her dream. She is too scared to share her wishes with her family, since she belongs to an orthodox family, where girls at best can pursue teaching as a career. When she tries telling her mother what she wants, she is firmly told that she can only do her B.Ed and can go to the coaching classes for these.

The above cited examples illustrate that learning is a universal phenomenon mediated by a number of factors, both personal and environmental in nature. The dictum "everybody learns" is as true as its corollary, i.e., everybody learns in accordance with his/her unique, individualized blend of personal and environmental factors.

For example, in case of Ravi, the desire to please his mother, striving to do well in his board exams and managing his Life situations appropriately constitute the key factors which influence him. For Rita Williams, it is her intrinsic desire to be a good tennis player which is paramount. She is not deterred by the lack of family support and continues to make efforts to promote her love for tennis on her own and fulfil her desire to be successful.

In case of Yuvraj, in spite of his innate capacity to study and perform well, his lack of achievement can be attributed to the emotional insecurity stemming from his parents' divorce. As far as Arti and Kavita are concerned, their special interests and talent in art and music respectively, seem to guide their activities. For Sayeeda, the home environment and family culture and values determine her professional choice. Her own inner interests, desires and wishes are not to be taken into cognizance.

In all the examples cited, you can find evidence of both personal and environmental factors influencing the process of learning. Learning can thus be defined as a function of the interaction of personal and environmental factors. L = f (EF x PF) L = learning; f = function; EF = environmental factors; PI? = personal factors. Personal factors are the intra individual factors like motivation, interests, abilities etc. which predispose an individual towards learning as in the case of Rita Williams, Arti and Kavita. Environmental factors on the other hand, are those contextual factors which highlight the role of the environment in learning, such as the socio-emotional, societal and cultural factors as seen in the case of Yuvraj and Sayeeda. Although the two factors represent different categories, they operate in a common system. The environmental factors provide the context within which the personal factors, operate. The learner and the learning process can only be completely understood with reference to the interaction of both environmental and personal factors.

Intelligence

One of the key factors which affects our ability to learn effectively is intelligence. There are wide variations across individuals and cultures as to what actually constitutes intelligence. Let us take a deeper look at what this statement means by engaging in the following analytical task.

Imagine a classroom in which there are ten students, each with a distinctive characteristic highlighting hislher ability. You have been asked to state which one among them you consider to be the most intelligent and why. How will you proceed in your judgement. The profiles of the ten students given to you are as follows:

- Manisha always comes first in class.
- Zubin is an ace chess player.
- Neha is the most popular girl in her class.
- Ashish can remember statistics about cricket from any time period. * Mumtaz never loses her cool and remains calm and even tempered even in difficult situations.
- Mark gets always called to arbitrate in peer disputes in his class.
- Zarina can organize any event, even at a short notice.
- Niloufer choreographs dances very well.
- Shrikant is a wizard in mental mathematics.
- Ayesha always gives novel and unique answers to routine questions.

In all probability, you will choose to identify some criteria which define intelligence and then, go case by case to consider who is the most intelligent. You will realize herein however lies your major difficulty of how to select the criteria? How to priorities their importance? How to assign ranking? In all likelihood, you will conclude that each student is intelligent in some way or the other, because some ability, competence or skill has been demonstrated by each one of them. Furthermore, this ability has optimised their performance or their existence in many ways. Thus two things may clearly strike you. First that there is no universal definition of the term intelligence. You will begin to realize that many possible definitions coexist. Secondly, it will become apparent to you, that irrespective of what intelligence is, it certainly augments learning, achievement and performance. You are thus likely to conclude that learning is greatly facilitated by intelligence.

To understand this you may like to take a brief look at some of the prominent views which attempt to conceptualize intelligence. The earliest among these was the psychometric tradition beginning with the work of Alfred Binet. This tradition is based on statistical analyses of conventional tests of intelligence, requiring students to show basic vocabulary, mathematical ability, reasoning and other skills. In a broad sense, intelligence is understood as a combination of several specific, component abilities. Binet for instance, suggested three main elements of intelligence: (1) direction, which involves knowing what has to be done and how to do it; *2)* adaptation or figuring out how to perform a task and (3) criticism, or the ability to critique one's own thoughts and actions.

British psychologist Charles Spearman suggested that intelligence can be understood in terms of two dimensions or factors. A single general factor (g factor), general mental ability, which would affect all tasks and activities, and specific factors (s factors) which affect performance in a single discrete area of mental ability, such as vocabulary, mathematics, reasoning etc.

The American psychologist Thurstone, however, argued that a single factor was an inadequate index of intelligence and suggested seven inter-related factors which he called primary mental abilities. According to him learning and p6rformance were the outcome of these seven primary mental abilities which, he labeled as: (i) Verbal comprehension, (ii) Verbal fluency, (iii) Inductive reasoning, (iv) Spatial visualization, (v) Number, (vi) Memory, and (vii) Perceptual speed. Other approaches to intelligence and learning view them as abilities to process information meaningfully (Sternberg) to adapt7to the demands of the environment (Piaget), to construct knowledge based on one's experiences (constructivism), and to be emotionally well adjusted and secure (Goleman). The conceptualization of intelligence, thus in these different frameworks is much broader and recognizes that children as well as adults can be intelligent in many different ways. The most dominant contemporary view in intelligence which has a marked influence on educational practice is the one proposed by Howard Gardener. He has advanced a theory of multiple intelligences in which there are eight distinct and relatively independent intelligences. Each is a separate system of functioning, although *i.* the various systems can interact to produce overall intelligent performance. The eight intelligences are:

- Linguistic intelligence
- Logical-mathematical intelligence
- Spatial intelligence
- Musical intelligence
- Bodily-kinesthetic intelligence
- Interpersonal intelligence
- Intrapersonal intelligence
- Naturalist intelligence.

The intelligence on which one is high in terms of manifestation will thus determine what one learns, how well one learns, and also influence the various ways in which one seeks engagement. Thus, irrespective of how we define intelligence, in relating it to learning, there is no doubt that it affects what, when and how we learn. Further, in operational terns, it definitely is a capacity or an ability for problem solving, thinking, reasoning, relating to others, dealing with emotions, developing interests, sense of right and wrong and living in consonance with our environment.

Aptitude

You must have wondered many times why individuals having the same level of intelligence do not necessarily show the same results when put to the same task or activity. Further, you must have heard persons saying when frustrated, "No matter what I do, I can't get my sums right", or "I just can't learn a foreign language", or "The cake I bake, never rises", or "I simply can't memorise the poem."

It is obvious from the above that no one finds all activities and tasks easy to master and learn. While some persons are good at languages or maths, some others simply can't cope with them although they are as bright as their counterparts. Similarly, some persons can learn to cook or play musical instruments with ease, while others struggle to get their recipes right or keep to the tunes and notes. This is because individuals vary greatly in their aptitudes or their specific capacities to do a task well or to profit from specific types of training. For example, if you are especially adept at assembling a new bicycle or fixing household appliances or gardening, you probably have a natural talent or ability for these activities. You obviously have manual and finger dexterity and scientific reasoning. These are your specific abilities. Likewise, if you are good at drawing, painting and music, you probably have an aptitude for beauty, aesthetics and creative expression.

An aptitude is thus best understood as a stable ability of an individual, that is readily available as a resource, which can be applied to specific tasks requiring this ability, thereby enhancing his/her potential for learning. Different jobs require different skills and their corresponding aptitudes. Recognising this, psychologists have developed may tests for assessing specific aptitudes so as to predict how an individual may perform on a specific skill. One of the most popularly used tests is the Differential Aptitude Test Battery (DATB) which measures aptitudes like verbal reasoning, abstract reasoning, numerical ability, mechanical reasoning, spatial ability, language ability and clerical speed and accuracy. These tests help to identify an individual's aptitudes, and to predict what he/she will learn and do with ease.

The knowledge about various types of aptitudes enables us to economise our efforts and maximise learning. For example, by selecting employees who demonstrate an aptitude for a particular kind of job, an employer is likely to benefit from sending them for advanced skill training. Likewise, teachers encourage students having an aptitude for scholastic ability to strive towards excellence and high achievement by providing them beneficial learning opportunities. Thus, an aptitude is a measure of the probable rate of learning, which results in interest and satisfaction. Aptitudes are often used synonymously with talents and specific abilities, which are actually manifested concepts, judged through performance parameters.

Goals

A goal is an outcome or attainment that an individual sets and strive to accomplish. Goals motivate people to act in order to reduce the discrepancy between 'what they are' and 'what they want to be'. They can be understood with reference to the vision of the future that each individual constructs for himself. Goals have been understood and classified in various ways. They can be short-term, long-term or personal or societal in nature and tangible or abstract. Let us now examine each one of these. Short term goals are those which seem achievable in the near future.

They involve less time as, the required time can be specified and it does not seem inordinate and endless. For a graduate, clearing the B.Ed or Journalism entrance examinations is an example of a short term goal.

For an overweight adolescent, losing weight by going on a regulatory diet and exercise schedule is an example of a short term goal. Long term goals are those which are distant and oriented towards the future. A child's wish to be a doctor or a teacher for example, are low term goals. For the rural girl, being able to pursue education and a suitable career at the end of it, are long term goals. Immediate goals are those which can be fulfilled quickly.

Resorting to crash dieting to lose weight within a week, is an example of an immediate goal. Studying for an exam only to pass it is another example of an immediate goal. Personal goals deal with the needs and motives of the individual and are self-rewarding. For example, wanting to be a good dancer, a good human being, maintaining good health, etc., are all illustrations of personal goals since they enable an individual to feel good about him/herself. Societal goals are those which are concerned with changes in society, such as wanting better gender equality, sensitivity towards the poor, developing a more broad-minded attitude towards social reforms among the rural folk, etc. Tangible goals are those which are clearly definable and achievable like wanting to be a doctor, or getting a distinction in the Board examinations. Abstract goals are those which deal with qualitative changes that are difficult to specify and measure quantitatively. For example, wanting to be a good human being, or a contented person are abstract goals, since 'good' and 'contented' are difficult to define or measure precisely.

Goals play a significant role in learning since they give strength and direction to it. When we learn only to meet the immediate goal of passing the examination, our leaning is usually temporary and ineffective and we forget it soon after the goal is accomplished. For effective learning to take place, we should be able to relate it to all that we learn. This will enable us to achieve our life goals. When learning is guided or motivated by long term goals, it helps us to reach newer heights and contributes productively and positively to our life. Thus, the types of goals that we set, influence the amount of motivation to achieve them. Further the nature of our goal setting activity has been found to be directly proportionate to improvement in our leaning and performance. This is because the goals help to direct our attention to the task at hand, they mobilize our effort, they increase our persistence at the task and they also help us to adopt new strategies when old ones fail to help us.

Educational psychologists like Murphy and Alexander (2000) have written about many goal orientations which help us to understand students' learning and performance. The important ones among these are, learning goals, performance goals and work avoidance. Learning goals are based on the personal intention to improve abilities and understand a concept, idea or issue, no matter what one's performance is. Thus the mistakes one makes are not important, since the intention is to learn or to improve. Performance goals are based on the personal intention to appear competent or perform well in the eyes of others. Students with performance goals are more concerned about winning, being toppers and outdoing other students. Some students don't want to learn or look smart or outshine others; they just want to avoid work. These students try to complete assignments and activities as quickly as possible without exerting much effort. These are the work avoidant learners. You can clearly see thus how knowledge about goals is extremely significant in the educational process to understand the student and his/her learning. Interests

You often hear teachers complaining to parents at the Parent Teacher Meetings that their children can do very well in studies, provided they take interest in them. You may have also heard students saying "Hindi is so boring"; "I just can't do physics-its subject matter doesn't interest me" or "why should I go for the cricket match when I am not interested in cricket!" Interest is one of the most important factors which mediates learning and which motivates to act. Without interest, as is evident from the examples cited above, there can be no learning. *An* interest is not the same as preference for some object, event or behaviour over others and which provides engagement and joy and is undertaken voluntarily. Interests are actually deep rooted constructs and are determined by the need structure of an individual. *An* individual with strong social needs such as belongingness, affiliation, and recognition will direct all his/her energies into activities which enable him/her to fulfil these needs such as meeting people, going to dubs, associations, parties, meetings etc. In theoretical terms, an interest may be defined as a learnt or acquired motive stemming from some inherent needs of the individual which drive him/her to act in a way that will sustain or satisfy his inner need structure.

Individuals differ greatly in their patterns of interests because their need structures vary. For some persons, social and emotional needs become the guiding forces, for others, aesthetic or higher cognitive needs may be the preponderant factors. Age variations are also visible. Young children have a need for activity, play, adventure etc. and thus they learn much better through a play-way approach. p his* arouses their interest in studies and helps to sustain their involvement in work. For adolescents and older learners, the needs for affiliatian and group belongingness are very high and thus they always show an interest in recreational group activities like parties, picnics, social outings etc. Interests are thus determined by both age related and human needs factors. They influence not only what one will learn best, but also serve to explain why learning sometimes flags or becomes inadequate. Interests are usually classified on the basis of the nature of activity involved, for example, spiritual interests, recreational interests, scholarly or academic interests, social interests etc.

Readiness to Learn and Maturation

As the tern suggests, there is an optimal or most appropriate time for each individual to learn a specific skill or concept with ease and efficiency. This appropriate time comes when ones physical, neural and intellectual aspects of development have advanced enough to enable one to perceive the problem and solve it with relative ease and comfort. For instance, seven month old child cannot walk since it lacks the physical maturation or level of development required to promote walking. Similarly, it is impossible for a five year old to comment on democracy or socialism as he/she is not 'ready' or cognitively adept at understanding these concepts. Maturation can be best interpreted as relatively permanent change in an individual- be it cognitive, emotional or physical, that occurs as a result of biological ageing, regardless of personal experience. Maturation is preprogrammed and occurs regardless of the interactions a child has with the environment. Most expert teachers in schools know that no matter how hard they work or how good they are, they cannot force a student to think or do what he/she is not biologically ready to do. Thus, cognitive 'coming of age', or maturation is another specific aspect of 'readiness to learn'. It implies that a child should have the requisite level of cognitive skills necessary for solving a problem or accomplishing a task set before her.

It is also important for you to understand that there are large individual differences in maturation. Some children for instance walk at nine months, while others, at two years. Some children speak a language quite competently at three years, while others may be as late as five years. Puberty comes to some girls at eleven while to others at fourteen. Maturation has to be thus understood as a natural process of unfolding of the development stages, resulting in functionally preparing an individual to acquire mastery over his/her environment.

It must have become clear to you that any attempt to teach things before an adequate level of readiness is acquired by the child is futile. This also serves to explain why non-performance on the part of learners or their inability to grasp a concept, can be attributed to lack of adequate maturation and readiness to learn. Since maturation determines the readiness for learning, it is critical for curriculum planners and teachers to take note of this. It enables them to decide what to teach, how to teach, when to teach and correspondingly be guide on what to expect from I their learners. You will now be able to appreciate why very young children should not J be encouraged to write. Similarly, if teenagers are undergoing mood swings, it is because of their developmental pattern-they are not pretending moods or deliberately misbehaving.

Interest (Emotion)

Interest is a feeling or emotion that causes attention to focus on an object or an event or a process. In contemporary psychology of interest, the term is used as a general concept that may encompass other more specific psychological terms, such as curiosity and to a much lesser degree surprise.

The emotion of interest does have its own facial expression, of which the most prominent component is having dilated pupils.

Curiosity

Curiosity (from Latin *curiosus* "careful, diligent, curious," akin to *cura* "care") is an emotion related to natural inquisitive behaviour such as exploration, investigation, and learning, evident by observation in human and many animal species. The term can also be used to denote the behaviour itself being caused by the emotion of curiosity. As this emotion represents a drive to know new things, curiosity is the fuel of science and all other disciplines of human study.

Causes

Although curiosity is an innate capability of many living beings, it should not be categorized as an instinct because it is not a fixed action pattern; rather it is an innate basic emotion because while curiosity can be expressed in many ways, the expression of an instinct is typically more fixed and less flexible.

Curiosity is common to human beings at all ages from infancy to old age, and is easy to observe in many other animal species. These include apes, cats, fish, reptiles, and insects; as well as many others. Many aspects of exploration are shared among all beings, as all known terrestrial beings share similar aspects: limited size and a need to seek out food sources.

Strong curiosity is the main motivation of many scientists. In fact, in its development as wonder or admiration, it is generally curiosity that makes a human being want to become an expert in a field of knowledge. Though humans are sometimes considered particularly curious, they sometimes seem to miss the obvious when compared to other animals. What seems to happen is that human curiosity about curiosity itself (i.e. meta-curiosity or meta-interest), combined with the ability to think in an abstract way, lead to mimesis, fantasy and imagination-eventually leading to an especially human way of thinking ("human reason"), which is abstract and self-aware, or conscious. Readers of this page who are curious about meta-curiosity are experiencing meta-meta-curiosity.

Brain

The degree to which a person says that they have curiosity about trivia questions links to activity in both in the Broca's area in their left inferior frontal gyrus, and the putamen in their basal ganglia. This suggests people that are curious activate both parts of their brain that comprehend and anticipates information, and those in which such information acts as a secondary reinforcer or reward.

Curiosity also increased activity in memory areas such as the hippocampus when subjects guessed trivia questions incorrectly and this suggests that it might act to enhance a person's long term memory for surprising new information. Such activation linked to curiosity predicted better recall of surprising answers one or two weeks later. Dopamine receptors in part of the hippocampus called the dentate gyrus contribute to the generation of curiosity in mice. These receptors are also important for plasticity and learning and therefore are proposed to represent a molecular link between intelligence and curiosity.

Teacher Enthusiasm

Since teachers can affect how students perceive the course materials, it has been found that teachers who showed enthusiasm towards the course materials and students can affect a positive learning experience towards the course materials. On teacher/course evaluations, it was found that teachers who have a positive disposition towards the course content tend to transfer their passion to receptive students. Teachers cannot teach by rote but have to find new invigoration for the course materials on a daily basis.

Teachers have to keep in mind that they are teaching new minds every term or semester. Otherwise, teachers will fall into the trap of having done this material again and start feeling bored with the subject which in turn bore the students as well. Students who had enthusiastic teachers tend to rate them higher than teachers who didn't show much enthusiasm for the course materials.

Teachers that exhibit enthusiasm can lead to students who are more likely to be engaged, interested, energetic, and curious about learning the subject matter. Recent research has found a correlation between teacher enthusiasm and students' intrinsic motivation to learn and vitality in the classroom. Controlled, experimental studies exploring intrinsic motivation of college students has shown that nonverbal expressions of enthusiasm, such as demonstrative gesturing, dramatic movements which are varied, and emotional facial expressions, result in college students reporting higher levels of intrinsic motivation to learn. Students who experienced a very enthusiastic teacher were more likely to read lecture material outside of the classroom.

There are various mechanisms by which teacher enthusiasm may facilitate higher levels of intrinsic motivation. Teacher enthusiasm may contribute to a classroom atmosphere full of energy and enthusiasm which feed student interest and excitement in learning the subject matter. Enthusiastic teachers may also lead to students becoming more self-determined in their own learning process. The concept of mere exposure indicates that the teacher's enthusiasm may contribute to the student's expectations about intrinsic motivation in the context of learning. Also, enthusiasm may act as a "motivational embellishment"; increasing a student's interest by the variety, novelty, and surprise of the enthusiastic teacher's presentation of the material. Finally, the concept of emotional contagion, may also apply. Students may become more intrinsically motivated by catching onto the enthusiasm and energy of the teacher.

Research shows that student motivation and attitudes towards school are closely linked to student-teacher relationships. Enthusiastic teachers are particularly good at creating beneficial relations with their students. Their ability to create effective learning environments that foster student achievement depends on the kind of relationship they build with their students. Useful teacher-to-student interactions are crucial in linking academic success with personal achievement. Here, personal success is a student's internal goal of improving himself, whereas academic success includes the goals he receives from his superior. A teacher must guide his student in aligning his personal goals with his academic goals. Students who receive this positive influence show stronger self-confidence and greater personal and academic success than those without these teacher interactions.

Students are likely to build stronger relations with teachers who are friendly and supportive and will show more interest in courses taught by these teachers. Teachers that spend more time interacting and working directly with students are perceived as supportive and effective teachers. Effective teachers have been shown to invite student participation and decision making, allow humour into their classroom, and demonstrate a willingness to play.

The way a teacher promotes the course they are teaching, the more the student will get out of the subject matter. The three most important aspects of teacher enthusiasm are enthusiam about teaching, enthusiasm about the students, and enthusiasm about the subject matter. A teacher must enjoy teaching. If they do not enjoy what they are doing, the students will be able to tell. They also must enjoy being around their students. A teacher who cares for their students is going to help that individual succeed in their life in the future. The teacher also needs to be enthusiatic about the subject matter they are teaching. For example, a teacher talking about chemsitry needs to enjoy the art of chemistry and show that to their students. A spark in the teacher may create a spark of excitement in the student as well. A enthusiatic teacher has the ability to be very influential in the young students life.

School and Classrooms

A school is an institution designed for the teaching of students (or "pupils") under the supervision of teachers. Most countries have systems of formal education, which is commonly compulsory. In these systems, students progress through a series of schools. The names for these schools vary by country (discussed in the *Regional* section below), but generally include primary school for young children and secondary school for teenagers who have completed primary education.

In addition to these core schools, students in a given country may also attend schools before and after primary and secondary education. Kindergarten or pre-school provide some schooling to very young children (typically ages 3–5). University, vocational school, college or seminary may be available after secondary school. A school may also be dedicated to one particular field, such as a school of economics or a school of dance. Alternative schools may provide nontraditional curriculum and methods.

There are also non-government schools, called private schools. Private schools may be for children with special needs when the government does not supply for them; religious, such as Christian schools, hawzas, yeshivas, and others; or schools that have a higher standard of education or seek to foster other personal achievements. Schools for adults include institutions of corporate training and Military education and training.

In homeschooling and online schools, teaching and learning take place outside of a traditional school building.

History and Development of Schools

The history of education is the history of teaching and learning. Each generation, since the beginning of human existence, has sought to pass on cultural and social values, traditions, morality, religion and skills to the next generation. The passing on of culture is also known as enculturation and the learning of social values and behaviours is socialization. The history of the curricula of such education reflects human history itself, the history of knowledge, beliefs, skills and cultures of humanity.

In pre-literate societies, education was achieved orally and through observation and imitation. The young learned informally from their parents, extended family and grand parents. At later stages of their lives, they received instruction of a more structured and formal nature, imparted by people not necessarily related, in the context of initiation, religion or ritual.

As the customs and knowledge of ancient civilizations became more complex, many skills would have been learned from an experienced person on the job, in animal husbandry, agriculture, fishing, preparation and preservation of food, construction, stone work, metal work, boat building, the making of weapons and defenses, the military skills and many other occupations.

With the development of writing, it became possible for stories, poetry, knowledge, beliefs, and customs to be recorded and passed on more accurately to people out of earshot and to future generations. In many societies, the spread of literacy was slow; orality and illiteracy remained predominant for much of the population for centuries and even millennia. Literacy in preindustrial societies was associated with civil administration, law, long distance trade or commerce, and religion. A formal schooling in literacy was often only available to a small part of the population, either at religious institutions or for the wealthy who could afford to pay for their tutors. The earliest known universities, or places of higher education, started teaching a millennium or more ago.

Universal education of all children in literacy has been a recent development, not occurring in many countries until after 1850 CE. Even today, in some parts of the world, literacy rates are below 60 per cent (for example, in Afghanistan, Pakistan, Bangladesh). Schools, colleges and universities have not been the only methods of formal education and training.

Many professions have additional training requirements, and in Europe, from the Middle Ages until recent times, the skills of a trade were not generally learnt in a classroom, but rather by serving an apprenticeship.

Nowadays, formal education consists of systematic instruction, teaching and training by professional teachers. This consists of the application of pedagogy and the development of curricula.

Education in Prehistory

Most of human history lies in prehistory, the period before the use of writing, and before written history. Throughout prehistory, most education was achieved orally and through observation and imitation.

From the origin of our species, thought by many anthropologists to have been around 20,000 years ago in the African savannah, until about 10,000 BC, most humans lived as hunter-gatherers. Some were settled in a given locale/region and others exhibited a nomadic lifestyle across a large territory.

These bands or tribes had traditions, beliefs, values, practices and local knowledge which was passed orally for generations from person to person. The young learned informally from their parents, extended family and kin. At later stages of their lives, they received instruction of a more structured and formal nature, imparted by people not necessarily related, in the context of initiation, religion or ritual.

Some forms of traditional knowledge were expressed through stories, legends, folklore, rituals, and songs, without the need for a writing system. Tools to aid this process include poetic devices such as rhyme and alliteration. These methods are illustrative of orality. The stories thus preserved are also referred to as part of an oral tradition.

The advent of agriculture prompted the Neolithic Revolution, when access to food surplus led to the formation of permanent human settlements, the domestication of some animals and the use of metal tools.

Settlement, agriculture and metalwork brought new knowledge and skills to be learned and taught by each generation. As communities grew larger, there was more opportunity for some members to specialize in one skill or activity or another, becoming priests, artisans, traders, builders or labourers. Many skills would have been learned from an experienced person on the job.

The increased size of communities also brought changes to methods of leadership, politics and organization, together with early institutions. Society became less egalitarian as chiefdoms, States, city states and early civilisations replaced the earlier bands and tribes. For example, the Uruk period (ca. 4000 to 3100 BC) saw the emergence of urban life in Mesopotamia. These early city-states had strong signs of government organization. The cities grew to cover up to 250 acres (1 km^2) and up to 10,000–20,000 people by the end of the period.

In large settlements, social stratification began to develop, a hierarchical arrangement of social classes or castes within the society. There might be a king and nobles. There were often priests or other religious leaders, because religious beliefs in deities or spirits often formed an important part of a culture. In some societies, the status of women was lower than that of men; in some there were slaves. A person's social class, caste or gender might in turn determine or limit the occupations which he or she might follow and the education that he or she would receive.

Before the development of writing, it is probable that there were already epic poems, hymns to gods and incantations (such as those later found written in the ancient library at Ninevah, and the Vedas), and other oral literature.

In ancient India, the Vedas were learnt by repetition of various forms of recitation. By means of memorization, they were passed down through many generations.

Education in Ancient Civilizations

The Development of Writing

Starting in about 3500 BC, various writing systems were developed in ancient civilizations around the world. These writ In Egypt fully developed hieroglyphs that could be read in rebus fashion were in use at Abydos as early as 3400 BC. Later, the world's oldest known alphabet was developed in central Egypt around 2000 BC from a hieroglyphic prototype. One hieroglyphic script was used on stone monuments, other cursive scripts were used for writing in ink on papyrus, a flexible, paper-like material, made from the stems of reeds that grow in marshes and beside rivers such as the River Nile.

The Phoenician writing system was adapted from the Proto-Canaanite script in around the 11th century BC, which in turn borrowed ideas from Egyptian hieroglyphics. This script was adapted by the Greeks. A variant of the early Greek alphabet gave rise to the Etruscan alphabet, and its own descendants, such as the Latin alphabet. Other descendants from the Greek alphabet include the Cyrillic alphabet, used to write Russian, among others. The Phoenician system was also adapted into the Aramaic script, from which the Hebrew script and also that of Arabic are descended.

In China, the early oracle bone script has survived on tens of thousands of oracle bones dating from around 1400-1200 BC in the Shang Dynasty. Out of more than 2500 written characters in use in China in about 1200 BC, as many as 1400 are identifiable as the source of later standard Chinese characters.

Of several pre-Columbian scripts in Mesoamerica, the one that appears to have been best developed, and the one to be deciphered the most, is the Maya script. The earliest inscriptions which are identifiably Maya date to the 3rd century BC, and writing was in continuous use until shortly after the arrival of the Spanish conquistadores in the 16th century AD.

Other surfaces used for early writing include wax-covered writing boards (used, as well as clay tablets, by the Assyrians), sheets or strips of bark from trees (in Indonesia, Tibet and the Americas), the thick palm-like leaves of a particular tree, the leaves then punctured with a hole and stacked together like the pages of a book (these writings in India and South east Asia include Buddhist scriptures and Sanskrit literature), parchment, made of goatskin that had been soaked and scraped to remove hair, which was used from at least the second century BC, vellum, made from calfskin, and wax tablets which could be wiped clean to provide a fresh surface (in Roman times).

Formal Education in Ancient Civilizations

In many early civilizations, education was associated with wealth and the maintenance of authority, or with prevailing philosophies, beliefs, or religion.

The Middle East

In what became Mesopotamia, the early logographic system of cuneiform script took many years to master. Thus only a limited number of individuals were hired as scribes to be trained in its reading and writing. Only royal offspring and sons of the rich and professionals such as scribes, physicians, and temple administrators, went to school. Most boys were taught their father's trade or were apprenticed out to learn a trade. Girls had to stay home with their mothers to learn housekeeping and cooking, and to look after the younger children. Later, when a syllabic script became more widespread, more of the Mesopotamian population became literate. Later still in Babylonian times there were libraries in most towns and temples; an old Sumerian proverb averred that "he who would excel in the school of the scribes must rise with the dawn." There arose a whole social class of scribes, mostly employed in agriculture, but some as personal secretaries or lawyers. Women as well as men learned to read and write, and for the Semitic Babylonians, this involved knowledge of the extinct Sumerian language, and a complicated and extensive syllabary. Vocabularies, grammars, and interlinear translations were compiled for the use of students, as well as commentaries on the older texts and explanations of obscure words and phrases. Massive archives of texts were recovered from the archaeological contexts of Old Babylonian scribal schools, through which literacy was disseminated. The Epic of Gilgamesh, an epic poem from Ancient Mesopotamia is among the earliest known works of literary fiction. The earliest Sumerian versions of the epic date from as early as the Third Dynasty of Ur (2150-2000 BC) (Dalley 1989: 41-42).

Ashurbanipal (685 – ca. 627 BC), a king of the Neo-Assyrian Empire, was proud of his scribal education. His youthful scholarly pursuits included oil divination, mathematics, reading and writing as well as the usual horsemanship, hunting, chariotry, soldierliness, craftsmanship, and royal decorum. During his reign he collected cuneiform texts from all over Mesopotamia, and especially Babylonia, in the library in Nineveh, the first systematically organized library in the ancient Middle East, which survives in part today.

In ancient Egypt, literacy was concentrated among an educated elite of scribes. Only people from certain backgrounds were allowed to train to become scribes, in the service of temple, pharaonic, and military authorities. The hieroglyph system was always difficult to learn, but in later centuries was purposely made even more so, as this preserved the scribes' status. The rate of literacy in Pharaonic Egypt during most periods from the third to first millennium BC has been estimated at not more than one percent, or between one half of one percent and one percent.

One thousand years later, in ancient Israel and Judah a basic education eventually became more widespread. The Torah (the fundamental religious text) includes commands to read, learn, teach and write the Torah, thus requiring literacy and study. In 64 AD the high priest caused public schools to be opened in every town and hamlet for all children above six or seven years of age (Babylonian Talmud, Bava Batra 21a). The expense was borne by the community, and strict discipline was observed. Raba fixed the number of pupils at twenty-five for one teacher; if the number was between twenty-five and forty an assistant teacher was necessary; and for over forty, two teachers were required. The standard education texts were all hand-written until the invention of printing. However significant emphasis was placed on developing good memory skills in addition to comprehension by practice of oral repetition. For details of the subjects taught, see History of education in ancient Israel and Judah. Although girls were not provided with formal education in the yeshivah, they were required to know a large part of the subject areas to prepare them to maintain the home after marriage, and to educate the children before the age of seven. Despite this schooling system, it would seem that many children did not learn to read and write, because it has been estimated that at least 90 percent of the Jewish population of Roman Palestine in the first centuries AD could merely write their own name or not write and read at all, or that the literacy rate was about 3 percent.

India

In ancient India, during the Vedic period from about 1500 BC to 600 BC, most education was based on the Veda (hymns, formulas, and incantations, recited or chanted by priests of a pre-Hindu tradition) and later Hindu texts and scriptures.

Vedic education included: proper pronunciation and recitation of the Veda, the rules of sacrifice, grammar and derivation, composition, versification and meter, understanding of secrets of nature, reasoning including logic, the sciences, and the skills necessary for an occupation. Some medical knowledge existed and was taught. There is mention in the Veda of herbal medicines for various conditions or diseases, including fever, cough, baldness, snake bite and others.

Education, at first freely available in Vedic society, became over time more discriminatory as the caste system, originally based on occupation, evolved, with the brahman (priests) being the most privileged of the castes.

The oldest of the Upanishads-another part of Hindu scriptures-date from around 500 BC. These texts encouraged an exploratory learning process where teachers and students were co-travellers in a search for truth. The teaching methods used reasoning and questioning. Nothing was labeled as the final answer.

The Gurukul system of education supported traditional Hindu residential schools of learning; typically the teacher's house or a monastery. Education was free, but students from well-to-do families paid "Gurudakshina," a voluntary contribution after the completion of their studies. At the Gurukuls, the teacher imparted knowledge of Religion, Scriptures, Philosophy, Literature, Warfare, Statecraft, Medicine, Astrology and History. The corpus of Sanskrit literature encompasses a rich tradition of poetry and drama as well as technical scientific, philosophical and generally Hindu religious texts, though many central texts of Buddhism and Jainism have also been composed in Sanskrit.

Two epic poems formed part of ancient Indian education. The Mahabharata, part of which may date back to the eighth century BC, discusses human goals (purpose, pleasure, duty, and liberation), attempting to explain the relationship of the individual to society and the world (the nature of the 'Self') and the workings of karma. The other epic poem, Ramayana, is shorter, although it has 24,000 verses. It is thought to have been compiled between about 400 BC and 200 AD. The epic explores themes of human existence and the concept of dharma.

An early centre of learning in India dating back to the 5th century BC was Taxila (also known as Takshashila), which taught the three Vedas and the eighteen accomplishments. It was an important Vedic/Hindu and Buddhist centre of learning from the 6th century BC to the 5th century AD.

China

During the Zhou Dynasty (1045 BC to 256 BC), there were five national schools in the capital city, Pi Yong (an imperial school, located in a central location) and four other schools for the aristocrats and nobility, including Shang Xiang. The schools mainly taught the Six Arts: rites, music, archery, charioteering, calligraphy, and mathematics. According to the Book of Rituals, at age twelve, boys learned arts related to ritual (i.e. music and dance) and when older, archery and chariot driving. Girls learned ritual, correct deportment, silk production and weaving.

It was during the Zhou Dynasty that the origins of native Chinese philosophy also developed. Confucius (551 BC – 479 BC) founder of Confucianism, was a Chinese philosopher who made a great impact on later generations of Chinese, and on the curriculum of the Chinese educational system for much of the following 2000 years.

During the Han Dynasty (206 BC-221 AD), boys were thought ready at age seven to start learning basic skills in reading, writing and calculation.

In 124 BC, the Emperor Wudi established the Imperial Academy, the curriculum of which was the Five Classics of Confucius. By the end of the Han Dynasty (220 AD) the Academy enrolled more than 30,000 students, boys between the ages of fourteen and seventeen years. However education through this period was a luxury. Later, during the Ch'in dynasty (246-207 BC), a hierarchy of officials was set up to provide central control over the outlying areas of the empire. To enter this hierarchy, both literacy and knowledge of the increasing body of philosophy was required: "....the content of the educational process was designed not to engender functionally specific skills but rather to produce morally enlightened and cultivated generalists". The Nine rank system was a civil service nomination system during the Three Kingdoms (220-280 AD) and the Southern and Northern Dynasties (420-589 AD) in China. Theoretically, local government authorities were given the task of selecting talented candidates, then categorizing them into nine grades depending on their abilities. In practice, however, only the rich and powerful would be selected. The Nine Rank System was eventually superseded by the Imperial examination system for the civil service in the Sui Dynasty (581-618 AD).

The Greek and Roman Empires

In the city-states of ancient Greece, most education was private, except in Sparta. For example, in Athens, during the 5th and 4th century BC, aside from two years military training, the state played little part in schooling. Anyone could open a school and decide the curriculum. Parents could choose a school offering the subjects they wanted their children to learn, at a monthly fee they could afford. Most parents, even the poor, sent their sons to schools for at least a few years, and if they could afford it from around the age of seven until fourteen, learning gymnastics (including athletics, sport and wrestling), music (including poetry, drama and history) and literacy. Girls rarely received formal education. At writing school, the youngest students learned the alphabet by song, then later by copying the shapes of letters with a stylus on a waxed wooden tablet. After some schooling, the sons of poor or middle class families often learnt a trade by apprenticeship, whether with their father or another tradesman. By around 350 BC, it was common for children at schools in Athens to also study various arts such as drawing, painting, and sculpture. The richest students continued their education by studying with sophists, from whom, they could learn subjects such as rhetoric, mathematics, geography, natural history, politics, and logic. Some of Athens' greatest schools of higher education included the Lyceum (the so-called Peripatetic school founded by Aristotle of Stageira) and the Platonic Academy (founded by Plato of Athens). The education system of the wealthy ancient Greeks is also called Paideia. In the subsequent Roman empire, Greek was the primary language of science. Advanced scientific research and teaching was mainly carried on in the Hellenistic side of the Roman empire, in Greek.

The education system in the Greek city-state of Sparta was entirely different, designed to create warriors with complete obedience, courage, and physical perfection. At the age of seven, boys were taken away from their homes to live in school dormitories or military barracks. There they were taught sports, endurance and fighting, and little else, with harsh discipline. Most of the population was illiterate.

The first schools in Ancient Rome arose by the middle of the fourth century BC. These schools were concerned with the basic socialization and rudimentary education of young Roman children. The literacy rate in the third century BC has been estimated as around one percent to two percent. We have very few primary sources or accounts of Roman educational process until the second century BC, during which there was a proliferation of private schools in Rome. At the height of the Roman Republic and later the Roman Empire, the Roman educational system gradually found its final form. Formal schools were established, which served paying students (very little in the way of fre . public education as we know it can be found). Normally, both boys and girls were educated, though not necessarily together. In a system much like the one that predominates in the modern world, the Roman education system that developed arranged schools in tiers. The educator Quintilian recognized the importance of starting education as early as possible, noting that "memory ... not only exists even in small children, but is specially retentive at that age". A Roman student would progress through schools just as a student today might go from elementary school to middle school, then to high school, and finally college. Progression depended more on ability than age with great emphasis being placed upon a student's *ingenium* or inborn "gift" for learning, and a more tacit emphasis on a student's ability to afford high-level education. Only the Roman elite would expect a complete formal education. A tradesman or farmer would expect to pick up most of his vocational skills on the job. Higher education in Rome was more of a status symbol than a practical concern.

It has been argued that literacy rates in the Greco-Roman world were seldom more than 20 percent; averaging perhaps not much above 10 percent in the Roman empire, though with wide regional variations, probably never rising above 5 percent in the western provinces, and that the literate in classical Greece did not much exceed 5 percent of the population.

Formal Education in the Middle Ages (500-1600 AD)

Europe

European Overview: During the Early Middle Ages, the monasteries of the Catholic Church were the centres of education and literacy, preserving the Church's selection from Latin learning and maintaining the art of writing. Prior to their formal establishment, many medieval universities were run for hundreds of years as Christian cathedral schools or monastic schools (*Scholae monasticae*), in which monks and nuns taught classes; evidence of these immediate forerunners of the later university at many places dates back to the early 6th century AD. The first medieval institutions generally considered to be universities were established in Italy, France, and England in the late 11th and the 12th centuries for the study of arts, law, medicine, and theology. These universities evolved from much older Christian cathedral schools and monastic schools, and it is difficult to define the date at which they became true universities, although the lists of studia generalia for higher education in Europe held by the Vatican are a useful guide.

Ireland became known as the island of saints and scholars. Monasteries were built all over Ireland and these became centres of great learning.

Northumbria was famed as a centre of religious learning and arts. Initially the kingdom was evangelized by monks from the Celtic Church, which led to a flowering of monastic life, and

Northumbria played an important role in the formation of Insular art, a unique style combining Anglo-Saxon, Celtic, Byzantine and other elements. After the Synod of Whitby in 664 AD, Roman church practices officially replaced the Celtic ones but the influence of the Anglo-Celtic style continued, the most famous examples of this being the Lindisfarne Gospels. The Venerable Bede (673-735) wrote his *Historia ecclesiastica gentis Anglorum* (Ecclesiastical History of the English People, completed in 731) in a Northumbrian monastery, and much of it focuses on the kingdom.

During the reign of Charlemagne, King of the Franks from 768 – 814 AD, whose empire united most of Western Europe for the first time since the Romans, there was a flowering of scholarship, literature, art, and architecture sometimes referred to as the Carolingian Renaissance. Brought into contact with the culture and learning of other countries through his vast conquests, Charlemagne greatly increased the provision of monastic schools and scriptoria (centres for book-copying) in Francia. Most of the surviving works of classical Latin were copied and preserved by Carolingian scholars.

Charlemagne took a serious interest in scholarship, promoting the liberal arts at the court, ordering that his children and grandchildren be well-educated, and even studying himself under the tutelage of Paul the Deacon, from whom he learned grammar, Alcuin, with whom he studied rhetoric, dialect and astronomy (he was particularly interested in the movements of the stars), and Einhard, who assisted him in his studies of arithmetic. His great scholarly failure, as Einhard relates, was his inability to write.

The English monk Alcuin was invited to Charlemagne's court at Aachen, and brought with him the precise classical Latin education that was available in the monasteries of Northumbria. The return of this Latin proficiency to the kingdom of the Franks is regarded as an important step in the development of mediaeval Latin. Charlemagne's chancery made use of a type of script currently known as Carolingian minuscule, providing a common writing style that allowed for communication across most of Europe. After the decline of the Carolingian dynasty, the rise of the Saxon Dynasty in Germany was accompanied by the Ottonian Renaissance. Cathedral schools and monasteries remained important throughout the Middle Ages; at the Third Lateran Council of 1179 the Church mandated that priests provide the opportunity of a free education to their flocks, and the 12th and 13th century renascence known as the Scholastic Movement was spread through the monasteries.

These however ceased to be the sole sources of education in the 11th century when universities, which grew out of the monasticism began to be established in major European cities. Literacy became available to a wider class of people, and there were major advances in art, sculpture, music and architecture. Large cathedrals were built across Europe, first in the Romanesque, and later in the more decorative Gothic style.

Islamic World

During the 6th and 7th centuries AD, the Academy of Gundishapur, originally the intellectual centre of the Sassanid empire and subsequently a Muslim centre of learning, offered training in medicine, philosophy, theology and science. The faculty were versed not only in the Zoroastrian and Persian traditions, but in Greek and Indian learning as well.

The House of Wisdom in Bagdad was a library, translation and educational centre from the 9th to 13th centuries AD. Works on astrology, mathematics, agriculture, medicine, and philosophy were translated. Drawing on Persian, Indian and Greek texts—including those of Pythagoras, Plato, Aristotle, Hippocrates, Euclid, Plotinus, Galen, Sushruta, Charaka, Aryabhata and Brahmagupta—the scholars accumulated a great collection of knowledge in the world, and built on it through their own discoveries. The House was an unrivalled centre for the study of humanities and for sciences, including mathematics, astronomy, medicine, chemistry, zoology and geography. Baghdad was known as the world's richest city and centre for intellectual development of the time, and had a population of over a million, the largest in its time.

The commonly accepted view is that the Islamic mosque school (better known as Madrasah), was an institution distinct from the medieval university, and that the university with all its facets, including the granting of academic degrees such as bachelor (Latin: *Baccalaureus*), master (*Magister*) and doctorate (*licentia docendi*), was a proper medieval European development unrelated to contemporaneous Islamic learning. This view is indirectly supported by the entry on the "Madrasa" in the Encyclopedia of Islam which draws no parallels between Islamic and Christian medieval institutions of higher learning and does not refer to any transmission process either way.

Also in the 9th century, Bimaristan medical schools were formed in the medieval Islamic world, where medical diplomas were issued to students of Islamic medicine who were qualified to be a practicing Doctor of Medicine. Al-Azhar University, founded in Cairo, Egypt in 975, was a *Jami'ah* ("university" in Arabic) which offered a variety of postgraduate degrees, had a Madrasah and theological seminary, and taught Islamic law, Islamic jurisprudence, Arabic grammar, Islamic astronomy, early Islamic philosophy and logic in Islamic philosophy.

Itas has been argued that the ijazah is the origin of the modern doctorate. However, The generally accepted view expounded by the internationally renowned Lexikon des Mittelalters is that the origin of the doctorate lies in European high medieval teaching with its roots going back to late antiquity and the early days of Christian teaching of the Bible. This view is indirectly supported by the entry on the "Madrasa" in the internationally renowned Encyclopedia of Islam which draws no parallels between Islamic and Christian medieval learning and does not refer to any transmission process either way.

Under the Ottoman Empire, the towns of Bursa and Edirne became major centers of learning. The Ottoman system of Kulliye, a building complex containing a mosque, a hospital, madrassa, and public kitchen and dining areas, revolutionized the education system, making learning accessible to a wider public through its free meals, health care and sometimes free accommodation.

In the 15th and 16th centuries, the town of Timbuktu in the West African nation of Mali became an Islamic centre of learning with students coming from as far away as the Middle East. The town was home to the prestigious Sankore University and other madrasas. The primary focus of these schools was the teaching of the Qur'an, although broader instruction in fields such as logic, astronomy, and history also took place. Over time, there was a great accumulation of manuscripts in the area and an estimated 100,000 or more manuscripts, some of them dated from pre-Islamic times and 12th century, are kept by the great families from the town. Their contents are didactic, especially in the subjects of astronomy, music, and botany. More than 18,000 manuscripts have been collected by the Ahmed Baba centre.

China

Although there are more than 40,000 Chinese characters in written Chinese, many are rarely used. Studies have shown that full literacy in the Chinese language requires a knowledge of only between three and four thousand characters.

In China, three oral texts were used to teach children by rote memorization the written characters of their language and the basics of Confucian thought.

The Thousand Character Classic, a Chinese poem originating in the 6th century AD, was used for more than a millennium as a primer for teaching Chinese characters to children. The poem is composed of 250 phrases of four characters each, thus containing exactly one thousand unique characters, and was sung in the same way that children learning the Latin alphabet may use the "alphabet song".

Later, children also learn the Hundred Family Surnames, a rhyming poem in lines of eight characters composed in the early Song Dynasty (i.e. in about the 11th century AD) which actually listed more than four hundred of the common surnames in ancient China.

From around the 13th century AD until the latter part of the 19th century, the Three Character Classic, which is an embodiment of Confucian thought suitable for teaching to young children, served as a child's first formal education at home. The text is written in triplets of characters for easy memorization. With illiteracy common for most people at the time, the oral tradition of reciting the classic ensured its popularity and survival through the centuries. With the short and simple text arranged in three-character verses, children learned many common characters, grammar structures, elements of Chinese history and the basis of Confucian morality.

After learning Chinese characters, students wishing to ascend in the social hierarchy needed to study the Chinese classic texts.

The early Chinese state depended upon literate, educated officials for operation of the empire. In 605 AD, during the Sui Dynasty, for the first time, an examination system was explicitly instituted for a category of local talents. The merit-based imperial examination system for evaluating and selecting officials gave rise to schools that taught the Chinese classic texts and continued in use for 1,300 years, until the end the Qing Dynasty, being abolished in 1911 in favour of Western education methods. The core of the curriculum for the imperial civil service examinations from the mid 12th century AD onwards was the Four Books, representing a foundational introduction to Confucianism.

Theoretically, any male adult in China, regardless of his wealth or social status, could become a high-ranking government official by passing the imperial examination, although under some dynasties members of the merchant class were excluded. In reality, since the process of studying for the examination tended to be time-consuming and costly (if tutors were hired), most of the candidates came from the numerically small but relatively wealthy land-owning gentry. However, there are vast numbers of examples in Chinese history in which individuals moved from a low social status to political prominence through success in imperial examination. Under some dynasties the imperial examinations were abolished and official posts were simply sold, which increased corruption and reduced morale.

In the period preceding 1040–1050 AD, prefectural schools had been neglected by the state and left to the devices of wealthy patrons who provided private finances. The chancellor of China at that time, Fan Zhongyan, issued an edict that would have used a combination of government funding and private financing to restore and rebuild all prefectural schools that had fallen into disuse and abandoned. He also attempted to restore all county-level schools in the same manner, but did not designate where funds for the effort would be formally acquired and the decree was not taken seriously until a later period. Fan's trend of government funding for education set in motion the movement of public schools that eclipsed private academies, which would not be officially reversed until the mid 13th century.

India

The first millennium and the few centuries preceding it saw the flourishing of higher education at Nalanda, Takshashila University, Ujjain, & Vikramshila Universities. Amongst the subjects taught were Art, Architecture, Painting, Logic, mathematics, Grammar, Philosophy, Astronomy, Literature, Buddhism, Hinduism, Arthashastra (Economics & Politics), Law, and Medicine. Each university specialized in a particular field of study. Takshila specialized in the study of medicine, while Ujjain laid emphasis on astronomy. Nalanda, being the biggest centre, handled all branches of knowledge, and housed up to 10,000 students at its peak.

Nalanda was a Buddhist centre of learning founded in Bihar, India around the 5th century AD and conferred academic degree titles to its graduates, while also offering postgraduate courses. It has been called "one of the first great universities in recorded history."

Vikramaúîla University, another important centre of Buddhist learning in India, was established by King Dharmapala (783 to 820) in response to a supposed decline in the quality of scholarship at Nâlandâ.

British records show that indigenous education was widespread in India in the 18th century, with a school for every temple, mosque or village in most regions of the country. The subjects taught included Reading, Writing, Arithmetic, Theology, Law, Astronomy, Metaphysics, Ethics, Medical Science and Religion. The schools were attended by students representative of all classes of society.

Japan

The history of education in Japan dates back at least to the sixth century, when Chinese learning was introduced at the Yamato court. Foreign civilizations have often provided new ideas for the development of Japan's own culture. Chinese teachings and ideas flowed into Japan from the sixth to the ninth century. Along with the introduction of Buddhism came the Chinese system of writing and its literary tradition, and Confucianism.

By the ninth century, Heian-kyo (today's Kyoto), the imperial capital, had five institutions of higher learning, and during the remainder of the Heian period, other schools were established by the nobility and the imperial court. During the medieval period (1185-1600), Zen Buddhist monasteries were especially important centers of learning, and the Ashikaga School, Ashikaga Gakko, flourished in the fifteenth century as a centre of higher learning.

Central and South American Civilizations

Aztec

Aztec is a term used to refer to certain ethnic groups of central Mexico, particularly those groups who spoke the Nahuatl language and who achieved political and military dominance over large parts of Mesoamerica in the 14th, 15th and 16th centuries, a period referred to as the Late post-Classic period in Mesoamerican chronology.

Until the age of fourteen, the education of children was in the hands of their parents, but supervised by the authorities of their *calpôlli*. Part of this education involved learning a collection of sayings, called *huçhuetlàtolli* ("sayings of the old"), that embodied the Aztecs' ideals. Judged by their language, most of the *huçhuetlatolli* seemed to have evolved over several centuries, predating the Aztecs and most likely adopted from other Nahua cultures.

At 15, all boys and girls went to school. The Mexica, one of the Aztec groups, were one of the first people in the world to have mandatory education for nearly all children, regardless of gender, rank, or station. There were two types of schools: the *telpochcalli*, for practical and military studies, and the *calmecac*, for advanced learning in writing, astronomy, statesmanship, theology, and other areas. The two institutions seem to be common to the Nahua people, leading some experts to suggest that they are older than the Aztec culture. Aztec teachers (*tlatimine*) propounded a spartan regime of education with the purpose of forming a stoical people. Girls were educated in the crafts of home and child raising. They were not taught to read or write. All women were taught to be involved in religion; there are paintings of women presiding over religious ceremonies, but there are no references to female priests.

Inca

Inca education during the time of the Inca Empire in the fifteenth and sixteenth centuries was divided into two principal spheres: education for the upper classes and education for the general population. The royal classes and a few specially-chosen individuals from the provinces of the Empire were formally educated by the *Amautas* (wise men), while the general population learned knowledge and skills from their immediate forbears. The Amautas constituted a special class of wise men similar to the bards of Great Britain. They included illustrious philosophers, poets, and priests who kept the oral histories of the Incas alive by imparting the knowledge of their culture, history, customs and traditions throughout the kingdom. Considered the most highly-educated and respected men in the Empire, the Amautas were largely entrusted with educating those of royal blood, as well as other young members of conquered cultures specially-chosen to administer the regions. Thus, education throughout the territories of the Incas was socially discriminatory, most people not receiving the formal education that royalty received. The official language of the empire was Quechua, although dozens if not hundreds of local languages were spoken. The Amautas did ensure that the general population learn Quechua as the language of the Empire, much in the same way the Romans promoted Latin throughout Europe; however, this was done more for political reasons than educational ones.

After the 15th Century CE

Europe

Modern systems of education in Europe derive their origins from the schools of the High Middle Ages. Most schools during this era were founded upon religious principles with the primary purpose of training the clergy. Many of the earliest universities, such as the University of Paris founded in 1160, had a Christian basis. In addition to this, a number of secular universities existed, such as the University of Bologna, founded in 1088. Free education for the poor was officially mandated by the Church at the Third Lateran Council (1179), which decreed that every cathedral must assign a master to teach boys too poor to pay the regular fee; parishes and monasteries also established free schools teaching at least basic literary skills. With few exceptions, priests and brothers taught locally, and their salaries were frequently subsidized by towns. Private, independent schools reappeared in medieval Europe during this time, but they, too, were religious in nature and mission.

The curriculum of the educational institutions of this period was frequently based around the trivium and quadrivium (the seven Artes Liberales or Liberal arts) and was conducted in Latin, the lingua franca of educated Western Europe throughout the Middle Ages and Renaissance.

In northern Europe this clerical education was largely superseded by forms of elementary schooling following the Reformation. In Scotland, for instance, the national Church of Scotland set out a programme for spiritual reform in January 1561 setting the principle of a school teacher for every parish church and free education for the poor. This was provided for by an Act of the Parliament of Scotland, passed in 1633, which introduced a tax to pay for this programme. Although few countries of the period had such extensive systems of education, the period between the 16th and 18th centuries saw education become significantly more widespread.

In Central Europe, the 17th century scientist and educator John Amos Comenius promulgated a reformed system of universal education that was widely used in Europe.

This growth resulted in increased government interest in education. In the 1760s, for instance, Ivan Betskoy was appointed by the Russian Tsarina, Catherine II, as educational advisor. He proposed to educate young Russians of both sexes in state boarding schools, aimed at creating "a new race of men". Betskoy set forth a number of arguments for general education of children rather than specialized one: "in regenerating our subjects by an education founded on these principles, we will create... new citizens." Some of his ideas were implemented in the Smolny Institute that he established for noble girls in Saint Petersburg.

Betskoy's work in Russia was soon followed by the Polish establishment in 1773 of a Commission of National Education (Polish: *Komisja Edukacji Narodowej*, Lithuanian: *Nacionaline Edukacine Komisija*). The commission functioned as the first government Ministry of Education in a European country.

Meanwhile, there was an increasing academic interest in education and the first attempts to create what might be considered academic rationales for teaching methods. This led, in the 1770s, to the establishment of the first chair of pedagogy at the University of Halle in Germany. Contributions to the study of education elsewhere in Europe included the work of Johann Heinrich Pestalozzi in Switzerland and Joseph Lancaster in Britain.

Under the guidance of Wilhelm von Humboldt a new university was founded in Berlin in 1810 which became the model for many research universities. Herbart developed a system of pedagogy widely used in German-speaking areas.

In the late nineteenth century, most of West, Central, and parts of East Europe began to provide elementary education in reading, writing, and arithmetic, partly because politicians believed that education was needed for orderly political behaviour. As more people became literate, they realized that most secondary education was only open to those who could afford it. Having created primary education, the major nations had to give further attention to secondary education by the time of World War 1.

In the 20th century, new directions in education included, in Italy, Maria Montessori's Montessori schools; and in Germany, Rudolf Steiner's development of Waldorf education.

France

While the French trace the development of their educational system to Charlemagne, the modern era of French education begins at the end of the nineteenth century. Jules Ferry, a lawyer holding the office of Minister of Public Instruction in the 1880s, is widely credited for creating the modern Republican school (*l'école républicaine*) by requiring all children under the age of 15—boys and girls—to attend. He also made public instruction free of charge and secular (*laïque*).

India

Education was widespread in the 18th century, with a schools in most regions of the country. The subjects taught included Reading, Writing, Arithmetic, Theology, Law, Astronomy, Metaphysics, Ethics, Medical Science and Religion.

The current system of education, with its western style and content, was introduced and founded by the British during the British Raj, following recommendations by Lord Macaulay. Traditional structures were not recognized by the British government and have been on the decline since. Gandhi, in a speech in London on October 20, 1931, described the traditional educational system as a beautiful tree that was destroyed during the British rule.

Japan

By 1603 Japan had been reunified by the Tokugawa regime (1600–1867), and by 1640 foreigners had been ordered out of Japan, Christianity banned, and virtually all foreign contact prohibited. The nation then entered a period of isolation and relative domestic tranquillity, which was to last 200 years. When the Tokugawa period began, few common people in Japan could read or write. By the period's end, learning had become widespread. Tokugawa education left a valuable legacy: an increasingly literate populace, a meritocratic ideology, and an emphasis on discipline and competent performance. Under subsequent Meiji leadership, this foundation would facilitate Japan's rapid transition from feudal country to modern nation.

One of the things that amazed Europeans that arrived in Japan at the end of the Edo period was that the Japanese were very well educated. It is estimated that the literacy rate was already over 80% for men and somewhere in the 60s or 70s for women and much higher in cities like Edo and Osaka.

Samurai curricula stressed morality and included both military and literary studies. Confucian classics were memorized, and reading and recitating them were common methods of study. Arithmetic and calligraphy were also studied. Most samurai attended schools sponsored by their han (domains), and by the time of the Meiji Restoration of 1868, more than 200 of the 276 han had established schools. Some samurai and even commoners also attended private academies, which often specialized in particular Japanese subjects or in Western medicine, modern military science, gunnery, or Rangaku (Dutch studies), as European studies were called.

Education of commoners was generally practically oriented, providing basic training in reading, writing, and arithmetic, emphasizing calligraphy and use of the abacus. Much of this education was conducted in so-called temple schools (terakoya), derived from earlier Buddhist schools. These schools were no longer religious institutions, nor were they, by 1867, predominantly located in temples. By the end of the Tokugawa period, there were more than 11,000 such schools, attended by 750,000 students. Teaching techniques included reading from various textbooks, memorizing, abacus, and repeatedly copying Chinese characters and Japanese script.

The origins of education in Japan are closely related to religion. Schooling was conducted at temples for youngsters who wanted to study Buddhism to become priests. Later, children who were willing to study started to meet at places called, "Tera-koya" (literally meaning temple huts) and learned how to read and write Japanese.

Norway

Organized education in Norway dates as far back as medieval times. Shortly after Norway became an archdiocese in 1152, cathedral schools were constructed to educate priests in Trondheim, Oslo, Bergen and Hamar.

After the reformation of Norway in 1537, (Norway entered a personal union with Denmark in 1536) the cathedral schools were turned into Latin schools, and it was made mandatory for all market towns to have such a school. In 1736 training in reading was made compulsory for all children, but was not effective until some years later. In 1827, Norway introduced the *folkeskole*, a primary school which became mandatory for 7 years in 1889 and 9 years in 1969. In the 1970s and 1980s, the *folkeskole* was abolished, and the *grunnskole* was introduced.

New Zealand

Education began with provision made by the provincial government, the missionary Christian churches and private education. The first act of parliament for education was passed in 1877, and sought to establish a standard for primary education. It was compulsory for children to attend school until the age of 14 years.

Imperial Russia and the Soviet Union

In Imperial Russia, according to the 1897 Population Census, literate people made up 28.4 percent of the population. During the 8th Party Congress of 1919, the creation of the new Socialist system of education was proclaimed the major aim of the Soviet government. The abolition of illiteracy became the primary task in the Russian SFSR.

In accordance with the Sovnarkom decree of December 26, 1919, signed by its head Vladimir Lenin, the new policy of likbez, was introduced. The new system of universal compulsory education was established for children. Millions of illiterate adult people all over the country, including residents of small towns and villages, were enrolled in special literacy schools. Komsomol members and Young Pioneer detachments played an important role in the education of illiterate people in villages. The most active phase of *likbez* asted until 1939. In 1926, the literacy rate was 56.6 percent of the population. By 1937, according to census data, the literacy rate was 86% for men and 65% for women, making a total literacy rate of 75%.

An important aspect of the early campaign for literacy and education was the policy of "indigenization" (korenizatsiya). This policy, which lasted essentially from the mid-1920s to the late 1930s, promoted the development and use of non-Russian languages in the government, the media, and education. Intended to counter the historical practices of Russification, it had as another practical goal assuring native-language education as the quickest way to increase educational levels of future generations. A huge network of so-called "national schools" was established by the 1930s, and this network continued to grow in enrollments throughout the Soviet era. Language policy changed over time, perhaps marked first of all in the government's mandating in 1938 the teaching of Russian as a required *subject* of study in every non-Russian school, and then especially beginning in the latter 1950s a growing conversion of non-Russian schools to Russian as the main medium of instruction.

Africa

Until at least 1900 AD, in most African countries south of the Sahara, children received traditional informal education on matters such as artistic performances, ceremonies, rituals, games, festivals, dancing, singing, and drawing. Boys and girls were taught separately to help prepare each sex for their adult roles. Every member of the community had a hand in contributing to the educational upbringing of the child. The high point of the African educational experience was the ritual passage ceremony from childhood to adulthood.

Nowadays, many sub-Saharan African countries have low rates of participation in formal education. Schools often lack basic facilities, and African universities may suffer from overcrowding and the difficulties of retaining staff attracted overseas by higher pay and better conditions.

Africa has more than 40 million children. According to UNESCO's *Regional overview on sub-Saharan Africa*, in 2000 only 58% of children were enrolled in primary schools, the lowest enrollment rate of any region. The USAID Centre reports as of 2005, forty percent of school-aged children in Africa do not attend primary school.

Recent World-wide Trends

Nowadays some kind of education is compulsory to all people in most countries. Due to population growth and the proliferation of compulsory education, UNESCO has calculated that in the next 30 years more people will receive formal education than in all of human history thus far.

Overall, illiteracy has greatly decreased in recent years. In some countries this has been the result of deliberate government action. For example, in Cuba the illiteracy rate was for many years less than that in the USA.

Illiteracy and the percentage of populations without any schooling have decreased in the past several decades. For example, the percentage of population without any schooling decreased from 36% in 1960 to 25% in 2000.

Among developing countries, illiteracy and percentages without schooling in 2000 stood at about half the 1970 figures. Among developed countries, figures about illiteracy rates differ widely. Often it is said that they decreased from 6% to 1%. However, the *National Adult Literacy Survey* of 1993 showed that more than 20% of the adults in the USA were functionally illiterate. These findings were confirmed in a 2003 follow-up study. Illiteracy rates in less economically developed countries (LEDCs) surpassed those of more economically developed countries (MEDCs) by a factor of 10 in 1970, and by a factor of about 20 in 2000. Illiteracy decreased greatly in LEDCs, and virtually disappeared in MEDCs. Percentages without any schooling showed similar patterns.

Percentages of the population with no schooling varied greatly among LEDCs in 2000, from less than 10% to over 65%. MEDCs had much less variation, ranging from less than 2% to 17%.

Regional Terms

The use of the term *school* varies by country, as do the names of the various levels of education within the country.

United Kingdom and Commonwealth of Nations

In the United Kingdom, the term *school* refers primarily to pre-university institutions, and these can, for the most part, be divided into pre-schools or nursery schools, primary schools (sometimes further divided into infant school and junior school), and secondary schools. Various types of secondary schools in England and Wales include grammar schools, comprehensives, secondary moderns, and city academies. In Scotland, while they may have different names, all Secondary schools are the same, except in that they may be funded by the state, or independently funded. It is unclear if "Academys", which are a hybrid between state and independently funded/controlled schools and have been introduced to England in recent years, will ever be introduced to Scotland. School performance in Scotland is monitored by Her Majesty's Inspectorate of Education. Ofsted reports on performance in England and Wales.

In the United Kingdom, most schools are publicly funded and known as state schools or maintained schools in which tuition is provided free. There are also private schools or independent schools that charge fees. Some of the most selective and expensive private schools are known as public schools, a usage that can be confusing to speakers of North American English. In North American usage, a public school is one that is publicly funded or run.

In much of the Commonwealth of Nations, including Australia, New Zealand, India, Pakistan, Bangladesh, Sri Lanka, South Africa, Kenya, and Tanzania, the term *school* refers primarily to pre-university institutions.

India

In ancient India, schools were in the form of Gurukuls. Gurukuls were traditional Hindu residential schools of learning; typically the teacher's house or a monastery. During the Mughal rule, Madrasahs were introduced in India to educate the children of Muslim parents. British records show that indigenous education was widespread in the 18th century, with a school for every temple, mosque or village in most regions of the country. The subjects taught included Reading, Writing, Arithmetic, Theology, Law, Astronomy, Metaphysics, Ethics, Medical Science and Religion.

Under the British rule in India, Christian missionaries from England, USA and other countries established missionary and boarding schools throughout the country. Later as these schools gained in popularity, more were started and some gained prestige. These schools marked the beginning of modern schooling in India and the syllabus and calendar they followed became the benchmark for schools in modern India. Today most of the schools follow the missionary school model in terms of tutoring, subject/syllabus, governance etc...with minor changes. Schools in India range from schools with large campuses with thousands of students and hefty fees to schools where children are taught under a tree with a small/no campus and are totally free of cost. There are various boards of schools in India, namely Central Board for Secondary Education (CBSE), Council for the Indian School Certificate Examinations (CISCE), Madrasa Boards of various states, Matriculation Boards of various states, State Boards of various boards, Anglo Indian Board, and so on. The typical syllabus today includes Language(s), Mathematics, Science-Physics, Chemistry, Biology, Geography, History, General Knowledge, Information Technology/Computer Science etc... Extra curricular activities include physical education/sports and cultural activities like music, choreography, painting, theater/drama etc...

Europe

In much of continental Europe, the term *school* usually applies to primary education, with primary schools that last between four and nine years, depending on the country. It also applies to secondary education, with secondary schools often divided between *Gymnasiums* and vocational schools, which again depending on country and type of school educate students for between three and six years. In Germany students graduating from Grundschule are not allowed to directly progress into a vocational school, but are supposed to proceed to one of Germany's general education schools such as Gesamtschule, Hauptschule, Realschule or Gymnasium. When they leave that school, which usually happens at age 15-19 they are allowed to proceed to a vocational school. The term school is rarely used for tertiary education, except for some *upper* or *high* schools (German: Hochschule), which describe colleges and universities.

North America and the United States

In North America, the term *school* can refer to any educational institution at any level, and covers all of the following: preschool (for toddlers), kindergarten, elementary school, middle school (also called intermediate school or junior high school, depending on specific age groups and geographic region), senior high school, college, university, and graduate school.

In the US, school performance through high school is monitored by each state's Department of Education. Charter schools are publicly funded elementary or secondary schools that have been freed from some of the rules, regulations, and statutes that apply to other public schools. The terms grammar school and *grade school* are sometimes used to refer to a primary school.

Universal Terms

In many countries, Business Schools are colleges providing instruction in business, business administration, and management. Boarding schools are schools where students live full-time amongst their peers in dormitories. Some boarding schools are separated by gender.

School Ownership and Operation

Many schools are owned or funded by states. Private schools operate independently from the government. Private schools usually rely on fees from families whose children attend the school for funding; however, sometimes such schools also receive government support (for example, through School vouchers). Many private schools are affiliated with a particular religion; these are known as parochial schools.

Components of most Schools

Schools are organized spaces purposed for teaching and learning. The classrooms, where teachers teach and students learn, are of central importance, but typical schools have many other areas, which may include:

- Cafeteria (Commons), dining hall or canteen where students eat lunch and often breakfast and snacks.
- Athletic field, playground, gym, and/or track place where students participating in sports or physical education practice
- Auditorium or hall where student theatrical and musical productions can be staged and where all-school events such as assemblies are held

- Office where the administrative work of the school is done
- Library where students consult and check out books and magazines and often use computers
- Specialized classrooms including laboratories for science education
- Computer labs where computer-based work is done and the internet accessed.

School Security

The safety of staff and students is increasingly becoming an issue for school communities, an issue most schools are addressing through improved security. After mass shootings such as the Columbine High School massacre and the Virginia Tech incident, many school administrators in the United States have created plans to protect students and staff in the event of a school shooting. Some have also taken measures such as installing metal detectors or video surveillance. Others have even taken measures such as having the children swipe identification cards as they board the school bus. For some schools, these plans have included the use of door numbering to aid public safety response. Other security concerns faced by schools include bomb threats, gangs, vandalism, and bullying.

School Health Services

School Health Services are services from medical, teaching and other professionals applied in or out of school to improve the health and well-being of children and in some cases whole families. These services have been developed in different ways around the globe but the fundamentals are constant... the early detection, correction, prevention or amelioration of disease, disability and abuse from which school aged children can suffer.

Unesco Tools

Unesco has published a set of tools, to support the FRESH framework, to guide those wishing to set up school health services around the world. Designed primarily for developing nations, these tools can be of universal use. The main emphasis of these tool is on:

- HIV/AIDS
- Food and nutrition
- Helminths and hygiene
- Malaria
- Violence
- Drugs, tobacco and alcohol.

United States

School health services are well developed in the United Sates. Central guidelines are provided by *Making Health Academic* but each state and within that each school board has adopted its own specific methods.

Making Health Academic

This is a five year project funded by CDC's Division of Adolescent and School Health (DASH) designed to enable all schools to be part of a co-ordinated school health program. The project is built around the fact that six preventable behaviours, mainly learned in childhood and youth, account for most of the serious illnesses and premature deaths in the United States; these are:

Examples of Existing Services

- Massachusetts. An example from a maritime state is where a typical mission statement starts "School Health Services fosters the growth, development and educational achievement of Massachusetts' students by promoting their health and wellbeing... "
- New Mexico. An example from a southern state is where an interesting "yucca model of coordinated school health" is used to help visualize the inter-relationship of the services.

United Kingdom

The health of children and youth in the UK is mainly the responsibility of the NHS, for example child health screening and advice for parents of overweight children. School based services are therefore more limited than in the US.

Other Countries

School health systems are expanding in low-and middle-income countries. Information on school health in these countries is collated on the Schools and Health website maintained by the Partnership for Child Development.

Online Schools/Classes

Some schools offer remote access to their classes over the Internet. Online schools also can provide support to traditional schools, as in the case of the School Net Namibia. Some online classes provide experience in a class so that when you take it you have already been introduced to the subject and know what to expect, and even more classes provide High School/College credit allowing you to take the class at your own pace. Many online classes cost money to use but some are offered free.

Stress

As a profession, teaching has levels of Work-Related Stress (WRS) that are among the highest of any profession in some countries, such as the United Kingdom. The degree of this problem is becoming increasingly recognized and support systems are being put into place. Teacher education increasingly recognizes the need to train those new to the profession to be aware of and overcome mental health challenges they may face.

Stress sometimes affects students more severely than teachers, up to the point where the students are prescribed stress medication. This stress is claimed to be related to standardized testing, and the pressure on students to score above average.

Discipline

Schools and their teachers have always been under pressure — for instance, pressure to cover the curriculum, to perform well in comparison to other schools, and to avoid the stigma of being "soft" or "spoiling" toward students. Forms of discipline, such as control over when students may speak, and normalized behaviour, such as raising a hand to speak, are imposed in the name of greater efficiency. Practitioners of critical pedagogy maintain that such disciplinary measures have no positive effect on student learning. Indeed, some argue that disciplinary practices detract from learning, saying that they undermine students' individual dignity and sense of self-worth—the latter occupying a more primary role in students' hierarchy of needs.

Classroom

A classroom is a room in which teaching or learning activities can take place. Classrooms are found in educational institutions of all kinds, including public and private schools, corporations, and religious and humanitarian organizations. The classroom attempts to provide a safe space where learning can take place uninterrupted by other distractions.

Typical Equipment

Most classrooms have a large writing surface where the instructor or students can share notes with other members of the class. Traditionally, this was in the form of a blackboard but these are becoming less common in well-equipped schools, and are replaced by flipcharts, whiteboards and interactive whiteboards. Many classrooms also have TVs, maps, charts, books, monographs and LCD projectors for presenting information and images from a computer.

Decor and Design

The layout, design and decor of the classroom has a significant effect upon the quality of education. Attention to the acoustics and colour scheme may reduce distractions and aid concentration. The lighting and furniture likewise influence study and learning.

Types of Classrooms

For lessons that require specific resources or a vocational approach different types of classrooms both indoors and outdoors are used. This is known as situated learning. Classrooms can range from small groups of five or six to big classrooms with hundreds of students. A large class room is also called a lecture hall. A few examples of classrooms are computer labs which are used for IT lessons in schools, gymnasiums for sports, and science laboratories for biology, chemistry and physics.

Challenges to the Classroom

While the classroom is clearly the dominant setting for learning, the flexibility of classroom instruction is often called into question. Instead of isolating learners in a classroom, many teachers are experimenting with integrating learning into a student's daily life. New learning technologies and mobile devices make it possible for learning to take place at any time, at any place, and (perhaps most importantly) at any pace that the learner desires.

According to the American Society for Training and Development, more than 40% of corporate training now takes place online and not in a classroom.

Education Infrastructure in India

Funding and Infrastructure

One study found out that 25% of public sector teachers and 40% of public sector medical workers were absent during the survey. Among teachers who were paid to teach, absence rates ranged from 15% in Maharashtra to 71% in Bihar. Only 1 in nearly 3000 public school head teachers had ever dismissed a teacher for repeated absence. A study on teachers by Kremer etc. found that 'only about half were teaching, during unannounced visits to a nationally representative sample of government primary schools in India.'.

A study of 188 government-run primary schools found that 59% of the schools had no drinking water and 89% had no toilets. 2003-04 data by National Institute of Educational Planning and Administration revealed that only 3.5% of primary schools in Bihar and Chhattisgarh had toilets for girls. In Madhya Pradesh, Maharashtra, Andhra Pradesh, Gujarat, Rajasthan and Himachal Pradesh, rates were 12-16%.

Curriculum Issues

Modern education in India is often criticized for being based on rote learning rather than problem solving. *BusinessWeek* denigrates the Indian curriculum saying it revolves around rote learning and ExpressIndia suggests that students are focused on cramming.

Peer Group

A peer group is a social group consisting of people who are equal in such respects as age, education or social class. Peer groups are an informal primary group of people who share a similar or equal status and who are usually of roughly the same age, tended to travel around and interact within the social aggregate Members of a particular peer group often have similar interests and backgrounds, bonded by the premise of sameness. However, some peer groups are very diverse, crossing social divides such as socioeconomic status, level of education, race, creed, culture, or religion.

Developmental Psychology

Developmental psychologists, Lev Vygotsky, Jean Piaget, Erik Erikson, and Harry Stack Sullivan, have all argued that peer relationships provide a unique context for cognitive, social, and emotional development, with equality, reciprocity, cooperation, and intimacy, maturing and enhancing children's reasoning abilities and concern for others. Modern research echoes these sentiments, showing that social and emotional gains are indeed provided by peer interaction.

Bonding and Functions of Peer Groups

- serve as a source of info.
- teaches sex roles.
- serves as a practicing venue to adulthood.
- teaches unity & collective behaviour
- discouraging discrimination.

Peer Pressure

The term peer pressure is often used to describe instances where an individual feels indirectly pressured into changing their behaviour to match that of their peers. Taking up smoking and underage drinking are two of the best known examples. In spite of the often negative connotations of the term, peer pressure can be used positively.

9

Intelligence and Learning

Intelligence is an umbrella term describing a property of the mind including related abilities, such as the capacities for abstract thought, understanding, communication, reasoning, learning, learning from past experiences, planning, and problem solving. Intelligence is most widely studied in humans, but is also observed in animals and plants. Artificial intelligence is the intelligence of machines or the simulation of intelligence in machines.

Numerous definitions of and hypotheses about intelligence have been proposed since before the twentieth century, with no consensus yet reached by scholars. Within the discipline of psychology, various approaches to human intelligence have been adopted, with the psychometric approach being especially familiar to the general public. Influenced by his cousin Charles Darwin, Francis Galton was the first scientist to propose a theory of general intelligence; that intelligence is a true, biologically-based mental faculty that can be studied by measuring a person's reaction times to cognitive tasks. Galton's research in measuring the head sizes of British scientists and laymen led to the conclusion that head-size is unrelated to a person's intelligence.

Alfred Binet, and the French school of intelligence, believed intelligence was an aggregate of dissimilar abilities, not a unitary entity with specific, identifiable properties.

Definitions

Scientists have proposed two major definitions of intelligence:

1. from *Mainstream Science on Intelligence* (1994), an editorial statement by fifty-two researchers:

   A very general mental capability that, among other things, involves the ability to reason, plan, solve problems, think abstractly, comprehend complex ideas, learn quickly and learn from experience. It is not merely book learning, a narrow academic skill, or test-taking smarts. Rather, it reflects a broader and deeper capability for comprehending our surroundings—"catching on," "making sense" of things, or "figuring out" what to do.

2. from *Intelligence: Knowns and Unknowns* (1995), a report published by the Board of Scientific Affairs of the American Psychological Association:

   Individuals differ from one another in their ability to understand complex ideas, to adapt effectively to the environment, to learn from experience, to engage in various forms of reasoning, to overcome obstacles by taking thought. Although these individual differences can be substantial, they are never entirely consistent: a given person's intellectual performance will vary on different occasions, in different domains, as judged by different criteria. Concepts of "intelligence" are attempts to clarify and organize this complex set of phenomena. Although considerable clarity has been achieved in some areas, no such conceptualization has yet answered all the important questions, and none commands universal assent. Indeed, when two dozen prominent theorists were recently asked to define intelligence, they gave two dozen, somewhat different, definitions.

Practical application — Furthermore, in clinical and therapeutic practice, such theoretic and academic definitions of intelligence might not apply to patients with borderline intellectual and adaptive functioning, whose treatments require comprehensive analysis of every diagnostic, testing, educational placement, and psychosocial factor.

The eighth (2005) and ninth (2009) editions of the *Kaplan & Sadock's Comprehensive Textbook of Psychiatry*, by Frank John Ninivaggi, MD, address these matters.

Human Intelligence

Theories of Human Intelligence

A popular theory of intelligence is based on psychometric testing, i.e. intelligence quotient (IQ) tests; however, some researchers' dissatisfaction with traditional IQ tests prompted their developing alternative theories of intelligence suggesting that intelligence results from independent capabilities that uniquely contribute to human intellectual performance.

Psychometric Approach

Despite the variety of concepts of intelligence, the approach to understanding intelligence with the most supporters and published research over the longest period of time is based on psychometric testing. Such intelligence quotient (IQ) tests include the Stanford-Binet, Raven's Progressive Matrices, the Wechsler Adult Intelligence Scale and the Kaufman Assessment Battery for Children. Charles Spearman is generally credited with defining general intelligence, which he reported in his 1904 *American Journal of Psychology* article titled "'General Intelligence,' Objectively Determined and Measured." Based on the results of a series of studies collected in Hampshire, England, Spearman concluded that there was a common function (or group of functions) across intellectual activities including what he called intelligence (i.e., school rank, which Spearman thought of as "present efficiency" in school courses; the difference between school rank and age, which was conceptualized as "native capacity;" teacher ratings; and peer ratings provided by the two oldest students, which was termed "common sense") and sensory discriminations (i.e., discrimination of pitch, brightness, and weight). This common function became known as "g" or general intelligence.

To objectively determine and measure general intelligence, Spearman invented the first technique of factor analysis (the method of Tetrad Differences) as a mathematical proof of the Two-Factor Theory. The factor analytic results indicated that every variable measured a common function to varying degrees, which led Spearman to develop the somewhat misleadingly named Two-Factor Theory of Intelligence. The Two-Factor Theory of Intelligence holds that every test can be divided into a "g" factor and an "s" factor. The g-factor measures the "general" factor or common function among ability tests. The s-factor measures the "specific" factor unique to a particular ability test. Spearman's g-factor account for positive correlations among any cognitive ability tests. However, the necessary condition for g-factor to exist is routinely violated in correlation matrices of cognitive tests, according to the work by Peter Schönemann and others. L.L. Thurstone extended and generalized Spearman's method of factor analysis into what is called the Centroid method and which became the basis for modern factor analysis. Thurstone demonstrated that Spearman's one common factor method (Spearman's method yielded only a single factor) was a special case of his multiple factor analysis. Thurstone's research led him to propose a model of intelligence that included seven orthogonal (unrelated) factors (i.e., verbal comprehension, word fluency, number facility, spatial visualization, associative memory, perceptual speed and reasoning) referred to as the Primary Mental Abilities.

In a critical review of the adult testing literature, Raymond B. Cattell found that a considerable percentage of intelligence tests that purported to measure adult intellectual functioning had all of the trappings of using college students in their development. To account for differences between children/adolescents and adults, which past theory did not address, Cattell proposed two types of cognitive abilities in a revision of Spearman's concept of general intelligence. Fluid intelligence (Gf) was hypothesized as the ability to discriminate and perceive relations (e.g., analogical and syllogistic reasoning), and crystallized intelligence (Gc) was hypothesized as the ability to discriminate relations that had been established originally through Gf, but no longer required the identification of the relation (commonly assessed using information or vocabulary tests). In addition, fluid intelligence was hypothesized to increase until adolescence and then to slowly decline, and crystallized intelligence increases gradually and stays relatively stable across most of adulthood until it declines in late adulthood.

With his student John L. Horn, Cattell indicated that Gf and Gc were only two among several factors manifest in intelligence tests scores under the umbrella of what became known as Gf/Gc Theory. General visualization (Gv; visual acuity, depth perception), general fluency (F, facility in recalling words), general speediness (Gs; performance on speeded, simple tasks) were among several cognitive ability factors added to Gf/Gc Theory. J.P. Guilford sought to more fully explore the scope of the adult intellect by providing the concept of intelligence with a strong, comprehensive theoretical backing. The Structure-of-Intellect model (SI model) was designed as a cross classification system with intersections in the model providing the basis for abilities similar to Mendeleev's periodic table in chemistry. The three-dimensional cube—shaped model includes five content categories (the way in which information is presented on a test; visual, auditory, symbolic, semantic, and behavioural), six operation categories (what is done on a test; evaluation, convergent production, divergent production, memory retention, memory recording, and cognition), and six product categories (the form in which information is processed on a test; units, classes, relations, systems, transformations, and implications). The intersection of three categories provides a frame of reference for generating one or more new hypothetical factors of intelligence.

John B. Carroll re-analysed 461 datasets in the single most comprehensive study of cognitive abilities. This analysis led him to propose the Three Stratum Theory, which is a hierarchical model of intellectual functioning. The strata represent three different levels of generality over the domain of cognitive abilities. At the bottom is the first stratum, which is represented by narrow abilities that are highly specialized (e.g., induction, spelling ability). The second stratum is represented by broad abilities that include moderate specializations in various domains. Carroll identified eight second-stratum factors: fluid intelligence, crystallized intelligence, general memory and learning, broad visual perception, broad auditory perception, broad retrieval ability, broad cognitive speediness, and processing speed (reaction time decision speed). Carroll has noted the similarity of his second stratum abilities and the Gf/Gc factors, although the Three-Stratum Theory does not incorporate the developmental trajectories associated with Gf/Gc Theory. Carroll accepted Spearman's concept of general intelligence, for the most part, as a representation of the uppermost third stratum.

More recently, an amalgamation of the Gf-Gc theory of Cattell and Horn with Carroll's Three-Stratum theory has led to the Cattell-Horn-Carroll (CHC) Theory of cognitive abilities.

CHC researchers have produced numerous studies that have influenced diagnostic issues and test development.

Intelligence tests are widely used in educational, business, and military settings due to their efficacy in predicting behaviour. *g* is highly correlated with many important social outcomes—individuals with low IQs are more likely to be divorced, have a child out of marriage, be incarcerated, and need long-term welfare support, while individuals with high IQs are associated with more years of education, higher status jobs and higher income. Intelligence is significantly correlated with successful training and performance outcomes, and *g* is the single best predictor of successful job performance.

Controversies

IQ tests were originally designed to identify mentally "defective" children. The inventors of the IQ did not necessarily believe they were measuring fixed intelligence. Despite this, critics argue that intelligence tests have been used to support nativistic theories which view intelligence as a qualitative object with a relatively fixed quantity. Critics of the psychometrics point out that intelligence is often more complex and broader in conception than what is measured by IQ tests. Furthermore, skeptics argue that even though tests of mental abilities are correlated, people still have unique strengths and weaknesses in specific areas. Consequently they argue that psychometric theorists over-emphasize *g*, despite the fact that *g* was defined so as to encompass all inter-correlated capabilities and skills.

Researchers in the field of human intelligence have encountered a considerable amount of public concern and criticism—much more than scientists in other areas normally receive. A number of critics have challenged the relevance of psychometric intelligence in the context of everyday life. There have also been controversies over genetic factors in intelligence, particularly questions regarding the relationship between race and intelligence and sex and intelligence. Another controversy in the field is how to interpret the increases in test scores that have occurred over time, the so-called Flynn effect.

Stephen Jay Gould was one of the most vocal critics of intelligence testing. In his book *The Mismeasure of Man* Gould argued that intelligence could not be quantified to a single numerical entity. He also challenged the hereditarian viewpoint on intelligence. Many of Gould's criticisms were aimed at Arthur Jensen, who responded that his work had been misrepresented. Gould also investigated the methods of 19th-century craniometry. Jensen stated that drawing conclusions from early intelligence research is like condemning the auto industry by criticizing the performance of the Model T.

Multiple Intelligences

Howard Gardner's theory of multiple intelligences is based on studies not only of normal children and adults but also by studies of gifted individuals (including so-called "savants"), of persons who have suffered brain damage, of experts and virtuosos, and of individuals from diverse cultures. This led Gardner to break intelligence down into at least eight different components: logical, linguistic, spatial, musical, kinesthetic, interpersonal, intrapersonal in 1983 and naturalist intelligences added in 1999. He argues that psychometric tests address only linguistic and logical plus some aspects of spatial intelligence. A major criticism of Gardner's theory is that it has never been tested, or subjected to peer review, by Gardner or anyone else, and indeed that it is unfalsifiable.

Triarchic Theory of Intelligence

Robert Sternberg proposed the triarchic theory of intelligence to provide a more comprehensive description of intellectual competence than traditional differential or cognitive theories of human ability. The triarchic theory describes three fundamental aspects of intelligence. Analytic intelligence comprises the mental processes through which intelligence is expressed. Creative intelligence is necessary when an individual is confronted with a challenge that is nearly, but not entirely, novel or when an individual is engaged in automatizing the performance of a task. Practical intelligence is bound in a sociocultural milieu and involves adaptation to, selection of, and shaping of the environment to maximize fit in the context. The triarchic theory does not argue against the validity of a general intelligence factor; instead, the theory posits that general intelligence is part of analytic intelligence, and only by considering all three aspects of intelligence can the full range of intellectual functioning be fully understood.

More recently, the triarchic theory has been updated and renamed the Theory of Successful Intelligence by Sternberg. Intelligence is defined as an individual's assessment of success in life by the individual's own (idiographic) standards and within the individual's sociocultural context. Success is achieved by using combinations of analytical, creative, and practical intelligence. The three aspects of intelligence are referred to as processing skills. The processing skills are applied to the pursuit of success through what were the three elements of practical intelligence: adapting to, shaping of, and selecting of one's environments. The mechanisms that employ the processing skills to achieve success include utilizing one's strengths and compensating or correcting for one's weaknesses.

Sternberg's theories and research on intelligence remain contentious within the scientific community.

Developmental Approach

Jean Piaget was the founder of the developmental approach to the study of intelligence. According to his theory of cognitive development, intelligence is the basic mechanism of ensuring equilibrium in the relations between the person and the environment. This is achieved through the actions of the developing person on the world. At any moment in development, the environment is assimilated in the schemes of action that are already available and these schemes are transformed or accommodated to the peculiarities of the objects of the environment, if they are not completely appropriate. Thus, the development of intelligence is a continuous process of assimilations and accommodations that lead to increasing expansion of the field of application of schemes, increasing coordination between them, increasing interiorization, and increasing abstraction. Piaget described four main periods or stages in the development towards completely equilibrated thought and problem solving. In the sensorimotor stage (0–2 years), thought is based on perceptions and external actions and their coordination. In the preoperational stage, sensorimotor schemes are internalized and thought occurs mentally rather than externally, through the manipulation of representations and symbols that stand for sensorimotor schemes and objects.

At the beginning, however, mental schemes are not coordinated. As a result, systematic logical reasoning is not possible (that, for example, A = C, if A = B and B = C). When mental schemes are coordinated, thinking enters the concrete operational stage. In this period, thinking is logical, but limited to the concrete aspects of the world. That is, children can grasp several important aspects of the world, such as the conservation of number, matter, length, weight, volume, etc. despite external transformation. Gradually, concrete operational schemes are coordinated with each other and cognitive development enters the final formal operational stage. In this period reality is subsumed to possibilities and reasoning becomes formal. As a result, abstract scientific concepts such as the concept of inertia, energy, algebra, and proportionality can be grasped and scientific experiments can be designed. All in all, for Piaget intelligence is not the same at different ages. It changes qualitatively, thereby allowing access to different levels of organization of the world. Research shows that Piagetian intelligence is correlated but it is not identical with psychometric intelligence and IQ.

The neo-Piagetian theories of cognitive development advanced by Case, Demetriou, Halford, and Pascual-Leone, attempted to integrate Piaget's theory with cognitive and differential theories of cognitive organization and development. Their aim was to better account for the cognitive factors of development and for intra-individual and inter-individual differences in cognitive development. They suggested that development along Piaget's stages is due to increasing processing efficiency which is defined in terms of speed of processing and working memory capacity. Moreover, Demetriou's theory ascribes an important role to hypercognitive processes of self-recording, self-monitoring, and self-regulation and it recognizes the operation of several relatively autonomous domains of thought. Overall, this approach suggests that there indeed is a general intelligence factor. This factor is geared on general processing efficiency functions that enable humans to represent and process information, that processing involves general inferential processes that are gradually constructed, and self-awareness and reflection are instrumental in this construction. The general understanding and problem solving ability associated with this factor changes qualitatively with age and this change is related to the succession of Piagetian stages. At the same time, individual differences in the state of the general efficiency factors may cause differences in the rate of intellectual development of different individuals and these differences may be reflected in psychometric measures of cognitive ability, such as the IQ tests. Moreover differences between individuals may come from differences in their predispositions or facility related to different domains of knowledge and problem solving.

Emotional Intelligence

Daniel Goleman and several other researchers have developed the concept of emotional intelligence and claim it is at least as "important" as traditionally proposed components of intelligence. These theories grew from observations of human development and of brain injury victims who demonstrate an acute loss of a particular cognitive function—e.g. the ability to think numerically, or the ability to understand written language—without showing any loss in other cognitive areas. Many researchers believe that emotional intelligence is a composite of general intelligence and agreeableness, one of the five dimensions of personality in the five-factor model of personality. In this model, an emotionally intelligent person would score higher than average in both dimensions, and vice versa. Moreover, an emotionally intelligent person cannot score high on only one of the two traits. For example, an individual with low general mental ability and high agreeableness would be impaired in his ability to produce emotionally intelligent behaviour despite his intentions, while an individual with high general mental ability and low agreeableness would be perfectly capable of being emotionally intelligent, but not inclined to do so.

PASS Theory

Pass theory has been offered as an alternative to general intelligence, and is based on a description of neuropsychological processes. These authors suggested that a unidimensional model with just intelligence fails to assist researchers and clinicians who study learning disabilities, disorders of attention, mental retardation, and interventions designed for special populations who face those challenges. The PASS model covers four kinds of competencies that are associated with areas of the brain.

1. The planning processes involve decision making, problem solving, and performing activities and requires goal setting and self-monitoring.

2. The attention/arousal component involves selectively attending to a particular stimulus, ignoring distractions, and maintaining vigilance.
3. Simultaneous processing involves the integration of stimuli into a group and requires the observation of relationships.
4. Successive processing involves the integration of stimuli into serial order.

The planning and attention/arousal components comes from structures located in the frontal lobe, and the simultaneous and successive processes come from structures located in the posterior region of the cortex.

Empirical Evidence

IQ proponents have claimed that IQ's predictive validity has been demonstrated, for example in predicting non-academic outcomes such as job performance, and that the various multiple intelligence theories have little or no such support. Meanwhile, it has been claimed that the relevance and existence of multiple intelligences have not been borne out when tested. A set of ability tests that do not correlate together would support the claim that multiple intelligences are independent of each other.

Evolution of Intelligence

Our hominid and human ancestors evolved large and complex brains exhibiting an ever-increasing intelligence through a long and mostly unknown evolutionary process. This process was either driven by the direct adaptive benefits of intelligence, or, alternatively, driven by its indirect benefits within the context of sexual selection as a reliable signal of genetic resistance against pathogens.

Factors Affecting Intelligence

Intelligence is an ill-defined, difficult to quantify concept. Accordingly, the IQ tests used to measure intelligence provide only approximations of the posited "real" intelligence. In addition, a number of theoretically unrelated properties are known to correlate with IQ such as race, gender and height but since correlation does not imply causation the true relationship between these factors is uncertain. Factors affecting IQ may be divided into biological and environmental.

Biological

The biological factors that correlate with IQ include ratio of brain weight to body weight and the volume and location of gray matter tissue in the brain. However, the basic mechanisms by which the brain produces complex phenomena such as intelligence are still poorly understood. Lesion studies indicate that general intelligence "draws on connections between regions that integrate verbal, visuospatial, working memory, and executive processes." Because intelligence appears to be at least partly dependent on brain structure and the genes shaping brain development, it has been proposed that genetic engineering could be used to enhance the intelligence of animals, a process sometimes called biological uplift in science fiction. Experiments on mice have demonstrated superior ability in learning and memory in various behavioural tasks.

Intelligence Quotient

An intelligence quotient, or IQ, is a score derived from one of several different standardized tests designed to assess intelligence. The term "IQ," from the German *Intelligenz-Quotient,* was devised by the German psychologist William Stern in 1912 as a proposed method of scoring children's intelligence tests such as those developed by Alfred Binet and Théodore Simon in the early 20th Century. Lewis Terman accepted that form of scoring, expressing a score as a quotient of "mental age" and "chronological age," for his revision of the Binet-Simon test, the first version of the Stanford-Binet Intelligence Scales. Although the term "IQ" is still in common use, the scoring of modern IQ tests such as the Wechsler Adult Intelligence Scale is now based on standard scoring of the subject's rank order on the test item content with the median score set to 100, and a standard deviation of 15, although not all tests adhere to that assignment of 15 IQ points to each standard deviation.

IQ scores have been shown to be associated with such factors as morbidity and mortality, parental social status, and, to a substantial degree, parental IQ. While the heritability of IQ has been investigated for nearly a century, controversy remains regarding the significance of heritability estimates, and the mechanisms of inheritance are still a matter of some debate. IQ scores are used in many contexts: as predictors of educational achievement or special needs, by social scientists who study the distribution of IQ scores in populations and the relationships between IQ score and other variables, and as predictors of job performance and income.

The average IQ scores for many populations have been rising at an average rate of three points per decade since the early 20th century, a phenomenon called the Flynn effect. It is disputed whether these changes in scores reflect real changes in intellectual abilities, or merely methodological problems with past or present testing.

History

Psychometrics

Englishman Francis Galton, influenced by Darwinism, founded eugenics (and later psychometrics) to measure differences between upper and lower classes. Galton argued that due to heredity, white aristocrats were intellectually superior to other humans; nurture, meanwhile, played a lesser role in intellectual capacity.

Clinical Diagnostics

French psychologist Alfred Binet gave more weight to nurture, arguing that intelligence could be improved. Binet and fellow French psychologist Théodore Simon later developed the Binet-Simon test for measuring intellectual development or mental age to diagnose French children in need of special assistance classes. Binet-Simon tasks were diverse in order to neutralize individual differences in types of intelligence and provide a general measure.

Intelligence Testing

English psychologist Charles Spearman, however, did not believe there were different types of intelligence. He devised a correlational formula to define a common intellective factor (which he called "general intelligence"), a factor that Binet argued did not exist.

Intelligence Quotient (IQ)

In 1910 the eugenics movement in the USA seized on the

Binet-Simon test as means to give them credibility in diagnosing mental retardation after American psychologist Henry H. Goddard published a translation of it that same year. American psychologist Lewis Terman revised the Binet-Simon scale, implementing German psychologist William Stern's intelligence quotient (I.Q.) ratio of mental age to chronological age and used the resulting Stanford-Binet scale as a measure of general intelligence.

World War I: Large Scale Testing

A team of psychologists led by eugenicist Robert Yerkes assisted the US army to rapidly assess and assign huge numbers of personnel. They developed two group-administered intelligence tests for this purpose: an alpha test for literate personnel; and a beta for the illiterate. They successfully tested 1,726,000 recruits. However, there was too little time for validity testing and not enough staff to administer tests correctly. Many officers distrusted the psychologists, accusing them of conducting research for their own purposes using culturally biased tests. Orders were issued that low test scores should not bar men from officer training and that a disability board should consider all discharges. The outcome was that 0.5% of recruits were discharged as mentally inferior, whilst Yerkes would have preferred to have discharged 3% whose results showed a mental age of under 10.

In contrast, another team of psychologists led by Walter Dill Scott defined intelligence as a diverse complex of capacities, as Binet had. They stressed an individual differences approach emphasizing environmental adjustments of mental qualities as functions. Soon they developed a rating scale to classify and place enlisted men according to how they used their intelligence, not their base levels of intelligence. The army was enthusiastic about Scott's classification of personnel. By the time the war ended they had already been incorporated into the military and had classified 3½ million men and assigned 973,858 to technical units.

Post War to 1929

The army abolished Yerkes' team after the war but employed two psychologists to continue intelligence testing research. However, a great deal of positive post war publicity on army psychological testing helped to make psychology a respected field. Subsequently there was an increase in jobs and funding in psychology. Group intelligence tests were developed for and became widely used in both primary and secondary schools, universities and industry. But controversy followed when one of Yerkes' team, Goddard, admitted that they had been guilty of bad logic in finding that 45% of army recruits had a mental age of 12 or less. In addition, there was no agreement on what the intelligence tests measured, and the publication of racial differences in scores led to much criticism that environmental influences on score had not been considered.

Wechsler's Innovation in Scoring

The modern IQ scale is a mathematical transformation of a raw score on an IQ test, based on the rank of that score in a normalization sample. This procedure was pioneered by David Wechsler. Modern scores are sometimes referred to as "deviation IQs," while older method age-specific scores are referred to as "ratio IQs." IQ scales of either kind are ordinal scales and thus IQ points are not units of measurement.

The two scoring methodologies yield similar results near the population median, but the older ratio IQs yielded far higher scores for high-scoring (gifted) children. Current IQ tests do not yield such high scores, as recent validation studies have shown that concerns about ceiling effects in identifying gifted children are exaggerated. In any event error of estimation is greatest for scores above the population median and likely to overestimate the true score (in the sense of formal testing theory) of a test-taker who obtains a score above the median.

Since the publication of the Wechsler Adult Intelligence Scale (WAIS), almost all intelligence scales have adopted the deviation method of scoring. The use of this scoring method makes the term "intelligence quotient" an inaccurate description, mathematically speaking, but the term "IQ" still enjoys colloquial usage, and is used to label the standard scoring of most cognitive ability tests currently in use.

Bibliography

Asch, M : *Abnormal and Developmental Psychology*, Ivy Pub, Delhi, 2003.

Barrows, H.: *Practice-Based Learning: Problem-Based Learning Applied to Medical Education*, Springfield, IL: Southern Illinois University School of Medicine, 1994.

Boring, E.G.: *A History of Experimental Psychology*. New York: The Century Company, 1929.

Boud, D., Feletti, G.: *The Challenge of Problem-based Learning*, London, Kogan, 1991.

Bridges, E., Hallenger, P.: *Problem-based Learning for Educational Administrators*, Oregon, ERIC Clearinghouse on Educational Management, 1992.

Burgess, R. L. : *Evolutionary Perspectives on Human Development*, Thousand Oaks, CA: Sage, 2004.

Damon, William : *Social and Personality Development, Infancy through Adolescence,* New York: Norton, 1983.

Dicken, P. : *Wheels of Change, the Automobile Industry*, London, 2007.

Dubey, K.C. : *Experimental and Developmental Psychology*, Omega Pub, Delhi, 2009.

Ellis, B.J., & Bjorklund, D.F.: *Origins of the Social Mind: Evolutionary Psychology and Child Development*, New York, Guilford Press, 2005.

Eysenck, Hans : *Psychoticism as a Dimension of Personality*, Pergamon, Elsevier Science Inc, Amsterdam, 1997.

Georgi, A. : *Psychology as a Human Science*, Harper & Row, New York, 1970.

Grace, G. : *School Leadership: Beyond Educational Development*, London, Falmer, 1995.

Gregory, S. : *Getting around Brown: Desegregation, Development, and the Columbus Public Schools*, Columbus, Ohio State University Press, 1998.

Hoy, W.K. : *Instructional Leadership: A Learning-centered Guide*, Boston, Allyn & Bacon/Longman, 2003.

Laub, D. : *Testimony, Crises of Witnessing in Literature, Psychoanalysis and History*, Routledge, New York, 1992.

Millican, J. : *Adult Literacy, A Handbook for Development Education*, Oxford, Oxfam, 1995.

Moustakas, S. : *Existential Psychotherapy and the Interpretation of Dreams,* J. Aronson, C., Northvale, NJ, 1994.

Murthy, J. Krishna : *Administration and Organisation of Physical Education and Sports*, Commonwealth, Delhi, 2005.

Rastogi, P.N. : *Management of Technology and Innovation : Competing Through Technological Excellence*, Response, Delhi, 2009.

Rathod, P B : *Dynamics of Political Psychology*, ABD Pub, Delhi, 2008.

Rogers, A. : *Adults Learning for Development*, London, Cassell, 1992.

Sen, Anuradha : *An Introduction to Developmental Psychology*, Indian Pub, Delhi, 2010.

Shen, Zheng : *Organizational Psychology: Foundations and Applications*. New York: Oxford University Press, 1998.

Smith, M.K. : *Local Education, Community, Conversation, Action*, Buckingham, Open University Press, 1994.

Sydney Ellen Schultz: *Psychology and Work Today*. Upper Saddle River, NJ: Prentice Hall, 1998.

Taylor, R. : *Learning Independence, A political outline of Indian Adult Education*, Leicester, National Institute of Adult Continuing Education, 1995.

Vaknin, Sam : *A Textbook of Organizational Psychology*, Dominant Pub, Delhi, 2010.

Verma, R.B. : *Developmental Psychology and Human Development*, Alfa, Delhi, 2006.

White, P. : *Civic Virtues and Public Schooling: Educating Citizens for a Democratic Society*, New York, Teachers College, 1996.

Index

□□□